JEWISI ... N

JEWISH LONDON

A COMPREHENSIVE GUIDEBOOK FOR VISITORS AND LONDONERS

RACHEL KOLSKY & ROSLYN RAWSON

Interlink Books

An imprint of Interlink Publishing Group, Inc.
Northampton, Massachusetts

Dedication
Rachel: To Ma and Pa, who instilled in me their love of London and Jewish heritage.
Roslyn: To my husband, Jon, and my mother Angela Davidson, whose input, love and
support I found invaluable.

First published in 2012 by
INTERLINK BOOKS
An imprint of Interlink Publishing Group, Inc.
46 Crosby Street, Northampton, Massachusetts 01060
www.interlinkbooks.com

Published simultaneously in Great Britain by New Holland Publishers (UK) Ltd

Library of Congress Cataloging-in Publication Data available

ISBN 978-1-56656-900-2

Publisher: Guy Hobbs
Project Editor: Clare Hubbard
Designer: Lucy Parissi
Picture Researcher: Rachel Kolsky
Cartographer: William Smuts
Production: Marion Storz

Printed and bound in China

Although the publishers have made every effort to ensure that information contained in this book
was researched and correct at the time of going to press, they accept no responsibility for any
inaccuracies, loss, injury or inconvenience sustained by any person using this book as reference.

To request our complete 48-page full-color catalog, please call us toll free at 1-800-238-LINK, visit
our website at www.interlinkbooks.com, or send us an e-mail: info@interlinkbooks.com

Picture Captions
Front cover top: *Children of the Kindertransport* by Frank Meisler; front cover bottom: West London
Synagogue; back cover: Hendon Reform Synagogue; page 2: Interior of New West End Synagogue,
Bayswater; page 5 from left to right: Selection of bagels, Hendon Bagel Bakery; Soup Kitchen for the
Jewish Poor; King's College Chapel, Strand, Science Faculty window with depiction of Rosalind Franklin;
Sandys Row Synagogue, photo – Jeremy Freedman.

contents

INTRODUCTION

The Jewish presence in London dates back to the 11th century. Today, there is a flourishing Jewish community numbering around 196,000. Whether you visit Golders Green with its bagel and falafel bars, Stamford Hill with its growing Orthodox community, Spitalfields with its memories of the Jewish East End, the City to trace civic emancipation through the lives of 19th-century financiers or stroll through leafy NW3 in the footsteps of refugees fleeing Europe in the 1930s, this book is the perfect guide to take with you to discover Jewish London through the centuries to the present day.

Divided into 11 chapters, the book includes 'Jewish London on Foot', a series of walking tours based upon Rachel Kolsky's experience as a Blue Badge London Tourist Guide. There are also chapters on exploring places of Jewish interest off the main tourist trail, an in-depth look at the Jewish Museum, features on Holocaust memorials, art and artists, literature and film, a calendar of cultural events and festivals and a chapter with suggested day trips from London. 'Jewish London Today' takes an independent look at contemporary Jewish London, providing listings for cafés and restaurants, shops, hotels, synagogues and religious amenities in the main Jewish areas within close proximity to Central London.

This book is for anyone who has an interest in Jewish life in London – past and present.

Enjoy!

Above: Wall of Scrolls, Czech Memorial Scrolls Museum (see pp. 122–3).
Right: Cable Street Mural, detail (see p. 44).

HOW TO USE THIS BOOK

Whether a local or a visitor, you will find *Jewish London* informative and easy to use. Every effort has been made to ensure that the information provided is up to date but restaurants and shops can close, galleries change their displays and opening hours and prices can vary. Basic opening-hours information for most listings is given but places often close on public holidays, Jewish festivals, etc. so call or consult websites before visiting. Unless otherwise stated, admission to the museums, galleries, etc. is free.

Telephone numbers provided are for calls made within the UK. For calls to the UK from outside the UK, the country code is 44 and the first '0' should be omitted. For example, a call to 020 8343 6255 from USA/Canada will be 011 44 20 8343 6255, and from Europe/Israel will be 00 44 20 8343 6255.

Some Hebrew terminology is included. Please refer to the Glossary on pp. 217–18.

West London Synagogue (see pp. 74–5).

CAFES, RESTAURANTS AND SHOPS

Most of the cafés, shops and restaurants listed in this book are kosher. In the listings we state which kashrut authorities provide their licences and supervision. They are shown by the following abbreviations:

LBD – London Beth Din Kashrut Division: affiliated to the United Synagogue (☎ *020 8343 6255; www.kosher.org.uk*).

SKA – Sephardi Kashrut Authority: under the auspices of the Sephardi Beth Din (☎ *020 7289 7663; www.sephardikashrut.org*).

Kedassia – the kashrut division of the Union of Orthodox Hebrew Congregations and Adath Yisroel representing the haredi communities in the UK (☎ *020 8349 9160; email: shechita@theproffice.com*).

KF – under the auspices of the kashrut division of the Federation of Synagogues Beth Din (☎ *020 8202 2263; www.kfkosher.org.uk*).

LBS – London Board for Shechita: licences kosher retail butchers to provide fresh meat and poultry, and provides kashrut seals for pre-packed kosher products (☎ *020 8349 9160; www.shechita.co.uk*).

For more information see *www.hechshers.info*.

The *Really Jewish Food Guide* published regularly by the London Beth Din provides a comprehensive guide to thousands of approved products, and monthly updates are available on *www.kosher.org*.

All the cafés and restaurants mentioned in 'Jewish London on Foot' (see pp. 13–94) are unsupervised unless otherwise stated.

SYNAGOGUES

Synagogues mentioned in this book are either independent or members of, or affiliated to, the following organizations:

United Synagogue: founded in 1870, this is the largest UK synagogal organization, currently comprising 62 Modern Orthodox synagogues (*www.theus.org.uk*).

Federation of Synagogues: established in 1887 as an umbrella organization for the growing number of small Orthodox immigrant communities. It currently comprises 23 Orthodox synagogues (*www.federationof synagogues.com*). (See p. 56.)

Union of Orthodox Hebrew Congregations: founded in 1926 to protect traditional Judaism, it acts as an umbrella organization for the Haredi Jewish community, including the Adath Yisroel synagogues.

Masorti: The New London Synagogue (see p. 193), established in 1964, was the first Masorti synagogue. Masorti Judaism is devoted to traditional Judaism combined with a modern understanding of religious thought and practice. There are 15 Masorti synagogues in the UK (*www.masorti.org.uk*).

Reform Judaism: established in 1840, and currently comprises 42 synagogues in the UK. It states that its roots are in ancient Jewish tradition but that Jewish law has to be freshly interpreted in every generation (*www.reform judaism.org.uk*).

Liberal Judaism: founded in 1902 and currently comprises over 30 synagogues in the UK. It states that it is the Judaism of the past in the process of becoming the Judaism of the future (*www.liberaljudaism.org*). (See p. 100.)

Visiting Synagogues and Cemeteries

Synagogues are not generally kept open for visits outside service times although visitors are always welcome to attend services.

When attending services at an Orthodox synagogue you should dress appropriately. Men should cover their heads and women should dress modestly wearing a skirt or dress, not trousers. Married women should wear a hat. For services at Masorti and Progressive synagogues, the dress code is more relaxed but you may want to contact individual synagogues in advance to clarify. To avoid compromising standards of kashrut in the synagogue, food and drink should not be taken in. On Shabbat, the use of mobile phones and cameras is not permitted.

As Jewish burial grounds are also sacred places, the above advice for dress and conduct should be followed. Additionally, it is forbidden to walk over or step on any grave. On leaving a cemetery it is customary to wash your hands and facilities are made available.

TRAVEL INFORMATION

For most listings, the nearest tube station and approximate walking times are shown. Transport for London (*www.tfl.gov.uk*) is an excellent resource for planning how to travel between two locations.

MAP KEY

- ▪▪▪ Walking route
- 🄯 Places of interest
- ⬥ Tube station
- ⬥ Overground station
- DLR Docklands Light Railway station
- ⇄ Mainline station
- 🚌 Bus stop
- ✡ Open synagogue – operating synagogue providing services and communal activities
- ✴ Closed synagogue – closed to membership but the building remains

HISTORICAL OVERVIEW

The UK Jewish community currently numbers around 280,000, with approximately 70 per cent living in London. Other cities have a rich Jewish heritage but with their communities now depleted, it is in London where the buildings, associations and personalities who have shaped the community are concentrated.

The text that follows is a condensed history of Jewish London, from the 11th century to the present day.

11th–17th CENTURIES

Following the invasion in 1066, William I is credited with first inviting Jews to England when he needed to establish a system of credit. Communities were established in county capital towns such as Norwich and Lincoln but the main concentration for medieval Jewry was in London, in the area that is now the City of London. They worked as moneylenders and merchants but the community was not a ghetto. Street and church names in the City, such as Old Jewry, Jewry Street and St Lawrence Jewry serve as reminders, as no buildings remain. It was very exciting when a 13th-century Mikvah was discovered in 2001.

Edward I expelled the Jewish community in 1290, which by then had dwindled in number. During the subsequent period, known as the Expulsion, a small secret community remained. Other Jews, often doctors and lawyers, who were given royal protection, were able to reside in England more openly.

Oliver Cromwell allowed Jews to return in 1656 and, following this Resettlement, Sephardi Jews and then Ashkenazi Jews settled to the east of the City and beyond, where they established cemeteries,

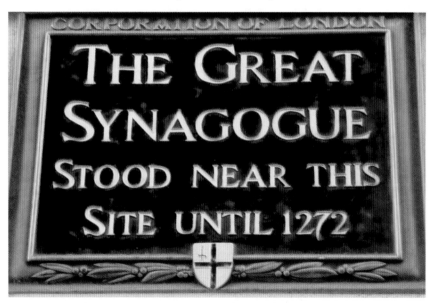

Great Synagogue plaque, Old Jewry, City of London (see p. 83).

synagogues, businesses, hospitals and schools. By the early 1700s, the area around Aldgate was nearly 25 per cent Jewish. The wealthy soon bought palatial homes and country estates mostly to the north and south of London in Highgate, Totteridge and Morden.

1800s–EARLY 1900s

The move westwards also began and an Anglo-Jewish aristocracy developed in the West End including the Rothschilds and Moses Montefiore. By the mid-1800s, branch synagogues were built in the West End and North and South London suburbs. By the 1870s all the key Jewish communal initiatives had been established including *The Jewish Chronicle*, Board of Guardians, Board of Deputies and the Jews' Free School (JFS).

In the 1880s, persecution of Jews in Eastern Europe led to tens of thousands of Jewish migrants arriving in London. They lived and worked near their point of arrival in the already crowded areas of Whitechapel and Spitalfields. A Jewish population of 125,000 with 65 synagogues was contained in 5sq km (2sq miles). It became the 'Jewish East End', with the sweated trades of tailoring, cap- and shoe-making, but vibrant street markets, youth clubs and Yiddish theatre also thrived. This life was replicated in the smaller community of Soho and Fitzrovia in London's West End.

To relieve overcrowding, the community was encouraged to move east to Stepney and north to Hackney, then green suburbs. There was a distinct hierarchy within the Jewish East End – moving eastwards reflected upward mobility and school and housing costs reflected this.

Hackney-born Jews did not consider themselves Jewish East Enders. Theirs was a close-knit community with several synagogues, Ridley Road street market and Hackney Downs School, which at one time was 50 per cent Jewish.

Daniel Mendoza plaque in grounds of Queen Mary College (see p. 51).

Stamford Hill and Stoke Newington also provided an escape from the East End. In the early 1900s, the furniture industry in Shoreditch and Bethnal Green moved northwards along the transport routes to Tottenham and Edmonton and new communities were established.

MID-1900s–21st CENTURY

The interwar years saw the first big changes to the Jewish community. Affordable housing built alongside new tube lines enabled an escape from the crowded East End to semi-detached suburbia. The Northern line to Golders Green and Finchley and the Central line to Gants Hill and Ilford formed two geographically distinct communities. East End synagogues closed down and new ones were

Hendon Reform Synagogue, stained-glass window (see p. 184).

established in these suburbs while businesses typically remained in East London.

The 1930s saw a new group of Jewish immigrants; Austrian and German émigrés escaping Nazi Europe. Urban, educated, professional and assimilated, they did not go east but settled in NW3 and NW6, where housing was then cheap and plentiful. They quickly replicated their shops, restaurants and more liberal form of worship. Today, there is still a large Jewish community in these areas.

Following WWII, with mass evacuation and the loss of housing, the disappearance of the Jewish East End continued. People moved to new housing estates in Essex or remained in their evacuation homes and the JFS relocated to Camden, North London. In the 1950s, additional large suburban communities were established in North-west London such as Stanmore, Kenton and Kingsbury.

By the early 1970s, with the second generation opting for the professions rather than working in 'the family business', the Jewish East End was nearly at an end. Soho and Fitzrovia followed the same pattern.

The late 20th century saw membership of North-west London synagogues decrease although the concentration of Jewish London facilities remains there. A proliferation of newer suburbs was established outside London including Bushey, Elstree, Radlett and Borehamwood, with a full range of facilities.

Into the 21st century Hackney hosts the vibrant and expanding ultra-orthodox community in Stamford Hill and inner suburbs such as Brondesbury and West Hampstead are experiencing a renaissance. One aspect unites the communities: they are composed, in the main, of the children and their descendants of the East European immigrants who were at the core of the Jewish East End.

JEWISH LONDON ON FOOT

London is a city best explored on foot. In many areas the networks of narrow streets provide the opportunity to discover less well-known buildings and the human stories behind them. This selection of self-guided tours is taken from the wide range that Rachel Kolsky has successfully led over the past 10 years. They focus on the East End, Central London and Hampstead; areas to which visitors and Londoners gravitate. On these walks, London's Jewish communities over the centuries will be brought to life.

The walks start and finish near tube stations and approximate durations and distances are provided. All the routes are flat, with only a few involving some steps. These are mentioned, where appropriate, together with suggestions for refreshments. Each walk has a map indicating the route and places mentioned in the text, but you should take a detailed city map with you as well. The map below provides an overview of the location of the walks (and also the areas featured in the 'Hidden Jewish London' chapter).

The East End is larger than most people imagine, so it has been split into four walks. Each contains vivid memories of the long-gone Jewish East End and three include synagogues that have survived. The mural by Beverley-Jane Stewart on pp. 14–15 captures the past and present of the Jewish East End, and incorporates many of the sites visited during the walking tours.

❶ Old Jewish East End Walk (see pp. 18–32)

❷ Angels and Radicals Walk (see pp. 33–9)

❸ An East End Village Walk (see pp. 50–55)

❹ In and Around Commercial Road – Jewish Whitechapel Walk (see pp. 40–49)

❺ Jewish City – A Walk of Jewish Firsts (see pp. 80–88)

❻ Fitzrovia and Soho Walk (see pp. 61–6)

❼ Mayfair and West End Walk (see pp. 67–73)

❽ Mittel Europe in NW3 Walk (see pp. 89–94)

❾ Notting Hill and Bayswater (see pp. 96–8)

❿ Holland Park and ⓫ Maida Vale (see pp. 102–5)

Overleaf: *Story of East End* by Beverley-Jane Stewart.

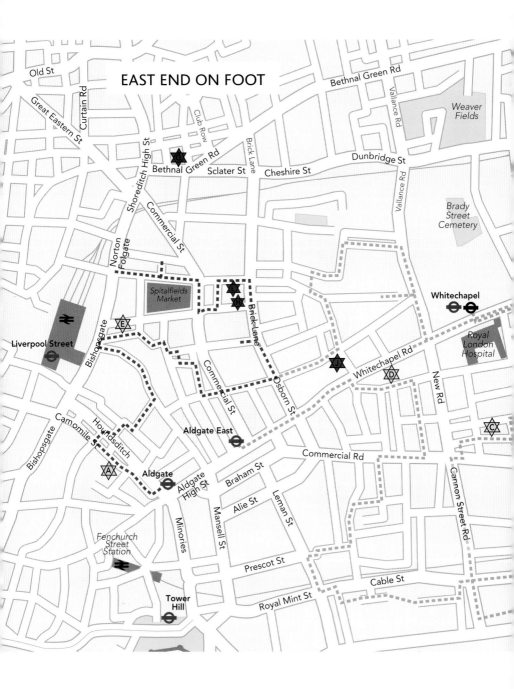

EAST END ON FOOT

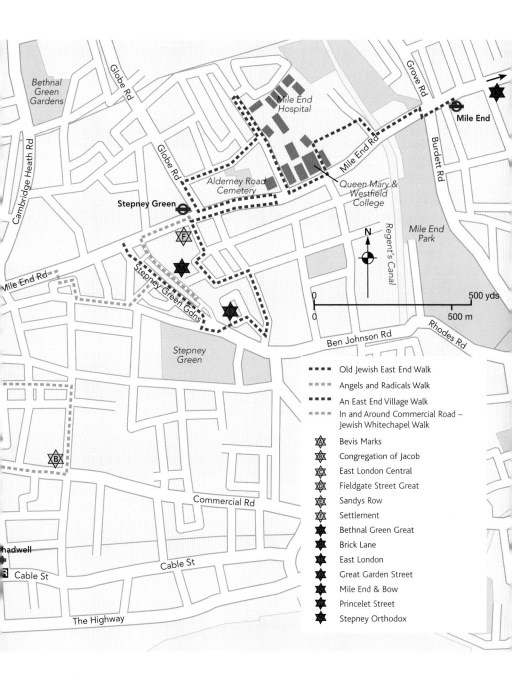

Bethnal
Green
Gardens

Globe Rd

Globe Rd

Cambridge Heath Rd

Mile End
Hospital

Alderney Road
Cemetery

Stepney Green

Stepney Green Gdns

Mile End Rd

Stepney
Green

Mile End Rd

Grove Rd

Mile End

Burdett Rd

Queen Mary &
Westfield
College

Regent's Canal

Mile End
Park

N

0
0

500 yds
500 m

Ben Johnson Rd

Rhodes Rd

Commercial Rd

hadwell

Cable St

Cable St

The Highway

Old Jewish East End Walk
Angels and Radicals Walk
An East End Village Walk
In and Around Commercial Road –
Jewish Whitechapel Walk

Bevis Marks
Congregation of Jacob
East London Central
Fieldgate Street Great
Sandys Row
Settlement
Bethnal Green Great
Brick Lane
East London
Great Garden Street
Mile End & Bow
Princelet Street
Stepney Orthodox

17

EAST END: OLD JEWISH EAST END WALK

This is the 'classic' old Jewish East End tour. Although the Jewish community may no longer live in Spitalfields, the streets and buildings still evoke memories of the synagogues, schools, shops and soup kitchens; not forgetting the street markets and the other immigrant communities who made this area their home.

▶ **START:** Aldgate tube (Circle, Metropolitan)

▶ **FINISH:** Spitalfields Market (near Liverpool Street station – Central, Circle, Metropolitan, Overground)

▶ **DISTANCE:** 3.6km (2¼ miles)

▶ **DURATION:** 1½–2 hours (allow longer if you want to browse the food shops on Brick Lane or visit Bevis Marks and/or Sandys Row synagogues)

▶ **REFRESHMENTS:** Androuet (*107b Commercial Street, E1 6BG;* ☎ *020 7375 3168; www.androuet.co.uk*) Specialist cheese and salads; **Leon** (*3 Crispin Place, E1 6DW;* ☎ *020 7247 4369, www.leonrestaurants.co.uk*) Budget organic food; Or one of the many **Bengali restaurants** on Brick Lane

🚶 On leaving Aldgate station, turn right and walk a few yards to the **Church of St Botolph Without Aldgate**. ❶ Enter the churchyard and walk up a couple of steps.

The church, named after the patron saint of travellers, St Botolph, was built in the 1740s outside Aldgate, one of the seven gates in the second-century Roman wall surrounding the City of London. The plaque indicating the original position of the gate is near the corner of Aldgate and Jewry Street, so named to remember the pre-Expulsion Jewish community.

In the right-hand corner of the churchyard is a bronze-like sculpture of a crouching figure below a curved canopy. Called *Sanctuary* ❶A by Naomi Blake, it evokes the feeling of both being in need and protected (see p. 129).

🚶 Retrace your steps and turn right out of the gateway of the churchyard. Pause by the **Mocatta Drinking Fountain**. ❶B

In 1859 Samuel Gurney, a wealthy Quaker banker, established the Metropolitan Drinking Fountain Association to make a safe drinking supply available via a series of fountains issuing filtered water, complete with chained cup. Many of the fountains were funded in memory of eminent people. This one commemorates **Frederick David Mocatta** (1828–1905).

The Mocattas were one of the first Sephardi families to move to London following the Resettlement, establishing Mocatta & Co. in 1671. The company dominated the gold bullion trade. Frederick David Mocatta retired aged 46, devoting the rest of his life to philanthropy, including education, housing and administration of the Jewish community. His book collection was given to University College London where it was named the Mocatta Library (now the Jewish Studies Library). When there were calls for the immigrants from Eastern Europe in the late 19th century to be barred from entry to Britain he fought on their behalf pleading, '*It is not for us as Englishmen to try and close the entrance into our country to any of our fellow creatures especially such as are*

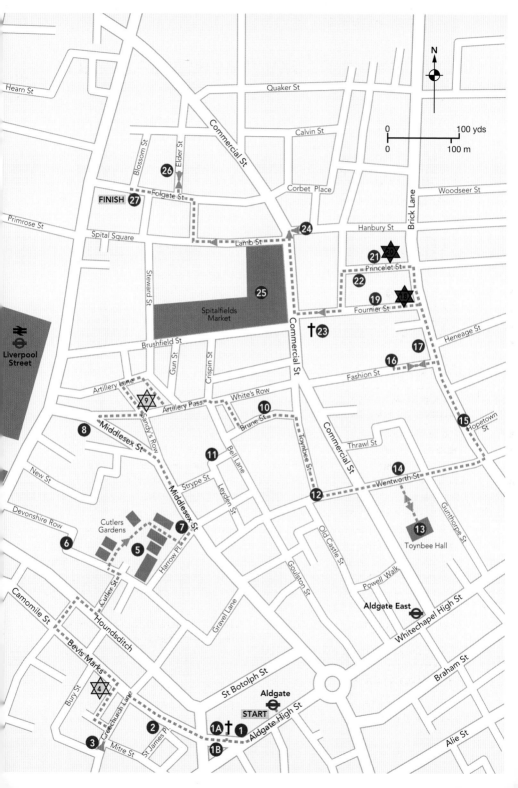

Mocatta Drinking Fountain.

oppressed. It is not for us as Jews to try and bar our gates against other Jews who are persecuted solely for professing the same religion as ourselves.' Ironically, he died in 1905, the year of the Aliens Act, which brought in measures to reduce immigration.

🚶 Cross the main road towards **Bevis Marks**. You will see Sir John Cass School. Turn right and continue to a large stone wall and look up. You will see a plaque to the **Great Synagogue, Duke's Place**. ❷

Today, modern office blocks predominate, but in the days of early Resettlement 'Duke's Place' was used as a euphemism for the Jewish area of London. By 1714 around 25 per cent of the area was Jewish. Over 11 per cent of them worked in the local citrus market.

The Ashkenazi community established its first synagogue in 1690 in rented rooms at Duke's Place. A purpose-built synagogue constructed in the 1720s was rebuilt in 1790 as a vast cathedral-like synagogue and, situated in a gated courtyard, had large plain glass windows on three levels. Membership included families such as the Rothschilds, and in 1809 three sons of King George III attended

a Sabbath morning service as guests of the Goldschmids. There could be up to five bar mitzvahs on the same Sabbath morning and on Sundays there were queues of brides awaiting their weddings. During the Blitz of WWII it was badly damaged and despite plans for rebuilding, the much-reduced community instead rented rooms in the Hambro Synagogue, Adler Street (see pp. 87–8). The synagogue officially closed in 1977.

🚶 Continue down Bevis Marks and turn left into **Creechurch Lane**. Continue until the junction of Bury Street and you will see **a plaque to the first synagogue established after the Resettlement**. ❸

By the end of 1656, the Sephardi community had acquired premises for use as a synagogue. Enlarged in 1674, it was used until new premises were built nearby in Bevis Marks. The 17th-century English diarist Samuel Pepys visited the synagogue on 14 October 1663 and his diary entry includes:
Thence home and after dinner my wife and I, ... to the Jewish Synagogue: ... Their service all in a singing way, and in Hebrew. ... But, Lord! To see the disorder, laughing, sporting, and no attention, but confusion in all their service, more like brutes than people knowing the true God, ... and indeed I never did see so much, or could have

Plaque to first synagogue following Resettlement.

imagined there had been any religion in the whole world so absurdly performed as this ...

He visited during Simchat Torah (Rejoicing of the Law) and would not have known such behaviour was unusual in a synagogue.

🚶 Retrace your steps down Creechurch Lane and turn left into Heneage Lane. At the end turn left into Bevis Marks. Continue until you see a pair of large gates on your left leading to the courtyard of **Bevis Marks Synagogue** ❹ and Restaurant. During opening hours, enter through the gates to visit the interior. If the gates are shut there is a good view of the exterior. (See pp. 22–3.) On leaving, turn left into Bevis Marks. At the next junction, turn right at the traffic lights down St Mary Axe and cross Houndsditch. Turn right and then turn left into Cutler Street and stand in front of the tall warehouses.

Cutlers Gardens ❺ was originally a complex of warehouses built between 1771 and 1820 for the East India Company. Plain high walls protected valuable goods such as coffee, cotton and spices. Following the closure of the docks in the late 1960s, the warehouses were converted into offices and restaurants. From the early 18th century several small markets developed around Cutler Street, many dominated by Jewish traders. By 1850 over 50 per cent of ostrich feather trade and the military stores market were in Jewish hands and they also dominated the local diamond trade.

Beyond Cutlers Gardens you will see **Devonshire Square** ❻. In 1859, the **Jewish Board of Guardians** was established at No. 13 'to attend to the relief of the strange and foreign poor'. The Board worked tirelessly to improve sanitation, prevent disease and promote self-sufficiency. Between 1869 and 1882 around 2,000 cases were dealt with annually. Between 1896 and 1956 it operated from nearby Middlesex Street and was renamed the Jewish Welfare Board in 1964. In 1990, having merged with the Jewish Blind Society (established 1819), it became known as Jewish Care, caring for over 5,000 members of the Jewish community. In 1982 the headquarters moved to Golders Green.

🚶 If open, walk through Cutlers Gardens, turning first right, passing through a small gateway and turning left into Harrow Place. If Cutlers Gardens is shut, continue down Cutler Street turning left into Harrow Place. Pause on the corner of **Middlesex Street**.

The famous **Petticoat Lane street market** ❼ is here every Sunday. Well established by the 1750s, you won't find the name on a map as the street was renamed Middlesex Street in 1830 to acknowledge the boundary between the City of London and the County of Middlesex. By the 1850s most of the goods

Cutlers Gardens looking towards Devonshire Square.

21

BEVIS MARKS SYNAGOGUE

Completed in 1701, Bevis Marks is the oldest operating synagogue in the UK. Its plain exterior and large, clear windows are both characteristics of Sir Christopher Wren's church architecture, and the architect, Joseph Avis, a Quaker, would have avoided ostentation. Above the central doorway are both the secular and Hebrew dates of opening, 1701/5462.

Step inside to see the wonderfully inviting interior, reminiscent of the Portuguese Great Synagogue of Amsterdam. The pews date from 1701 and there are original wooden benches from the Creechurch Lane Synagogue. Most striking are the seven brass chandeliers, lit by candle. It is believed that the largest was donated by the Amsterdam Sephardi community. Candle-lit services are still held for High Holy Days and special occasions. The large windows and chandeliers provided much needed light in the days before electricity. To the east, there is the Ark in a wooden cabinet resembling a church reredos. In front of the Tevah (Bimah) there is a grand chair for the Haham, the senior rabbi for the Sephardi community. To the side there are boxed and canopied pews for the wardens, unusual in English synagogues. Also visible are 10 large brass candlesticks and 12 pillars resembling marble, which are actually painted wood.

In front of the Ark there is a chair with a rope across it. This was the seat of **Moses Montefiore** (1784–1885), the congregation's most famous worshipper and only members of the Montefiore family, with rare exceptions, may use it. Montefiore made his fortune on the stock exchange. He retired in 1824 and devoted the rest of his life to philanthropic, communal and civic duties. His marriage to Judith Barent-Cohen in 1812 was groundbreaking as she was Ashkenazi. They were a pious devoted couple, with a home in Park Lane, Mayfair and a country estate in Ramsgate where they are buried (see pp. 211–13).

Another famous congregant was the young **Benjamin Disraeli** (1804–81), son

Exterior of Bevis Marks Synagogue.

Interior of Bevis Marks Synagogue.

of writer Isaac D'Israeli. However, following a disagreement between his father and the community, Isaac took his family in 1817, the year that would have been Benjamin's bar mitzvah, to the Church of St Andrew Holborn where the children were baptized as Christians. This changed Benjamin's life (see pp. 76–9).

Climb the stairs to the ladies' gallery for a wonderful view of the interior. There are also painted boards listing previous presidents and wardens – many of the names remain in the community today such as Sassoon, Sebag and Montefiore. There is also a collection of beautiful mantle covers for the Torah scrolls. One is made from the silk of the wedding dress of Judith Barent-Cohen when she married Moses Montefiore.

There are still regular services at Bevis Marks (see pp. 198–9). A new extension houses a kosher restaurant (see p. 198).

sold were second-hand clothes. Cheap, mass-produced clothes predominated by the late 19th century, when the market was 95–100 per cent Jewish. On weekdays it sold general household goods. However, the Sunday market was unregulated and did not trade officially until 1936. In its heyday, the traders' sales banter was like street theatre. The Sunday market covers an area embracing Middlesex Street, Cobb Street and Wentworth Street. Get there early, it begins to close down around 2pm.

🯅 After browsing the stalls (if the market is open), continue up **Middlesex Street**, and stop outside the Shooting Star pub. A plaque to the **Jewish Board of Guardians ❽** indicates its second home after leaving Devonshire Square. Turn right into **Widegate Street**. At **No. 31** see reliefs of bakers at work – a reminder of when the premises were once used by Levy Bros, matzah-makers established in 1710.

Sandys Row Synagogue. Photo Jeremy Freedman.

Continue, then at the junction turn left into **Sandys Row**. Stop in front of **Sandys Row Synagogue ❾** on your right.

Founded in 1854 by economic migrants from Holland, this is London's oldest Ashkenazi community. It is still functioning while almost all the other East London synagogues have closed (see pp. 56–60).

🯅 Continue to the end of Sandys Row. Turn right into **Artillery Lane** and turn right into **Parliament Passage**. Turn left into **Artillery Passage**, a narrow 17th-century alleyway, lined with cafés and shops. The hanging signs give an air of 'ye olde England'. Exiting the alley into **Artillery Lane**, see **Providence Row**, on the left. Now student accommodation, the original building was established in 1866 as a refuge run by Catholic nuns. **Raven Row Gallery**, with shopfronts dating from the 1750s, is to your right at No. 56. Cross **Bell Lane**, turn right into **Tenterground**, where early Flemish immigrants set their cloth out to dry, pulled taut over tenter pegs. Hence the phrase 'to be on tenterhooks' when feeling tense. Turn left into **Brune Street**. Stop opposite the **Soup Kitchen for the Jewish Poor**. ❿

Previous premises were in Leman Street – where it was founded in 1854, Black Lion Yard and Fashion Street. The terracotta facia displays the secular and Hebrew year of building, 1902/5662. For Jewish immigrants who spoke only Yiddish, the relief of a steaming tureen of soup over the door indicates its purpose. Post WWII, the kitchen also provided a meals-on-wheels service to the elderly and infirm and finally closed in 1990. The premises have been converted for residential and commercial use. On the wall

Jewish Soup Kitchen.

🚶 Continue down **Brune Street**. Turn right into **Toynbee Street**. Stop on the corner of **Wentworth Street**. ⑫

Wentworth Street remains part of the Petticoat Lane market complex and is open on weekdays. At the height of the Jewish East End it was also full of delis, kosher butchers (there were 15 in 1901), bakeries, costumiers and furriers, many remaining beyond the 1960s. The business names live on in the collective memory of London Jewry: Mossy Marks's deli with Mr Mendel, the salmon cutter; Ostwinds the bakers, Bonn's and Goide's, both caterers; Shapiro Valentine, booksellers; and Bloom's sausage factory.

opposite the Soup Kitchen colourful panels celebrate the past Jewish and the current Bengali communities. Included are receipts for donations to the Soup Kitchen and extracts from Yiddish songs and Yiddish newspapers.

🚶 Facing the Soup Kitchen, to your left you will see a tall, blue, glass building. This was the site of the **Jews' Free School**. ⑪

Developed from the Talmud Torah established by the Great Synagogue Duke's Place in 1732, a new school opened in 1820 on Bell Lane. It was largely funded by the Rothschilds, who also provided 'suits and boots', spectacles and regular practical assistance such as teaching. By the early 1900s the school had become the largest in Europe, with over 4,000 pupils. Famous alumni include the writer Israel Zangwill, Professor Selig Brodetsky and the founder of De Beers, Barney Barnato. Most of the school was evacuated to Ely during WWII but did not return here. Re-established at Camden Town in 1958, it moved to North-west London in 2002, with the uniform still in the Rothschild family colours of deep blue and gold. (See *www.jfsalumni. com/history.*)

🚶 Turn left and cross Commercial Street. Turn right into the gateway with the black-and-white 'Tree of Life' sign. This leads to **Toynbee Hall**. ⑬ Walk through to the courtyard. (Note: this gate is sometimes locked.)

Opened in 1884 by Samuel and Henrietta Barnett, Toynbee Hall provided much needed resources to the predominantly Jewish local community. Classes including English, art and dressmaking were provided alongside free legal aid, country holiday funds and a toy library. Oxford University students were social workers living on site, hence it became known as a settlement. It was home to the world's first Jewish Scout troop and they donated the small clock tower as a 'thank you'. For over 75 years, until 2011, the Friends of Yiddish met here every Saturday afternoon. During WWII the Jewish market traders donated food and clothes to the distribution depot at Toynbee Hall and a plaque to Jimmy Mallon, a much-loved warden, can be seen. Toynbee Hall continues as a settlement in addition to social welfare activities. It was named after Arnold Toynbee, a

Charlotte de Rothschild Dwellings arch.

Charlotte de Rothschild Dwellings by John Allin.

noted historian at Oxford and a friend of the Barnetts who died young, a year before Toynbee Hall opened. In 1892 the Barnetts opened the Whitechapel Library and in 1902, the Whitechapel Art Gallery (see pp. 47–8).

🚶 Retrace your steps and leave Toynbee Hall. Cross Wentworth Street and stop at the **red brick arch**. ⓮

The arch with the inscription 'Erected by the Four Per Cent Industrial Dwellings Company – 1886' is all that remains of the first tenement block funded by Lord Nathaniel Rothschild's housing initiative, named after the financial return on the investment. The block was called **Charlotte de Rothschild Dwellings** in memory of his mother and the first residents arrived in 1887. They were mainly, but not exclusively, Jewish. Built in plain yellow stock brick around a courtyard, the six-storey blocks were forbidding, and known locally as 'The Buildings'. There was running water on all floors and the rent was affordable. An immediate success, they were quickly followed by the Brady (1890), Nathaniel (1892) and Stepney Green Dwellings (1896). By 1901, 4,600 people were housed in 'Four Per Cent' dwellings. Of the original four blocks only Stepney Green Dwellings (now Court) survives on its original site (see p. 55). By the 1960s 'The Buildings' were in a bad state of repair and were demolished in 1976. They were replaced by the current social housing in 1984. Read the full story in Jerry White's *Rothschild Buildings*.

🚶 Continue down Wentworth Street and turn left on to **Brick Lane**. ⓯ Stop by the arch.

Named after bricks originally made in the area, Brick Lane has for centuries been the backbone of immigrant communities. Erected in 1997 and painted in the colours of the Bangladeshi flag, the arch indicates you are now in 'Banglatown'. Note the street signs in English and Bengali. Where you see Bengali shops and businesses, imagine when the street was almost entirely Jewish in character. Nicknamed the 'Bond Street of the East End', by the 1930s Brick Lane contained gown-makers, corset-makers, hosiers, boot and shoe dealers, milliners, tailors, trimming merchants

Brick Lane.

and mantle-makers. Food establishments included Bloom's at Nos. 2 and 58 and the 'bagel ladies', Esther and Annie, selling their wares straight from the sack.

🚶 Continue down Brick Lane. On the right, opposite the junction with Fashion Street, No. 54 is **Epra Fabrics**, the last remaining Jewish textile business, here from 1956 and still run

by the Epstein family. Turn left into **Fashion Street.** ⑯

Fashion Street has an ornate fascia, reminiscent of a Moorish bazaar, along its east side. This was the initiative, in 1905, of Abraham Davis, who wanted to provide a dry and warm shopping environment for the local street vendors. However, they preferred the outdoor life and the buildings reverted to wholesale, remaining as such until the recent renovation.

Fashion Street was home to two important Anglo-Jewish writers. **Israel Zangwill** (1864–1926) in his 1892 best-seller, *Children of the Ghetto*, vividly brings to life the Jewish East End of the late 19th century – the people, the festivals, the life cycle and the food. Zangwill was also a staunch supporter of womens' rights (see also p. 205). **Arnold Wesker** (b.1932), lived as a boy at No. 43 in the 1930s. Like Zangwill, he also wrote about the immigrant experience in his late 1950s trilogy of plays *Chicken Soup with Barley, I'm Talking About Jerusalem* and *Roots. Chicken*

Fashion Street.

Soup with Barley, in particular, emotionally portrays life in the East End, exposing unrealized hopes and aspirations. His prolific output is often linked to political ideals. He was instrumental in establishing Centre 42, in 1964, putting into practice the trade union desire for access for all to arts and culture. (See also p. 205).

🚶 Retrace your steps. Turn left into Brick Lane. Pass **Christ Church School** ⓱, rebuilt in 1873 with a drinking fountain in the wall. On the pavement is a replica manhole cover depicting crayons, one of several installed by the local council relating to cultural and social heritage. You will see more on the

tour. Look up to see a drainpipe with a **Star of David**, a delightful memory of the Jewish community.

Stop on the corner opposite **Brick Lane Jamme Masjid (Mosque)**. ⓲

This building captures the essence of the changing communities in Brick Lane. Look up and you will see a sundial dated 1743 with the inscription 'Umbra Sumus' ('We are shadows'). It was built as a chapel for the French Huguenots (Protestants), who arrived fleeing persecution following the Revocation of the Edict of Nantes in 1685. After they moved west to Soho, the chapel was used from 1809 to 1819 by the London Society for Promoting Christianity Amongst the Jews. Unsuccessful, the society moved on and Methodists took over the building in 1819. In 1898 it became the Spitalfields Great Synagogue for the ultra-orthodox Machzikei Haddas ve Shomrei Shabbat (Strengtheners of the Law and Guardians of the Sabbath) congregation. With services almost around the clock, the congregation was renowned for its piety and strict adherence to orthodoxy. There was a Talmud Torah school next door on Brick Lane attended by over 500 boys. By 1970, the congregation had dwindled and the building became a mosque. No evidence remains of the synagogue but across the street, Stars of David are depicted in the fencing of Bangla City.

🚶 Turn left into **Fournier Street** ⓳ and stop halfway down.

Built in the 1720s, these were homes for French Huguenots. With many working in the silk industry, the attic windows along the width of the houses, replicated at the back, formed large, light rooms for the silk looms. The detailing of the doorways and shutters is wonderful. Irish residents followed the French

Brick Lane Mosque.

Spitalfields' houses.

and in the late 19th century the Jewish community moved in. In each house several families could have been trying to eke out a living from the sweated tailoring trade. Post WWII, the businesses were mostly fur and leather. Following their closure, impoverished artists needing large but cheap light-filled studios arrived. No. 14, Howard House, dating from 1726, has an elaborate porch. Look also for the bobbin dangling between two windows on the first floor. One of several hung in 1985 by the council on houses known to have been lived in by a Huguenot family, it commemorates the 300th anniversary of the Revocation of the Edict of Nantes. No. 27 is one of the largest houses in Spitalfields. Between 1829 and the 1940s it was owned by the London Dispensary, becoming a garment factory until 1977. No. 29 was used

CH N. Katz.

as a synagogue. See the name sign of S. Schwarz at No. 33a.

🚶 Retrace your steps to Brick Lane.

Opposite the junction with Fournier Street was Schewzik's, the Russian Vapour Baths, named after the reverend who ran it. The busiest day was Friday for the men's pre-Sabbath bathe.

🚶 Turn left into Brick Lane.

At No. 92 was **CH N. Katz**, which sold paper bags and string. It survived until the 1990s and the incoming art gallery has preserved the fascia.

🚶 Continue down Brick Lane and at Princelet Street look north and see **Truman's Brewery**. Opened in 1669 and brewing until the 1970s, the site is now a complex of galleries and cafés. Beyond, on a Sunday, you will find Brick Lane street market and an array of designer-makers and food outlets. Towards the top of Brick Lane at No. 159 is the **24 Hour Beigel Bake** (see p. 173). Turn left into Princelet Street (previously Princes Street) and stop opposite **No. 19**. ⑳ See p. 31.

Next door, **No. 17 Princelet Street** has a plaque to **Miriam Moses** ㉑ (1886–1965) who was born here. She became the first female mayor of Stepney in 1931 and the UK's first Jewish

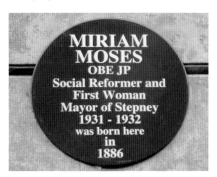

Miriam Moses, birthplace.

female mayor. She is most fondly remembered, however, for founding Stepney Jewish Girls' Club in the mid-1920s (see pp. 34 and 38).

🚶 Continue up the road and stand outside **No. 6** ㉒, built in 1928. On the pavement you will see another manhole cover, depicting a violin.

The first purpose-built Yiddish theatre in London was established here. In 1883 Jacob Adler, a Yiddish actor, fled Russia for London. He established the **Hebrew Dramatic Club**, which performed in rented rooms but he wanted a permanent home. With funding from a local butcher his new theatre opened in 1886. It seated 500 and included a bar and reading room. It was successful but only until January 1887. During a sell-out performance, someone yelled 'fire' and in the haste to escape 17 people lost their lives; but there was no fire. Adler moved to New York, but often returned to London to perform in the Yiddish theatre.

🚶 Continue to **No. 2** on the corner. On the first floor of this beautifully renovated house you will see a plaque to Anna Maria Garthwaite, an important silk designer of the 1700s. At **No. 4** the exterior looks poorly maintained but is left deliberately like that for use by film-makers needing a decrepit Dickensian house.

Turn left into Wilkes Street to see a last vestige of the 'schmatte' trade, the wall sign for **H Suskin, Trimming Merchants**. At one time, almost every building would have proclaimed a business, together with vacancy boards alongside the doorways.

Turn right into Fournier Street. Stop at **Christ Church Spitalfields**. ㉓

Designed by Nicholas Hawksmoor and consecrated in 1726, Christ Church dominates the skyline with its 68.5m (225ft) steeple. It was underused, as immigrant communities built their own places of worship and following damage during WWII, it was derelict by the 1960s. It would have been demolished but for a successful campaign to save it. If open, do go inside. The restored interior is magnificent. In the vestibule are some interesting wall memorials pertaining to the work of the mission dedicated to converting Jews to Christianity, relocated from the Episcopal Chapel, Bethnal Green.

🚶 Turn right into Commercial Street then turn right into Hanbury Street. Stop outside **No. 12, Rosa's Café**. ㉔

A plaque indicates the birthplace of **Bud Flanagan** (1896–1968), born Chaim Reuben Weintrop. He was a popular entertainer, naming himself after his bully of a sergeant during WWI. Teaming up with Chesney Allen

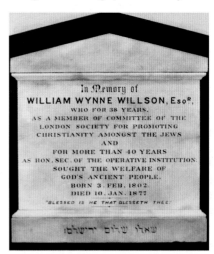

London Society for Promoting Christianity Amongst the Jews, memorial stone in Christ Church.

19 PRINCELET STREET

No. 19, built in 1718, is believed to be the oldest house in the street. It was originally home to a Huguenot family, the Ogiers, hence the bobbin above the door. In 1869, a synagogue was built over the back garden for the Loyal United Friends Friendly Society, linked to a small and poor Jewish community. Long and narrow, with a ladies' gallery on the first floor, it has delicately coloured tinted glass in the skylight. It was typical of the many small Orthodox synagogues relying on donations from wealthy patrons. They held cheap or free marriage ceremonies for those who could not afford the United Synagogue fee. Remaining until 1963, the community merged with Bethnal Green Synagogue. A caretaker lived on site and a reclusive young man, David Rodinsky, lived in the attic.

It became a forgotten building until 1983 when the Spitalfields Housing Trust bought it and No. 17 next door. The new owners were astonished when entering for the first time. The synagogue was still intact though very much decayed and upstairs the attic was full of books, papers, gramophone records and atlases, a table set for dinner and an unmade bed, but there was no David Rodinsky. The mystery of why Rodinsky seemed to have vanished has entered Spitalfields folklore. He died in 1969, aged 44, at the Long Grove asylum in Surrey. Read more in *Rodinsky's Room* by Rachel Lichtenstein and Iain Sinclair. Today the building is owned by a trust and called the Museum of Immigration. It is open by appointment only and during special events. See *www.19princeletstreet. org.uk* for open days.

Top: Princelet Street Synagogue, interior.
Above: 19 Princelet Street today.

32 Elder Street.

gabled buildings with green paintwork date from the 1880s when Robert Horner, formerly a market worker, redeveloped the site. The market traded here until 1991, when it relocated to Temple Mills. Today there is a vibrant mix of offices, retailers and restaurants together with a varied selection of markets that come alive on a Sunday. On Brushfield Street, some of the earlier houses remain.

The recent market refurbishment included eight gates named after people or events associated with the area. Montagu Gate honours banker Sir Samuel Montagu, MP for Whitechapel from 1890 to 1905 and founder of the Federation of Minor Synagogues in 1887.

🚶 Walk down **Lamb Street**. Turn right into **Nantes Passage**, then left into **Folgate Street** and right into **Elder Street**. Stop outside **No. 32**. ㉖

The blue plaque indicates the home of **Mark Gertler** (1891–1939) (see pp. 48, 134, 151), a talented East End artist who was given patronage by the Bloomsbury Group (see p. 134).

from 1926, they became members of the 1930s Crazy Gang. His trademark costume was an oversize shabby fur coat and battered boater and hit songs included 'Underneath the Arches' and 'Run Rabbit Run'. In 1968 he gained a new audience, singing the theme tune to the TV series *Dad's Army*.

🚶 Retrace your steps. Look across Commercial Street to **Old Spitalfields Market**. ㉕

Established in 1682, Spitalfields was a wholesale fruit and vegetable market. The

🚶 Retrace your steps to Folgate Street, turn right and stop opposite No. 18.

This is **Dennis Severs' House** ㉗ (*18 Folgate Street E1 6BX;* ☎ *020 7247 4013; www. dennissevershouse.co.uk; see website for opening times & booking info; adm. fee*), named after the American who relocated to London and created a time capsule in his home with rooms representing the different generations of an imaginary family, the Gervais. Open to the public, it is more of a theatrical experience than a museum.

🚶 The tour ends here.

EAST END: ANGELS AND RADICALS WALK

Walking the lesser-known area east of Brick Lane uncovers the stories of radicals, revolutionaries and those who devoted their lives to improving the working and living conditions of the Jewish East End.

▶ **START:** Stepney Green tube (District, Hammersmith & City)

▶ **FINISH:** Brick Lane (southern end) (near Aldgate East tube station – District, Hammersmith & City)

▶ **DISTANCE:** 3.8km (2⅓ miles)

▶ **DURATION:** 1 hour

▶ **REFRESHMENTS: Poppies** (*6–8 Hanbury Street, E1 6QR;* ☎ *020 7247 0892; www.poppiesfishandchips.co.uk*) Traditional fish and chips, eat in or take away; one of the many eateries in Spitalfields Market; one of the **Bengali restaurants** on Brick Lane; **Whitechapel Art Gallery Café** (see p. 40)

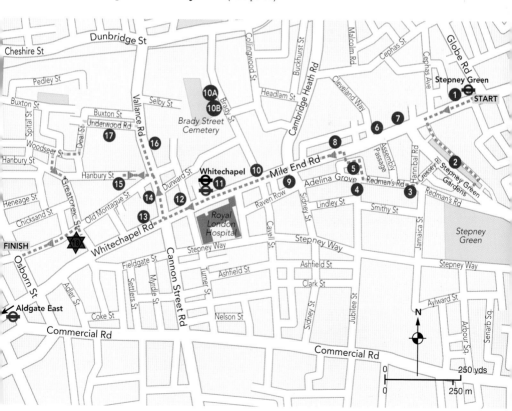

🚶 Exit Stepney Green tube station, turn right and walk along the Mile End Road, passing a white stone building, the old **Stepney Public Baths**. ❶

Opened in 1932 by Miriam Moses, then mayor of Stepney (see pp. 29 and 30), they are now used by the HIV charity, THT.

🚶 Continue and pause outside two large houses, **Nos 133–35 Mile End Road**.

Built in 1740, Malpaquet House is on the right. By the 1990s it was in a ruinous state but renovated by the current owners, it serves as a reminder of when this area was 'Millionaires' Row'.

Dunstan House, Stepney Green.

🚶 Cross Mile End Road and go down Hayfields Passage, named after the Whitechapel hay market held between 1708 and 1928. You will enter **Stepney Green Gardens** (see pp. 54–5 for details of sites). ❷

Turn right into **Cressy Place**, passing Cressy House. Cross a small roundabout and continue into **Redmans Road**. ❸

Redmans Road Talmud Torah School operated from the Redmans Road Synagogue from 1901 until 1961. The headmaster was Rev. J. K. Goldblum, who pioneered learning Ivrit b'Ivrit (Hebrew in Hebrew). English was forbidden! Classes were held every evening Monday to Thursday and Sunday afternoons. This was on top of the students' five-days-a-week general schooling.

🚶 Continue and stop opposite the corner of **Jubilee Street**. ❹

In 1902, a federation of Jewish anarchist clubs was formed with its headquarters established in 1906 at No. 165 Jubilee Street (demolished). Named the **Arbeiter Freund (Workers'**

Friend) Club and Institute, Rudolph Rocker was its leader (see also pp. 55, 66). Supported by leading anarchists such as Malatesta and Kropotkin, it became central to social, trade union and intellectual activities. During WWI Rocker was interned as an enemy alien and subsequently deported. The Jewish anarchist movement never fully recovered and most of its members became Zionists or communists. Rocker returned to Germany and died in the USA.

🚶 Turn into **O'Leary Square**. On your right is **Rinkoff Bakery**. ❺

Established in 1911 by Russian immigrants, Rinkoff still makes traditional Jewish bread, challot and bagels. Although it is a wholesale business, you can buy bagels here and at No. 79 Vallance Road, a few minutes walk away.

🚶 Turn left on to **Mile End Road**. Stop and look to your right at the large Portland stone building with a tower. ❻

This was **Wickhams** department store, built in 1928 and nicknamed the 'Harrods of the East End'. Mr Wickham ideally needed to purchase all the shops on the block but one shopkeeper,

Mr Spiegelhalter, a German jeweller at No. 81, would not sell. You will see a dip in the building where it, and later Carmel wine merchants, traded. Wickhams closed in the 1960s but a Spiegelhalter is still trading in the west of England. Today the building has been refurbished as shops, offices and a party venue.

To the right of Wickhams is the **Genesis Cinema**. ❼ Established as Lusby's Musical Hall and later renamed the Paragon Theatre of Varieties, the young Charlie Chaplin performed here and also Louis Winogradsky (Lord Grade). After converting to a cinema it was owned for a while by the Bernstein family, who later founded the Granada chain. Renamed the ABC in 1963, it became an independent cinema in 1999.

Wickhams Department Store.

🚶 Cross the road, turn left and stop by the statue of **William Booth**. In 1865 he began preaching here for the salvation of the underclass. From his first East End Mission, he founded the Salvation Army in 1868, now a global organization.

SIDNEY STREET SIEGE

Following a bungled burglary on 16 December 1910 at Exchange Buildings, Houndsditch, when three policemen were killed, the burglars took flight. They were believed to be Eastern European anarchists as such a crime could not be 'English'. One assailant had been shot during the gunfight and later died in their hideout in Grove Street, where radical literature found seemed to confirm the burglars' anarchist origins. Despite a wide search they were not found but in January 1911 were recognized by a Mrs Gershon, who rented a room to them at No. 100 Sidney Street. On 3 January 1911, surrounded by police and the Scots Guard, and with the Horse Artillery on alert, the siege began. Winston Churchill, then Home Secretary, watched, in top hat and fur-collared overcoat, together with hundreds of locals. Shots rang out, the building went up in smoke and two bodies were subsequently found. Peter Piatkov (known as Peter the Painter), a famous anarchist, was expected to be a third victim but he seemingly disappeared and speculation continues regarding the full story. Professor William Fishman tells the definitive version in his book *East End Jewish Radicals 1875–1914*.

Memories of the Sidney Street Siege.

Trinity Green.

Turn left and continue. Through a wooden gate, on your right, you will see a set of almshouses and a chapel set around a communal lawn. **8**

This is **Trinity Green**, originally built in 1695 as almshouses by Trinity House 'for decayed masters and commanders of ships and widows thereof'. Trinity House was founded in 1514 to administer the coastline and lighthouses around Great Britain. See the ships above the gateways.

🚶 Continue and stop on the corner of **Cambridge Heath Road**. Across the road is **Sidney Street**, site of the Sidney Street Siege (see p. 35). **9**

Continue and stop on the corner of **Brady Street**. **10** There is no need to turn right unless you have arranged a visit to **Brady Street Cemetery**, which is on the left-hand side (see p. 156). **10**A

Brady Street was also home to two of the Four Per Cent Company housing blocks (see pp. 26 and 146). Brady Street Dwellings, built in 1890 were demolished in the 1970s but **Mocatta House 10**B, a small block of flats named after David Mocatta and built in 1905 remains. Sainsbury's is on the site of the Mann, Crossman & Paulin Albion brewery.

🚶 Continue along **Whitechapel Road** to Whitechapel tube station. **11**

Opposite is the **Royal London Hospital**. A little further along is the **drinking fountain** erected in 1911 to honour King Edward VII and funded by the local Jewish community. For more details of both, see p. 40.

🚶 Continue down **Whitechapel Road**. Stop on the corner of **Fulbourne Street**. **12**

Premises here housed the **Jewish Socialist Club**, officially the International Workers' Education Association. This was one of numerous socialist groups in the Jewish East End including the Hebrew Socialist Union, the Social Democrats, the General Jewish Workers' Union known as 'The Bund', the Workers' Circle and the Jewish Anarchist Club. In 1907 Lenin, Stalin and Trotsky all attended meetings at the Socialist Club for the fifth Congress of the Russian Social Democratic party. Stalin lodged for a time in Tower House on Fieldgate Street (see p. 46) and in digs at No. 75 Jubilee Street. Jewish trade unions also proliferated for a short while rising from 12 in 1896 to 32 by 1902. Ranging from trouser-makers to vest-makers it was the London Jewish Bakers Union that survived the longest, lasting to 1970.

🚶 Continue and cross **Vallance Road**. Stop in front of **Nos 191–193**

Whitechapel Road (a building site at time of writing). ⓭

This is the site of the **Pavilion Theatre**, a place of entertainment since 1828. It was vast, seating over 2,600 people, earning the nickname 'The Drury Lane of the East'. Yiddish theatre began as matinees in the 1890s and predominated between 1906 and 1935. Famous actor-managers working with the resident company included Sigmund Feinman, Maurice Moscovitch and Fanny Waxman. Productions ranged from Yiddish plays to classics and the audiences were noisy, appreciative but critical too, shouting from the gallery. It closed in 1935 and the Yiddish

theatre found a new home at the Grand Palais (see p. 43). The building was damaged in the Blitz, demolished in 1962 and, unusually for this regenerated area, the site has remained empty.

🚶 Turn around and turn left into **Vallance Road**. Stop opposite **Durward Street** (previously Buck Row). ⓮

In the distance is what was Buck Row School, now converted to apartments. The flat roof with railings was typical of London School Board buildings where lack of space at ground level necessitated playground facilities on the roof. The street was also home to the Brady

London Jewish Bakers Union banner.

Brady Centre, Hanbury Street.

This was opened in 1935 by the Duchess of York (later Queen Elizabeth), as purpose-built premises for Miriam Moses's Brady Girls' Club and Settlement (see also pp. 29–30). Established in 1925 at Buxton Street School, activities included dressmaking and elocution. Moses famously never left the East End during the Blitz and the club provided refuge for those who lost homes and family. The Boys' Club moved in post WWII and by the 1950s the centre offered a crèche and clubs for both youths and seniors. The Brady Club closed in 1976 and today the Brady Centre is home to a wide range of social facilities. Brady had a renaissance in the 1990s, with a new club opening in Edgware, North-west London.

Street Boys' Club for working lads. Established in 1896 and supported by the Rothschilds, the facilities at the clergy house of St Mary's (demolished) included boxing and debating. It was not specifically a Jewish club but the strong Jewish presence in the area led it to become so. From WWII, the boys shared the girls' Brady Centre on Hanbury Street.

🚶 Continue. Turn left at the pedestrianized area into **Hanbury Street**. Stop outside **No. 192, the Brady Centre**. ⓯

Miriam Moses.

🚶 Retrace your steps. Turn left into **Vallance Road**. Stop when you see the sign **Hughes Mansions** on a block of flats on the right-hand side. ⓰

Built in 1928, it is named after the social worker, Quaker, local councillor and magistrate, Mary Hughes. She lived opposite from 1926 to 1941, in a converted pub, renamed the Dew Drop Inn. Hughes Mansions revives memories of one of the most tragic events for the Jewish East End during WWII.

On 27 March 1945, the last V2 rocket fell on Central London, hitting the block of flats at 7am, when families were preparing for the day ahead, the eve of Passover. The flats were full of visiting relatives. Of the 134 people killed, 120 were Jewish and some families were completely destroyed. King George VI and Queen Elizabeth visited the site in May 1945.

🚶 Turn left into **Underwood Road**. Stop outside the brick buildings to the left (at time of writing, awaiting redevelopment). ⓱

This was the **Jewish Maternity Hospital**, opened in 1911. Founded by Alice Model (see

Hughes Mansions.

also p. 53) and funded by Jewish philanthropists, it provided maternity care, training facilities for midwives and an infant welfare centre. Extended in 1928, by the 1930s approximately 800 children a year were born here. It is remembered as Mother Levy's after the long-serving superintendent. After relocating to Stoke Newington it reopened as the Bearsted Memorial Hospital in 1947. This closed in 1974 amid protests and subsequently the site was redeveloped as social housing.

🚶 Continue. Turn left into **Deal Street**, passing Victoria and Albert Cottages erected in the 1850s and 1860s by the Metropolitan Association for Improving the Dwellings of the Industrious Poor. Turn right into **Woodseer Street** and then left into **Daplyn Street**. On the corner is **Vollasky House**, named in memory of a local Jewish alderman who lost his life at Hughes Mansions. Turn left at **Hanbury Street** and immediately right into **Greatorex Street**. Stop at **Nos 7–15**. ⓲

At one time in **Great Garden Street (now Greatorex Street)** almost every business and

home was a Jewish one. Within a few minutes walk, there were 12 synagogues including Dunk Street, the Beis Hamedrish Hagodol, the Djikever Shtiebel, Mile End New Town, the Chevra Shass and **Great Garden Street Synagogue** at Nos 7–15. This opened in 1896, closed around 1996 and is now used as a Business Development Centre. Ask to see the courtyard that displays wall plaques rescued from the synagogue. The synagogue was also the headquarters for the Federation until 1996 and for several years, home to the Kosher Luncheon Club.

🚶 Retrace your steps and turn left into **Old Montagu Street**. Continue until you reach **Brick Lane**. The junction was nicknamed **'Bloom's Corner'** when the restaurant moved here in the early 1930s before relocating to the High Street in 1952. The tour ends here. Turn right to reach restaurants and shops. Turn left for Whitechapel Road and Aldgate East tube station.

Mother Levy's.

EAST END: IN AND AROUND COMMERCIAL ROAD – JEWISH WHITECHAPEL WALK

Around Commercial Road you can still find reminders of the vibrant Jewish community who lived and worked there including the synagogues, street markets, medical missions and Yiddish theatre. You will also visit Cable Street, site of the battle against the fascists and home to the 'Angel of Cable Street', Hannah Billig.

▶ START: Whitechapel tube (District, Hammersmith & City, Overground)

▶ FINISH: Aldgate East tube (Circle, Metropolitan)

▶ DISTANCE: 5km (3 miles)

▶ DURATION: 1¾ hours (allow longer if you include a visit to the Whitechapel Art Gallery, Nelson Street Synagogue or Fieldgate Street Synagogue)

▶ REFRESHMENTS: Whitechapel Art Gallery Café (*77–82 Whitechapel High Street, E1 7QX;* ☎ *020 7522 7888; www.whitechapelgallery.org*) Perfect for a quick coffee, sandwich or cake; **Bengal Cuisine** (*12 Brick Lane, E1 6RF;* ☎ *020 7377 8405; www.bengalcuisine.net*) An excellent long-established Bengali restaurant; **Spitalfields Market** (see p. 18 for a selection of eateries)

🚶 **Whitechapel Road**, with its very wide pavements, was a social hub for the Jewish East End, perfect for the daytime market and Saturday evening promenades. On leaving the station turn right, walk alongside the Whitechapel Market (if open) and stop at the **drinking fountain. ❶**

Erected in 1911 and funded by the local Jewish community, this was a 'thank you' to King Edward VII for providing a refuge from persecution. There is a depiction of the king, and four delightful cherubs – one sewing a piece of cloth with the others holding a book, a ship and, a sign of modernity, a car.

Edward VII fountain.

🚶 Look across the road and see the **Royal London Hospital. ❷**

Founded in 1740 as the London Infirmary, it moved to Whitechapel in 1753. By 1837 it was providing kosher food and special visiting arrangements for Jewish patients. Jewish wards followed and by the late 19th century these facilities and more were ensured by the friendship between Lord Rothschild and Viscount Knutsford, the Chair of Governors. Wards and operating theatres

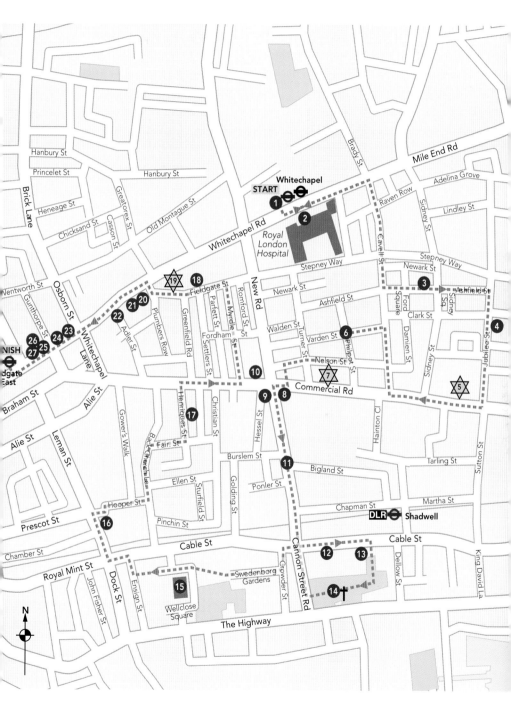

were funded by Jewish benefactors such as Bearsted and Levy. It was here that Joseph Merrick, 'The Elephant Man', was given refuge from 1886 until his death in 1890. The hospital is also home to the Helicopter Emergency Medical Service. Look up and you will see the helipad.

🚶 Retrace your steps to the crossing. Cross the road and turn left. Turn right into Cavell Street, named after the nurse Edith Cavell, who trained at the London Hospital. She later worked in Belgium and during WWI she was executed for helping Allied soldiers escape into Holland. Turn left into Ashfield Street. Stop at **No. 91**. ❸

Sir Jack Cohen's childhood home.

A plaque commemorates the childhood home of **Sir Jack Cohen** (1898–1979), the founder of Tesco, a global supermarket retailer. In 1919, he began trading in a Hackney street market selling military surplus. The Tesco brand was born in 1924, when he merged his surname with that of his tea merchant, T. E. Stockwell. The first Tesco store opened in 1931 and, at the time of writing, there are over 2,400 stores in the UK. (See also p. 151.)

🚶 Continue to **Jubilee Street**, home of the Jewish Anarchist Club (see p. 34). ❹ Turn right and then left into **Commercial Road**, built between 1802 and 1810 to connect the East and West India Docks to Whitechapel. It was extended in 1870. Once, almost every business was Jewish. Today, the businesses are mostly wholesale clothing but Bengali owned. Stop at **No. 351**, the **Synagogue of the Congregation of Jacob**. ❺

Built in 1920–21, it is one of the five remaining synagogues in the East End (see also pp. 58 and 199).

Synagogue of the Congregation of Jacob.

🚶 Continue. Turn right into Cavell Street and left into Varden Street. Stop on the corner of **Philpott Street**. ❻

This street comprises 19th-century housing, interwar homes for medical staff and post-WWII reconstruction. There were at one time two synagogues, Philpott Street Sefardish and the Philpott Street Great Synagogue.

There was also a **Medical Mission to the Jews**, one of nine in the East End between 1880 and 1935. They provided free medical assistance in return for attending Christian services. The ultimate aim was conversion. With so many synagogues nearby, it is said that the Jewish community would receive medicine, drink a cup of tea, leave and then attend their own synagogue services.

🕴 Turn left into **Philpott Street** and turn right into **Nelson Street**. Stop outside **East London Central Synagogue**. ❼

Built in 1923, and better known as Nelson Street Synagogue, this was the last purpose-built synagogue to be built in the East End. In 1982 it amalgamated with 17 other synagogues, which ensured its survival (see also pp. 59 and 199).

🕴 Continue. Turn left at New Road. Turn right into Commercial Road. Stop opposite **No. 162**, which is on the corner of Cannon Street Road. This was **Frumkins**. ❽

Nicknamed 'The House of Weddings', Frumkins was founded in 1893 by Russian immigrants Ariyeh and Sarah Frumkin. By the 1920s, the family firm made liqueurs, raisin wine and supplied liquid refreshments for up to 30 weddings a week. In the 1950s, they opened in Great Titchfield Street and the North London suburb, Edgware. All their stores are now closed. The current Chief Rabbi, Lord Jonathan Sacks, is the grandson of Sarah Frumkin.

🕴 Across the road you will see **Hessel Street**. ❾

Famous for its poultry market, you could also buy other foodstuffs and household goods. In 1962, following much WWII damage, it was due for demolition. Robert Vas made a poignant film called The Vanishing Street about its last days (see p. 204).

🕴 Cross **Commercial Road** and look across to see **Flick Fashions**, with its small porch above the doorway. ❿

This was the **Grand Palais**. Previously a wedding hall, it became a Yiddish theatre in 1935 following the closure of the Pavilion in Whitechapel Road. Its biggest hit was the King of Lampedusa in 1943, based on the true story of RAF pilot Sydney Cohen, a tailor from Hackney, who crash-landed on the Mediterranean island of Lampedusa and the islanders surrendered to him, hence the title. The famous actors who played here include father and daughter Meir and Anna Tzelniker, Bernard Mendelovitch and Harry Ariel. It closed in 1970.

🕴 Turn to your right. Turn right into **Cannon Street Road** and stop outside **No. 125**, with the painted signage, **Raine's Boys' School**. ⓫

Founded in 1719 as a charity school in Wapping, it relocated here in 1875, moving to Arbour Square in 1912 and to its current site in Bethnal Green in 1985. Many Jewish boys, who have since become household names, were pupils, including Sidney Bloom of Bloom's (see

East London Central Synagogue.

Battle of Cable Street mural.

p. 48); Ronald Schatt, better known as jazz musician Ronnie Scott (see p. 65); and the actor-playwright Stephen Berkoff.

🚶 Continue to the end of the street. Turn left into **Cable Street**. It is long and straight having been a rope-making area. Stop outside **No. 198** with a plaque to **Hannah Billig** (1901–87). ⑫

Known as the 'Angel of Cable Street', Hannah was born in Hanbury Street, qualified as a doctor in 1925 and established her GP practice here in 1935, often providing medical services free of charge. Her bravery during WWII in London assisting the heavy rescue squads, and her work in India, was rewarded with the George Medal and MBE. She emigrated to Israel in 1964, where she is buried.

🚶 Continue down the street until you reach the old town hall. Turn right to face the mural commemorating the **Battle of Cable Street**. ⑬

On 4 October 1936, Oswald Mosley planned for his British Union of Fascists (the 'Blackshirts') to march through the Jewish East End for a victory parade at Victoria Park. Anglo-Jewish leaders asked Jewish residents to stay away, but they, and the local communists and dock workers, prepared to prevent the march. Over 6,000 police were there to clear the way for the Blackshirts and this 1970s mural depicts the barricades and crowds that halted the march. Note the marbles under the horses' hooves, mattresses and missiles thrown from windows and caricatures of Hitler and Mosley. A law banning political marches was passed soon after and the event has inspired poems, songs and plays ever since.

🚶 Turn right into the churchyard of **St George's in the East**. ⑭

Built in 1729 by Nicholas Hawksmoor, it is one of his six London churches. The churchyard contains the tomb of Henry Raine, of Raine's School. Walk through to the front of the church. It was nearly destroyed during WWII and the new church has been built inside the old nave.

🚶 Leave the church precinct and turn right into **Cannon Street Road**. Turn left on to **Cable Street**, left into **Crowder Street** and then turn right and walk through the housing estate of **Swedenbourg Gardens** to **Wellclose Square**. ⑮

Following the Resettlement, many wealthy Jews lived here including Judith Levy, daughter of Moses Hart, a benefactor of the Great Synagogue, Duke's Place. Her house became home to **Samuel Falk** (unknown–1782), the reknowned mystic and Kabbalist. Around 1742, he escaped Germany as he was to be burned as a sorcerer. Once in London he amassed wealth and established a private synagogue. His powers became legendary. An incantation could fill a cellar with coal and he seemingly prevented the synagogue at Duke's Place being burnt to the ground, writing four Hebrew letters on the door-posts. He is buried in Alderney Road Cemetery (see p. 155). He left annuities and his travelling silver scrolls (known as Kandler Scrolls) to Duke's Place, which are now in the Jewish Museum (see pp. 114 and140).

🚶 To your right, you will see a sign for **Wilton's Music Hall**.

(*Graces Alley E1 8JB;* ☎ *020 7702 2789; www. wiltons.org.uk; see website for opening times & access.*) This is the world's oldest grand music hall. Built by John Wilton in 1858 behind his pub, the Prince of Denmark, it held 1,500 people who heard the top artists of the day. In 1880 it became the East End Mission of the Methodist Church and served as the headquarters for the 1936 Battle of Cable Street. In 1956 it became a clothing warehouse and was saved from demolition in the 1960s. It is now an arts centre.

🚶 Turn right. Turn left into **Cable Street**. Turn right under the Docklands Light Railway into **Leman Street**. Walk and stop near **Hooper Street**. ⓰

At **No. 84** was the site of the **Poor Jews' Temporary Shelter.** Established by a local baker, Simcha Becker, in 1895, it provided temporary accommodation, food and advice to newly arrived immigrants, often both penniless

and hungry. In 1928 it moved to No. 63 Mansell Street and later, in 1973, moved to Brondesbury Park where it remains as a Jewish Care home.

🚶 Cross the road, turn into **Hooper Street**. Turn left into **Back Church Lane**, noting the renovated warehouses, turn right into **Fairclough Street** and then turn left into **Henriques Street** (previously Berner Street).

Bernhard Baron Settlement.

Stop outside the **Bernhard Baron Settlement**. ⓱ Once a school and now converted to apartments, this was the **Oxford and St George's Settlement**. Established in 1914 as a boys' club in Cannon Street Road by **Sir Basil Henriques** (1890–1961) (see also p. 152), it merged with a girls' club founded in 1915 in Betts Street by Rose Lowy. Basil and Rose married in 1917 and in 1919 founded the St George's Settlement Synagogue, as both Reform and Liberal, in a disused hostel at 26a Betts Street. The club and synagogue relocated here in 1929 and became the largest Jewish settlement, with 125 rooms for sport, recreation and prayers. In 1973 the synagogue moved to the Brady Centre and subsequently the Stepney Jewish Day Centre, Beaumont Grove (see pp. 53 and 59), although it is formally part of the South West Essex Reform Synagogue (see pp. 59 and 199). The club relocated to Totteridge, North London.

Henriques was influential in the National Association of Boys' Clubs, being awarded a knighthood for his youth work. In 1963 the street was renamed in his honour.

The building is named after the generous Russian-Jewish philanthropist Bernhard Baron, a tobacco magnate, who funded the purchase. See the stones on the front.

No. 41 Berner Street was the headquarters of the Hebrew Socialist Union founded by Aaron Lieberman in 1876 before he moved to New York. The members were known as the 'Berner Streeters'.

🚶 Continue to the end of the road passing a school on your left with original London School Board signage. Cross **Commercial Road**. Turn left into **Myrdle Street**. Turn left into **Fieldgate Street**. No. 89, now a Pakistani restaurant, was originally used as a synagogue. The Samuel Lewis buildings, now Fieldgate Mansions, date from 1905–06.

The large brick building with the small windows is **Tower House**. 🔞 It was built in 1902 as one of six Rowton Houses funded by Montagu Corry, Lord Rowton, private secretary to Benjamin Disraeli. They provided cheap, clean accommodation for thousands of working men in London. Only two survive. Arlington House in Camden Town is still used for its original purpose and Tower House is now apartments. Famous people who stayed

FIELDGATE STREET
GREAT SYNAGOGUE.
COMMUNAL CENTRE
THIS FOUNDATION STONE WAS LAID BY
Mr NATHAN ZLOTNICKI
PRESIDENT OF THE SYNAGOGUE.
נחום בן ר' גרשון יהודה
JULY 12th 1959. ר' תמוז תשי"ט
TAMMUZ 6th 5719.

Fieldgate Street Great Synagogue, post-WWII foundation plaque.

here include the author Jack London in 1902, Stalin in 1907 and George Orwell in 1933.

🚶 Continue and stop opposite **Fieldgate Street Great Synagogue**. ⑲

Founded in 1899, it used the word 'Great' to distinguish it from the other smaller synagogues in the street (see also pp. 59 and 199).

On the left-hand side is a small plaque commemorating **Grodzinski's**, one of the longest-established kosher bakeries in London. Founded in 1888 by immigrants from Vilnius, Lithuania, the business flourished, producing more than 20,000 loaves a week. In the 1930s, they opened a big bakery in Stamford Hill and outlets in new Jewish suburbs such as Willesden, Cricklewood and Golders Green. During WWII, the bakery was demolished by the same bomb that nearly destroyed the adjoining synagogue. The business is still in family hands today (see p. 169).

The synagogue is now surrounded by the **East London Mosque and London Muslim Centre**. Opened in 1985, it is on the site of Wonderland, a popular entertainment venue, famous for boxing matches, which later became the Rivoli Cinema, demolished during the Blitz.

🚶 Continue and stop by the mosaic plant holder, called **Oasis**, decorated with bells, Islamic symbols and a Star of David. Opposite, on the corner of **Plumbers Row**, is the **Whitechapel Bell Foundry**. ⑳

(*32–34 Whitechapel Road, E1 1DY;* ☎ *020 7247 2599; www.whitechapelbellfoundry.co.uk; museum display & foundry store open Mon–Fri 9am–4.15pm; tours on selected Sat & Wed, book in advance, payable.*) Founded in 1570 this is believed to be the oldest registered company in England. Here, since 1738, bells made include the Liberty Bell, Philadelphia, USA and 'Big Ben' in the clock tower at the Palace of Westminster.

🚶 Turn right and then left on to Whitechapel Road. Stop outside **No. 150**. ㉑

Leaving Poland aged 18, **Boris Bennett** (1900–85) arrived in London, via Paris, in 1922, and his first photographic studio here proved an instant success. Following their marriage ceremonies, thousands of Jewish couples immediately visited Boris for their wedding photographs. Whatever their background the brides and grooms always looked glamorous and locals gathered outside to see the procession of couples, sometimes 60 in one day.

🚶 Across the road is **Black Lion House**.

This name remembers **Black Lion Yard**, an enclave of courtyards that contained over 20 shops including bookshops, shtiebels and a dozen jewellers. A dairy here famously proclaimed 'Milch, frish fun din ku', Yiddish for 'Milk, fresh from the cow'.

🚶 Continue to **Adler Street**. ㉒

It is named after Chief Rabbi, Hermann Adler (1839–1911), who succeeded his father Nathan (1803–1890), in the same role. Between them they led the Anglo-Jewish community for 65 years. An office block now stands on the site of Adler Hall, home between 1943 and 1947 to the New Yiddish Theatre. The last Yiddish production in England of the *Merchant of Venice* was produced here, with Meier Tzelniker playing Shylock and his daughter Anna playing Portia.

Altab Ali Park, to your left, remembered by many as 'Itchy Park', is named after a young Bengali tailor who was murdered nearby in 1978. Look at the grass and you will see the outline of the Church of St Mary Matfelon. It was whitewashed in the 1200s and

nicknamed the White Chapel, hence the name of this area. It was destroyed during WWII.

🚶 Cross the road, turn left and continue along **Whitechapel Road**. Cross **Osborn Street** and stand outside what was **Whitechapel Library**, now part of the Whitechapel Art Gallery. (See p. 49.) ㉓

A plaque commemorates **Isaac Rosenberg** (1890–1918). A talented writer and artist, he attended Stepney Green Art School and later Slade School of Art, funded by supporters. He was killed in action during WWI and is one of 14 WWI poets commemorated at Westminster Abbey due to his highly regarded 'Poems from the Trenches'. You can find his art in Tate Britain and Ben Uri collections.

🚶 Next door is **Whitechapel Art Gallery**, ㉔ a contemporary art space with changing exhibitions.

Established by Samuel and Henrietta Barnett in 1901 and designed in art nouveau style by Charles Harrison Townsend, its aim was 'to bring great art to the people of the East End of

Whitechapel Art Gallery.

Jewish Daily Post, offices on Whitechapel Road.

London'. It opened on Sunday afternoons to enable local Jewish residents to visit and gained a reputation for launching the careers of many 20th-century artists. Those from the Jewish East End, later known as the Whitechapel Boys (actually seven men and one woman), included David Bomberg (see p. 133), John Rodker and **Mark Gertler** (1891–1939). Gertler, born in Gun Street, Spitalfields, and nurtured by the socialite Lady Ottoline Morrell, was on the fringes of the Bloomsbury Set. Many of his paintings depict memories of East End life but ultimately he seemed neither comfortable with his Jewish heritage or the artistic circles in which he lived. He committed suicide in 1939. (See also pp. 32, 134, 151).

The gallery has a room dedicated to the Whitechapel Library, whose premises it now incorporates. For more information on visiting the gallery see p. 134.

🚶 Either visit the gallery at this point or continue to the last few sites and return later. Continue along Whitechapel High Street reaching Angel Alley **㉕** on your right. Enter and stop opposite the **mural** on the left.

The radicals commemorated here are depicted in anarchic fashion by first name. Many were influential in East London, such as Rudolph Rocker and Peter Kropotkin. Next

Anarchists in Angel Alley.

door is the **Freedom Press** which since 1886 has been publishing *Freedom*, the only UK regular national anarchist newspaper.

🚶 Retrace your steps, turn right and continue to the corner of **Gunthorpe Street** at **No. 88 Whitechapel High Street**. **㉖**

The **Star of David** above the shop, designed in 1935 by Arthur Szyk, indicates the publishing house for the *Jewish Daily Post*, a short-lived 1930s Yiddish paper.

🚶 Continue to **No. 90**, Burger King. **㉗**

In 1952, Sidney Bloom opened **M Bloom (Kosher) & Son** restaurant, named after his father Morris, who had established the sausage factory on Wentworth Street. It became the most famous kosher restaurant in London if not the world. Renowned for its brusque waiters, Bloom's became 'the' place to get a salt beef sandwich, and royalty and celebrities including Princess Margaret, Frank Sinatra and Barbra Streisand all ate here. A Golders Green branch opened in 1965. Both branches are now closed.

🚶 The tour ends here, near Aldgate East tube station.

WHITECHAPEL LIBRARY

Opened in 1892, an initiative of Samuel and Henrietta Barnett, and funded by John Passmore Edwards (see the inscription), it was the first free public library in Whitechapel. Open on Sunday afternoons to serve the local Jewish community, it became a place for study, homework and vibrant political discussion. Many early readers became famous, including writers Isaac Rosenberg, Bernard Kops and Arnold Wesker, mathematician Selig Brodetsky and child psychologist Jacob Bronowski. It housed a substantial Yiddish book collection, later replaced by books in Bengali and Somali. It closed in 2005, reopening nearby as an Idea Store. Many people mourned its closing and its significance was perfectly captured by Bernard Kops, in his poem 'Whitechapel Library, Aldgate East'.

Whitechapel Library, Aldgate East

How often I went in for warmth and a doze
The newspaper room whilst my world outside froze
And I took out my sardine sandwich feast.
Whitechapel Library, Aldgate East.
And the tramps and the madman and the chattering crone.
The smell of their farts could turn you to stone
But anywhere, anywhere was better than home.

The joy to escape from family and war.
But how can you have dreams?
you'll end up on the floor.
Be like your brothers, what else is life for?

You're lost and you're drifting, settle down, get a job.
Meet a nice Jewish girl, work hard, earn a few bob.
Get married, have kids; a nice home on the never
and save up for the future and days of rough weather.

Come back down to earth, there is nothing more.
I listened and nodded, like I knew the score.
And early next morning I crept out the door.

Outside it was pouring
I was leaving forever.

I was finally, irrevocably done with this scene,
The trap of my world in Stepney Green.
With nowhere to go and nothing to dream

A loner in love with words, but so lost,
I wandered the streets, not counting the cost.
I emerged out of childhood with nowhere to hide
when a door called my name
and pulled me inside.

And being so hungry I fell on the feast.
Whitechapel Library, Aldgate East.

And my brain explodes when I suddenly find,
an orchard within for the heart and the mind.
The past was a mirage I'd left far behind

And I am a locust and I'm at a feast.
Whitechapel Library, Aldgate East.

And Rosenberg also came to get out of the cold
To write poems of fire, but he never grew old.
And here I met Chekhov, Tolstoy, Meyerhold.
I entered their worlds, their dark visions of gold.

The reference library, where my thoughts were to rage.
I ate book after book, page after page.
I scoffed poetry for breakfast and novels for tea.
And plays for my supper. No more poverty.
Welcome young poet, in here you are free
to follow your star to where you should be.

That door of the library was the door into me

And Lorca and Shelley said "Come to the feast."
Whitechapel Library, Aldgate East.

© Bernard Kops

EAST END: AN EAST END VILLAGE WALK

Walking from Mile End, Stepney Green comes as a revelation to visitors with its attractive terraced houses and green spaces. Memories of the Jewish community abound including historic cemeteries, Stepney Jewish School and Rothschild Dwellings.

▶ **START:** Mile End tube (Central, District, Hammersmith & City)

▶ **FINISH:** Stepney Green tube (District, Hammersmith & City)

▶ **DISTANCE:** 4.5km (2¾ miles)

▶ **DURATION:** 1 hour 15 minutes (allow longer if you have arranged to visit a cemetery)

▶ **REFRESHMENTS: Stepney Jewish Day Centre** (*2–8 Beaumont Grove, E1 4NQ;* ☎ *020 7790 6441*) Supervised sandwiches and salads; **The Half Moon** (*213 Mile End Road, E1 4AA;* ☎ *020 7790 6810*) Inviting J D Wetherspoon pub in a converted 1900 Methodist chapel

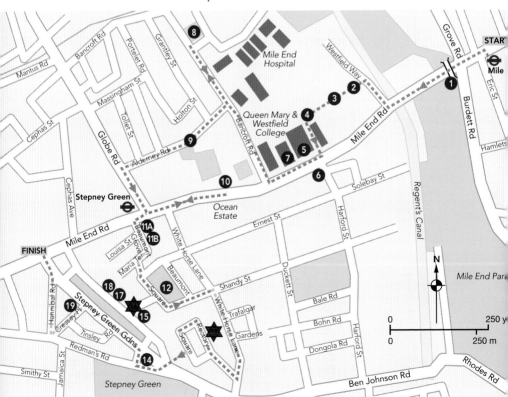

Queen Mary College, main entrance.

🚶 On leaving Mile End tube station, turn left and cross Burdett Road. Walk up the stairs to your left and cross over the 'green bridge'. ❶ In reality the bridge is yellow but it is environmentally green; it was part of a millennium project linking two sides of **Mile End Park**. Walk down the steps on the other side and turn right and right again under the bridge. Continue until you come to the entrance of **Queen Mary College, East Gate** at Westfield Way. Enter and turn left at the first opportunity. Stop at the **Harold Pinter Studio** on your left, at the Arts Faculty. ❷

Harold Pinter (1930–2008) was born in Hackney. After an early acting career he became a noted playwright. His plays, including *The Birthday Party* (1957) and *The Caretaker* (1959), invoke a certain mood, described as 'the comedy of menace', where little is said but a sense of unease prevails. He was an atheist, political activist, cricket fan and was awarded the Nobel Prize for Literature in 2005.

🚶 Continue down the narrow alleyway. Pause when you see a cemetery to your right. There is a good view over the locked gate. This is the **Nuevo (New) Sephardi Cemetery**. ❸

Opened in 1733, extended in 1855 and closed in 1936, this was the second cemetery for the London Sephardi community (see p. 154).

Nuevo (New) Sephardi Cemetery.

🚶 Continue down the alleyway until the end. Turn right. On the wall to your right you will see a plaque commemorating **Daniel Mendoza**. ❹

Regarded as the father of scientific boxing, Mendoza (1764–1836) was a Sephardi, born and brought up on the Mile End Road. Apprenticed to a butcher, his first prizefight was in 1784. Billed as 'Mendoza the Jew', he later became world heavyweight boxing champion between 1791 and 1795 and was popular with the rich and poor. In 1789 he opened a boxing academy at Capel Court in the City but eventually died in poverty. His home at 3 Paradise Row, Bethnal Green is also commemorated with a plaque.

Subsequent Jewish boxing champions from the East End include Samuel Elias (1775–1816), billed as 'Dutch Sam'; Jack 'Kid' Berg (1909–91) (see also p. 147) and Harry Mizler (1913–90), both British lightweight champions; and Ted 'Kid' Lewis (1893–1970), world welterweight champion (see also p. 149).

🚶 Facing the plaque, turn to your left and then turn to your right, passing the statue of Clement Atlee on your right. Continue through the college precinct and turn left through a gap in the brick wall. Turn left and then at the end of the passageway turn right. You will be in front of the main entrance of **Queen Mary College**. ❺

Francis Bancroft, a draper, funded almshouses, a hospital and a school on this site through a trust established following his death in 1727. Administered by the Drapers' Company who were also responsible for the later legacy of artist John Barber Beaumont, the two trusts were merged. The school relocated to Woodford in 1886 and the People's Palace opened providing educational and recreational facilities for the local working population. Subsequent mergers and name changes have resulted in Queen Mary College, part of University of London.

The clock tower in the forecourt was funded by Herbert de Stern in honour of his father, Baron Hermann de Stern, a German-Jewish immigrant of Portuguese descent, who headed the bank, Stern Brothers.

🚶 As you leave look across the road to see **Silvermans**, military stores. **❻**

Established in 1896 it is still in family hands with 'Mr S' being the fifth generation. Originally in Alderney Road and here since 1970, this is where the armed forces, police and fire brigade obtain their boots and equipment. The Royal Warrant for providing footwear to HM Forces is displayed above the entrance.

🚶 Look to your right and see the **People's Palace**. **❼**

Opened in 1936, the reliefs by Eric Gill represent recreation, drama, music, fellowship, dance and sport, which, appropriately, depicts boxing.

🚶 Turn right into **Bancroft Road**. The Velho Cemetery is found within the campus to your left but is behind a brick wall and not visible. Continue, passing **Tower Hamlets Local History Library** to your right which has a comprehensive collection of maps, photographs and other materials for

further research (☎ *020 7364 1290*). Continue down the road and stop at **Bancroft Road Cemetery**. **❽**

Established by the Western Synagogue in 1810, it closed in the 1920s (see p. 155).

🚶 Retrace your steps and turn right into **Alderney Road**. On your left you will see a long, plain, brick wall. Behind is **Alderney Road Cemetery**. **❾**

Established in 1696 and closed in 1852, this is the oldest Ashkenazi cemetery in the UK (see p. 155).
Between 1960 and 2002, No. 32 Alderney Road was the site of the **L. Goldstein** salmon smokery (see p. 172).

🚶 Turn left into **Globe Road** and left on to **Mile End Road**. Continue, walking past the **Half Moon pub** and a delightful cul-de-sac on your left, **Mile End Place**, until you reach **Albert Stern House** on your left. **❿**

Albert Stern House.

This was built in 1912 on the site of the Hospital for Sick and Lying-In Women established by the Sephardi community in 1665. In 1747, an old-age home opened in Leman Street and from 1790 both operated from this site. In 1977, by then an old-age home only, it moved to Wembley, North-west London. Today it is student accommodation and behind, but not visible from the road, is the Velho Cemetery and some almshouses also built in 1912 and funded by the Mocatta family (see p. 18).

Opposite is the Ocean Estate built in the 1960s to alleviate the housing shortage in Stepney, post-WWII.

🚶 Retrace your steps towards Stepney Green tube station, cross the road and turn left into **Beaumont Grove**. Stop by **Phyllis Gerson House**, the **Stepney Jewish Day Centre. ⑪A**

(2–8 Beaumont Grove, E1 4NQ). Originally the B'nai Brith Centre, it was renamed in honour of **Phyllis Gerson** (1903– 90), the warden who for 45 years, until 1975, managed the Stepney Jewish Girls' Club and Settlement. During WWII she worked extensively for the Jewish Relief Unit abroad. A pioneer of social work, she transformed the youth club into a centre providing for all ages, including the kosher meals-on-wheels service that originated here in 1958. The complex currently houses the East London branch of the South West Essex and Settlement Reform Synagogue (see pp. 59–60).

🚶 Next door is the **Alice Model Nursery. ⑪B**

Alice Model (1856–1943) devoted her life to the provision of mother and child care. She was instrumental in setting up the Sick Rooms Help Society in 1895, providing home help when mothers were ill; opening the Jewish Day Nursery in 1897 in Spitalfields;

and the Jewish Maternity Hospital in 1912 in Underwood Road. The nursery moved to New Road in 1901, remaining there until 1943. Open from 8am–7pm for 2d per day, facilities for the 50 children included daily medical checks, defumigating the children's clothes to prevent the spread of disease, subsidized meals and a fund for mothers' dinners enabling them to eat with their children. The nursery relocated to Beaumont Grove in 1956 and was renamed in honour of its founder (see also p. 38).

Alice Model Nursery

🚶 Continue and turn right and then left into **Beaumont Square. ⑫**

The London Independent Hospital is on the site where John Barber Beaumont (1774–1841) founded his New Philosophical Institute. After it moved to Mile End Road in 1879, the site became home to Stepney Jewish Girls' Club and later, a nurses' home for the **London Jewish Hospital**. The hospital began in 1907 as an initiative by local Jewish barber Isidore Berliner. It opened on Stepney Green in 1919 after a long battle to raise money. The initiative was not supported by the Anglo-Jewish establishment, who feared funds would be diverted from the nearby London Hospital. In 1958 Ernst Freud, son of Sigmund and father of Lucian, designed the hospital synagogue. The hospital became part of the NHS in 1948 but closed in 1979 and has been demolished.

Stepney Green Dwellings (now Court).

🚶 Continue around the square. Turn right into **Whitehorse Lane**. Turn right into **Rectory Square**. Stop outside **Temple Close**, previously **East London Synagogue**. ⑬

Designed by Davis & Emanuel and opened in 1873, this was the first synagogue to be built under the auspices of the United Synagogue. Its aim was to encourage new Jewish immigrants to follow established Anglo-

Jewish traditions rather than continue establishing small chevrot. Plain brick on the outside, the interior had coloured brick banding with ornate surrounds to the Ark. Reverend Stern was minister for 40 years from 1887 and it is said that 20,000 weddings took place here. In the mid-20th century membership increased as local smaller synagogues closed, but by 1987 the building was abandoned and in 1996 it was converted into apartments.

🚶 Turn left and walk through to **Stepney Green Gardens**. One of London's urban farms is glimpsed ahead. Turn right and continue to the clock tower.

The clock tower was erected in 1913 in honour of Alderman Stanley Atkinson. Alongside is the **Leonard Montefiore Memorial Fountain**. ⑭ Erected in 1884 at Rutland Street School, it was moved to Stepney Green in 1939. The great-great-nephew of Sir Moses Montefiore, Leonard (1853–1879), was the brother of

STEPNEY JEWISH SCHOOL

Established in 1865 in a house, a purpose-built school was built in 1872 and later extended in 1906. See the gable inscription. Like the dwellings, the school in Stepney was a little more expensive than the Jewish Free School in Bell Lane, reflecting the higher incomes of the local residents. The school relocated to Ilford in 1970. Pupils included Louis and Barnet Winogradsky (later impresarios, lords Grade and Delfont) and the writer Bernard Kops (b.1926), who lived in the Dwellings next door. Inspired by the Whitechapel Library (see pp. 47 and 49), he became a writer and his first success was the 1959 play *The Hamlet of Stepney Green*. He moved to West Hampstead and has continued to write movingly of his memories of the Jewish East End.

Claude Montefiore. He devoted himself to study, philanthropy and supporting the feminist movement, but died, aged 27, while in New York.

🚶 Continue further into **Stepney Green Gardens**.

Stepney Green Gardens were laid out in 1872. The large tenement block is **Stepney Green Dwellings** (now Court). ⓯ Built in 1896, it is the earliest surviving block built by the Four Per Cent Industrial Dwellings Company (see pp. 26 and 146). Designed by N. S. Joseph, they were a higher standard than earlier blocks with facilities such as constant hot water, a clubhouse and laundry and no shared toilets and sculleries. It remains rental property and is managed by the Industrial Dwellings Society (IDS), the successor to Four Per Cent.

Next door, the brick building with a green gate decorated with initials 'SJS' was **Stepney Jewish School**. ⓰ (See left.)

🚶 Walk through the gardens and stop opposite the **Rosalind Green Hall**. ⓱

In 1916, after a disagreement at the East London Synagogue over a mixed choir, the Orthodox members established **Stepney Orthodox Synagogue** in a disused Methodist chapel on Stepney Green. Badly damaged during WWII, it was rebuilt in 1958, closed in 1980 and is now home to the Arbour Youth ABC.

🚶 Continue through the gardens and stop outside **No. 37**. ⓲

Built in 1694, it is the oldest house in Stepney Green and indicates the wealth of those who lived here in the late 17th and early 18th centuries. Residents of the house included merchants of the East India Company, the Charrington brewing family and from 1875–1907 it was a Jewish old-age home.

37 Stepney Green.

Subsequently a craft school and local authority offices, it has recently been restored to a family home.

🚶 On the other side of the gardens you will see **Dunstan House**. ⓳

Built in 1899 by the East End Dwellings Company, the housing initiative of Henrietta and Samuel Barnett, Flat 33 was home to **Rudolph Rocker** (1873–1958), the German gentile who moved to London and aligned himself with the Jewish workers. He led their anarchists club; edited their Yiddish newspapers, such as *Arbeiter Fraint* and *Die Zeit*; encouraged trade union membership; and campaigned for better working conditions. He lived in 'free union' with Millie Witcop, a Russian-Jewish immigrant. Jewish trade unions in London would have been very different if they had been man and wife. In 1897 they were refused entry into New York as they were unable to provide a marriage certificate and had to return to London. Read more in *East End Jewish Radicals* by Professor William Fishman.

🚶 Leave Stepney Green via Hannibal Road to reach Mile End Road, where this tour ends. Opposite is the Anchor Retail Park, named after the Charrington Anchor Brewery. Turn right to return to Stepney Green tube station.

EAST END SYNAGOGUES

By the mid 19th century an increasing number of poorer immigrants, to whom the large City synagogues did not appeal, established their own. By 1854, research indicates there were already three in East London. The United Synagogue, established in 1870, built its first new synagogue in East London, part of a concerted effort by community leaders to encourage both accepted Anglo-Jewish practice and migration further east to Stepney. Migration westwards was also underway with Great Portland Street and Bayswater synagogues opening in 1855 and 1863, and in 1870 the flagship Reform Synagogue opened in Upper Berkeley Street.

However, between 1881 and 1914 over 100,000 new Jewish immigrants arrived in London from Eastern Europe and they mostly lived in East London. They established a proliferation of chevrot, small congregations based on Friendly Societies providing facilities for prayer, charity and study, and income at times of mourning. Each community centred around families from the same place of origin. Synagogue names, such as Plotsker, Kovno and Poltava, evoked the Eastern Europe they had left behind.

Eventually there were over 65 small synagogues in an area of 5sq km (2sq miles). However, most of them did not have the means to provide fully for their communities. Samuel Montagu, MP for Whitechapel, suggested that they be grouped together and in 1887 the Federation of Minor Synagogues was established, with 16 founding communities. By 1911 there were 51 and the word 'minor' was dropped. By 1939, over 60 existed, almost all of them in the East End. At the time of writing, there are 13 constituent and 10 affiliated members. Of the five surviving East End synagogues, three retain Federation membership.

For travel and service details see pp. 198–9. Map references refer to the map on pp. 16–17.

Sandys Row Synagogue

4a Sandys Row, E1 7HW; ☎ *020 7377 6196; www.sandysrow.org.uk; open for services Mon–Thur 1.30pm; contact synagogue to arrange visits outside these hours; voluntary donation appreciated.* Ⓔ

Visiting the oldest Ashkenazi synagogue in London, and the last remaining in

Poltava Synagogue, Spital Square.

Sandys Row Synagogue. Photo: Jeremy Freedman.

Spitalfields, helps to understand its website banner: 'Cherishing the past – embracing the future'. The site was built in 1766 as a French Huguenot chapel, l'Eglise de l'Artillerie. From 1786 it was let to the Baptists.

In 1854, 50 Dutch Ashkenazi Jewish economic migrants founded a chevra, 'The Society for Loving-Kindness and Truth'. By 1867, it had grown to 500 members and acquired the leasehold of the chapel, having outgrown rented premises in Mansell Street. This site was particularly suitable having been built with a balcony, for use by the ladies, and an east-west axis. However, the entrance was on the eastern side, where the Ark was to be sited. N. S. Joseph remodelled the interior to close the original entrance and create a new entrance on Sandys Row. A new three-storey building provided offices and accommodation.

The Chief Rabbi, Nathan Adler, opposed its establishment and refused to acknowledge it, so, in 1870, it was consecrated by the rabbi of nearby Sephardi Bevis Marks. In 1887, Sandys Row was the largest of the founding congregations of 'the Federation'. Seeking religious independence it left the Federation in 1899, becoming an Associate of the United Synagogue in 1922. In 1949 it returned to independent status and has remained so ever since.

The warm orange and white interior is evocative of the small East End chevrot. Many original artefacts remain including a Dutch silver ewer for hand washing. There is also a genizah, most likely the oldest in London. In 2010 there were around 200 members, many being descendants of previous congregants. Midweek Mincha services attract up to 80 worshippers, mostly from nearby offices and a renaissance has gathered momentum with a variety of communal, cultural and social events including Friday night dinners, Yiddish classes and heritage exhibitions. In late 2010 the synagogue embarked on the largest building programme in its history, with a new roof and interior renovation throughout.

Congregation of Jacob (Kehillas Ya'akov)

351–53 Commercial Road, E1 2PS; ☎ *020 7790 2874; www.congregation ofjacob.org; to visit, contact synagogue; voluntary donation appreciated.* Ⓑ

Built in 1920–21 by Lewis Solomon, the building is reminiscent of Eastern European synagogue design. Established in 1903 by immigrants from Lithuania and Poland, early services were held in a family home on Commercial Road. The interior includes folk-art-style painted panels depicting the seven-branched menorah, the Four Species – palm, etrog, willow and myrtle, seven species of Israeli fruit and grain and musical instruments. These were most likely added in the 1950s by artist Philip Steinberg, a synagogue member. It is still active and is an affiliated member of the Federation.

Congregation of Jacob, above the Ark.

58

East London Central Synagogue

30–40 Nelson Street, E1 2DE; ☎ *020 7790 9809; to visit, contact synagogue; voluntary donation appreciated.* **C**

Better known as Nelson Street Synagogue, it was built in 1923, by Lewis Solomon. This is the last purpose-built synagogue in East London. The modest exterior hides a light and homely interior with paintwork in pastel blue and white. The collection of foundation stones and donation boards belonging to the 18 small local synagogues which merged in 1982, including Chevra Shass, Bels, Berdichower and Buroff Street, include donor surnames such as Samuel and Aronson and relate to Anglo-Jewish aristocracy who funded their foundation. Services follow the Nusach Sephardish, which is not Sephardi but derived from the Chassidic form of worship. The synagogue is still active and is a constituent member of the Federation.

Fieldgate Street Great Synagogue, donation boards.

Fieldgate Street Great Synagogue

41 Fieldgate Street, E1 1JU; ☎ *020 7247 2644; to visit, contact synagogue; voluntary donation appreciated.* **D**

The congregation was established in 1899 but the current building dates from the 1950s rebuilding following WWII. The word 'Great' in its name singles it out as the largest of the three synagogues once in Fieldgate Street. Painted boards indicate donations from the rich and the poor and prayer books survive in Cyrillic script. The much-loved Rev. Gayer arrived from Poland in 1934 and remained the religious leader here until his death in 1992.

The synagogue is still active and is an affiliated member of the Federation. The neighbouring mosque and London Muslim Centre are testament to the continuing cultural diversity of the area.

Settlement Synagogue

2 Beaumont Grove, E1 4NQ; ☎ *020 8599 0936.* **F**

Established in 1919 at the Oxford & St George's Settlement and Youth Club founded by Basil and Rose Henriques, it was, unusually, linked to both the Reform and Liberal movements. In 1929, it

East London Central Synagogue.

moved with the club to the Bernhard Baron Settlement in Berners Street, Whitechapel. Before WWII it was one of the largest non-Orthodox congregations in the UK and a prayer book written specifically for the congregants is still used today. The Whitechapel Art Gallery was used for High Holy Days services with much improvisation – the Ark was a wardrobe and silver teaspoons were used for rimonim. It was one of the six founding synagogues of the Reform Synagogues of Great Britain

(RSGB) in 1942 but the rapid depopulation of East London necessitated the closure of the centre. The synagogue moved to the Brady Centre (see p. 38) and when that closed in 1976 it moved to the present site at Stepney Jewish Day Centre and subsequently merged with the South West Essex Reform Synagogue. **Note:** These synagogues are open on the **European Day of Jewish Culture and Heritage** (see p. 202). For details of services, see pp. 198–9. Several are used for new purposes:

Closed East End Synagogues

Bethnal Green Great Synagogue
11–15 Bethnal Green Road, E1. **G**
Closed after 1966, the building became a clothing warehouse and more recently a an artist's living space and studio. The Star of David on the exterior remains.

Brick Lane (Machzikei Hadass) Synagogue
59 Brick Lane. E1 6PU. **H**
Closed in 1970, now a mosque (see p. 28).

East London Synagogue
52 Rectory Square, E1 3NU. **I**
Closed in the 1980s, this is now apartments (see p. 54).

Great Garden Street Synagogue
7–15 Greatorex Street, E1 5NF. **J**

Closed around 1996, this is now a business development centre (see p. 39).

Mile End & Bow District Synagogue
Harley Grove, E3 2AT. **K**
Closed in 1977, this is now a Sikh gurdwara.

Princelet Street Synagogue
19 Princelet Street, E1 6QH. **L**
Closed in 1963, but with access to the public on specified open days (see p. 31).

Stepney Orthodox Synagogue
53 Stepney Green, E1 3LE. **M**
Closed in 1980 and now Arbour Youth ABC (see p. 55).

Bethnal Green Great Synagogue.

Mile End & Bow District Synagogue.

CENTRAL: FITZROVIA AND SOHO WALK

Discover Jewish connections in Fitzrovia and Soho where the rich social history includes the West Central Lads' and Girls' Clubs, Westminster Jews Free School, synagogues and the Fitzroy Tavern, one of London's most famous literary pubs once run by Jewish landlords.

▶ **START:** Warren Street tube (Northern, Victoria)

▶ **FINISH:** Berwick Street, near Oxford Street (10 minutes from Oxford Circus tube station – Bakerloo, Central, Victoria, and Tottenham Court Road tube – Central, Northern)

▶ **DISTANCE:** 2.8km (1¾ miles)

▶ **DURATION:** 1½ hours (allow longer if you would like to stop for a drink in the Fitzroy Tavern)

▶ **REFRESHMENTS: Princi** (*135–37 Wardour Street, W1F 0UT;* ☎ *020 7478 8888; www.princi.co.uk*) Mouth-watering breads, pizza and cakes; **Mildreds** (*45 Lexington Street, W1F 9AN;* ☎ *020 7494 1634, www.mildreds.co.uk*) Long-established mostly vegetarian café; There are also several of the better chain cafés and sandwich bars in the area such as **Pret A Manger** and **EAT**

🚶 Leaving Warren Street tube station, turn right into Warren Street, turn left into Fitzroy Street to reach **Fitzroy Square. ❶**

Fitzroy Square is named after Henry Fitzroy. The surname 'Fitzroy' derives from '*fils roi*', meaning 'son of the king'. Henry was one of Charles II's illegitimate sons. The south and east sides of the square were built in the 1780s and the north and west sides from 1828. From the 1800s the area was inhabited by artists, writers and musicians.

By the late 19th and early 20th centuries, there was already a considerable Jewish presence in the West End of London. Wealthy Jews had made their homes in Mayfair but the Jewish community was concentrated in Soho and Fitzrovia, numbering, at the height of the Jewish West End in the mid-1920s, around 25,000. Their work and family life was similar to

that in the Jewish East End, but they appeared better off as their homes bordered on the glitz and glamour of London's theatres and clubland.

🚶 Stand in front of No. 38. **❶A**

In 1898 the **West Central Lads' Club**, for boys and youths, began here in the basement and ground floor. It followed the same principles as

Fitzroy Square.

the earlier **West Central Girls' Club** founded in 1893. Activities included gymnastics, boxing, evening concerts and debates. It was funded by wealthy benefactors such as the Montefiores. It moved to No. 39 during WWII then to Woburn House and Hanway Place. Young people came from all over London for the club and the dances. Winding up in the 1950s, it formally closed in 1986. Its reputation for drama was such that many of the 'lads' went on to forge careers in entertainment. **Michael Klinger** (1920–89), producer and director, made *The London Nobody Knows* (1967) and a series of 'Confessions of ...' films in the 1970s. **Lewis Gilbert** (b.1920) directed seminal British films including *Reach For The Sky* in 1956, *Alfie* in 1966, 1970s Bond films and *Educating Rita* and *Shirley Valentine* in the 1980s.

The open space is one of London's private key gardens. The sculpture with the hole is *View* by artist **Naomi Blake**. ❶B (See p. 129.)

No. 33 ❶C was home to the **Omega Workshops** between 1913 and 1920, the initiative of Roger Fry, artist and art critic, who wanted to remove what he saw as the false division between fine and decorative art. Key members were Vanessa Bell, Duncan Grant and also the American-Jewish artist **Jacob Epstein** (1880–1959). His sculptures were strong and powerful, exhibiting a primitive sexuality, and the public were often shocked by his work (see pp. 134, 136).

🚶 Turn right into **Fitzroy Street** and turn left into **Maple Street**. Stop and stand opposite No. 32, the **Montagu Centre**. ❷

Named after **Lily Montagu** (1886–1963) (see pp. 99–101), this post-WWII site houses the West Central Liberal Synagogue (see p. 164), once aligned to the West Central Girls' Club, which

Montagu Centre.

Montagu established in 1893. Lily was also instrumental in the foundation of the Jewish Religious Union in 1902, now Liberal Judaism, which has its headquarters here (see p. 100).

🚶 Turn right into **Whitfield Street** and right into **Howland Street**. Turn left into **Charlotte Street**. Stop outside **Saatchi & Saatchi** (now part of Publicis). ❸

Nathan Saatchi, a successful textile merchant in Iraq, moved to England in 1946 with his family, including young sons Charles and Maurice who rose to prominence in the 1970s with their advertising agency Saatchi & Saatchi. Maurice later became co-chairman of the Conservative Party between 2003 and 2005 and Charles is now a well-known art collector. His Saatchi Gallery opened in Chelsea in 2008. A synagogue funded by the family opened in 1998. It currently holds prayers in the premises of St. John's Wood Synagogue (see pp. 192 and 194).

🚶 Continue walking and stop on the corner of **Scala Street**. ❹

This was the site of the Scala Theatre, built in 1904 on the site of nine previous theatres and a Salvation Army hostel. Famous for its Christmas productions of *Peter Pan*, the

Jewish community used it for High Holy Day services, fundraising events for the West Central Clubs and Yiddish film shows.

At the height of the Jewish West End, there were numerous Jewish businesses in **Charlotte Street** including Rudin, the trimming merchants, Resnick the butcher, Kahn's salt beef bar, drapers, dairies, hosiers and tobacconists. Italians opened Bertorellis restaurant in 1912 and the French, l'Etoile in 1904.

🚶 Continue. Stop outside the **Fitzroy Tavern** on the corner of **Windmill Street** (see below). ❺

Opposite is the Charlotte Street Hotel, opened in 2000. The upper levels used to be occupied by Cottrell Dental Factory, and Schmidt's restaurant was on the ground floor. Opened as a German deli in 1901, the owner Frederick Schmidt added the restaurant after WWI and it became the 'in place' of the area, closing in the 1970s. The spy

Donald Maclean allegedly spent his last night in England here before fleeing the UK in 1951.

🚶 Walk down **Windmill Street** and cross **Tottenham Court Road** into **Store Street**. Turn left into Alfred Place. Stop at **Nos 31/32 Remax House**. ❻

This was the site of the **Western Synagogue**, **Lily Montagu's West Central Synagogue** and **West Central Girls' Club**. During WWII it was a settlement, offering shelter from the Blitz. Tragically 27 girls died when it was destroyed by a bomb on 16 April 1941. (See also pp. 99–101.)

🚶 Retrace your steps and turn left into **Tottenham Court Road**. Cross the road. Turn right into **Hanway Street** and turn right into **Hanway Place**. ❼

You will see a terracotta inscription **'Westminster Jews' Free School'** (WJFS). Established in 1811 by the independent

FITZROY TAVERN

The **Fitzroy Tavern** site was a coffee house in 1883 and converted to a pub in 1887. **Judah Kleinfeld**, a Polish-Jewish immigrant, arrived in the United Kingdom in 1886, trained as a tailor and became landlord here in 1919. He welcomed the bohemian residents of the area including Albert Pierrepoint, executioner; Nina Hamnett and Augustus John, both artists; and Dylan Thomas, the poet. Kleinfeld had a novel way of encouraging charity.

Customers threw money to the ceiling on darts. It was taken down annually, counted and the 'pennies from heaven' were used to give local children a fun day out. His daughter and son-in-law took over in the 1930s, running the pub to the 1950s. Inside, a collection of photographs brings back memories from its heyday, when it was known as Kleinfelds.

Western Synagogue, it was formalized in 1820. After several homes in Soho it moved to these purpose-built premises in 1883. At its peak there were 700 pupils, much smaller than the JFS in the East End, with over 4,000. The last pupil joined in 1939. It closed following WWII.

🚶 Continue down Hanway Place and on reaching Oxford Street, look to your right to **Rathbone Place**. ❽

Harry Errington, ex-WJFS boy, Savile Row tailor and a WWII auxiliary fireman, saved two fellow firemen here who were trapped in a basement hit by an incendiary bomb. He received the George Cross, the highest civilian bravery award, which his family donated to the Jewish Museum (see pp. 111–16).

🚶 Cross Oxford Street, continue into Soho Street. Enter the garden of **Soho Square**. ❾

Soho was named after the hunting cry 'so ho' when the area was open land in the 1530s. Developed in the late 17th century, the area remained fashionable but soon became a haven for European immigrants, notably the French and later the Greeks and Italians. Jewish immigrants were also attracted here in the late 19th century and the Orthodox needed small chevrot here just as they did in the East End.

Bet Hasefer was established at No. 26a Soho Square and the **Bikkur Holim** nearby at No. 41 Brewer Street. Both were founded in 1910 but ultimately merged with the Talmud Torah Synagogue in Manette Street.

🚶 Exit Soho Square into Greek Street. Turn left into **Manette Street**. Stand outside Foyles looking at the detached white building opposite. ❿

A workhouse in 1771, it subsequently became a mission house and industrial school. In 1916,

Westminster Jews' Free School.

the Talmud Torah Synagogue, established above a shop in 1880 in Green Court, moved here, merging with Bikkur Holim, becoming known as **Manette Street Synagogue**. It was a modest poor community where 60 per cent of the members were tailors. In 1948 it merged with Bet Hasefer, moved to Dean Street and was renamed the West End Great Synagogue.

🚶 Retrace your steps and turn left into **Greek Street**, then right into **Bateman Street**, passing Bateman's Buildings. Continue to **Frith Street** and pause. ⓫

No. 47 houses **Ronnie Scott's Jazz Club**. Born Ronald Schatt (1927–96), he was brought up in Whitechapel, spent his pocket money on a soprano saxophone and aged 20 blew his savings on a trip to New York for the jazz. After returning, he opened a club on Gerrard

Manette Street Synagogue.

65

West End Great Synagogue, architect drawing.

was sold in Savile Row bespoke businesses, worn on stage in theatre and revues or at ceremonies at court. Several apartments here included workrooms. Associated businesses in the area supplied trimmings, embroidery and buttons. Conditions were hard and in 1912, 1,500 skilled West End tailors, mostly immigrants from many different countries, went on strike. Encouraged by Rudolph Rocker (see p. 55), over 12,000 Jewish East End tailors went on strike in support, bringing success to the campaign and also an end to the sweated system.

Street in 1959, moving to Frith Street in 1965. It became, and has remained, the pre-eminent jazz venue in Soho (see also p. 44).

🚶 Continue to Dean Street. Turn right and stop opposite **Quo Vadis**. ⓬

The blue plaque commemorates No. 28, the home, between 1848 and 1856, of socialist writer **Karl Marx**. His family lived in abject poverty. When his wife inherited a legacy they were able to relocate to Haverstock Hill in Belsize Park.

From here you can see the **Soho Theatre**. ⓭ A plaque in the foyer indicates that this was previously the site of the **West End Great Synagogue**. The original building was rebuilt as a new synagogue in 1964, incorporating halls used for dances and by the Labour Friends of Israel. The **Ben Uri Gallery**, founded in 1915 to harness and support the creativity of East End artists, relocated here in the 1970s, remaining until 1996 (see p. 133).

🚶 Retrace your steps down Dean Street. Turn right into **Meard Street**.

Royalty Mansions ⓮, named after the now demolished Royalty Theatre, were built in 1908. The predominant local industry was tailoring and much of the clothing made here

🚶 Walk to the end of the street and pause on **Wardour Street**.

Once the centre for British film production and distribution, numerous Jewish cinema owners and film distributors worked here.

🚶 Cross the road into Peter Street. Turn right into **Berwick Street**. Stop opposite the shops with V Falber and The Silk House on their facades. ⓯

Street-market stalls in **Berwick Street** date back to the 1770s, but the market was officially recognized in 1892. Originally specializing in second-hand clothes, this trade ended due to the fear of cholera. Later, the street became known for Jewish-owned specialist shops and stalls, and in the 1930s businesses included drapers, trimming merchants, costumiers and lace dealers. A Jewish presence remained in the area until the 1980s with Grodzinskis, the bakers in Brewer Street and Grahame's Seafare in nearby Poland Street.

🚶 The tour ends here. Continue up Berwick Street to reach Oxford Street. Turn right for Tottenham Court Road tube station or turn left for Oxford Circus tube station.

CENTRAL: MAYFAIR AND WEST END WALK

This tour provides an opportunity to stroll through the residential Grosvenor Estate of Mayfair, discovering the associations with Jewish financiers, politicians and communal leaders including the Rothschilds (see pp.141–6) and Disraeli (see pp. 76–9). Crossing Oxford Street you reach prominent synagogues for today's community.

▶ **START:** Hyde Park Corner tube, exit 1 (Piccadilly)

▶ **FINISH:** Near Marble Arch tube (Central)

▶ **DISTANCE:** 4.4km (2¾ miles)

▶ **DURATION:** 1 hour (allow longer if you want to browse Shepherd Market and the shops en route or visit the West London Reform Synagogue)

▶ **REFRESHMENTS:** **L'Artiste Muscle** (*1 Shepherd Market, W1Y 7HS;* ☎ *020 7493 6150*) Authentic French bread, cheese and salads; **Maroush Express** (*68 Edgware Road, W2 2EG;* ☎ *020 7224 9339; www.maroush.com*) Their coffee and meze are legendary (*other branches nearby at 21, 43 & 45 Edgware Road, 62 Seymour Street*)

🚶 On exiting the station, follow directions to Piccadilly and you will see **Apsley House ❶**, a honey-coloured detached mansion.

(*149 Piccadilly, W1J 7NT;* ☎ *020 7499 5676; www.english-heritage.org.uk; tube: Hyde Park Corner (Piccadilly); check website for opening times; adm. fee.*) The address was originally No.1 London, being the first house reached from the west. It was designed by the Adam brothers in the 1770s for Baron Apsley. Later the home of Arthur Wellesley, Duke of Wellington, it remains the Wellesley London residence and is open to visitors.

🚶 Look ahead down **Piccadilly ❷**.

In the mid 19th century there was a series of aristocratic town houses facing Green Park. On what is now Park Lane, between Apsley House and the Intercontinental Hotel, was No. 148 Piccadilly, the home of Lionel de Rothschild and later, his son Nathaniel.

Further along were Nos 142 and 143, homes to Alice and Ferdinand de Rothschild. On the current site of the Park Lane Hotel was No. 107, home of Nathan Mayer Rothschild, and the first of the homes on what became known as 'Rothschild Row'. All of these houses have been demolished. (See also pp. 143–4.)

🚶 Cross the road, continue and turn left into **Hamilton Place**. Stop outside No. 5, **Les Ambassadeurs**. ❸

5 Hamilton Place, five arrows detail.

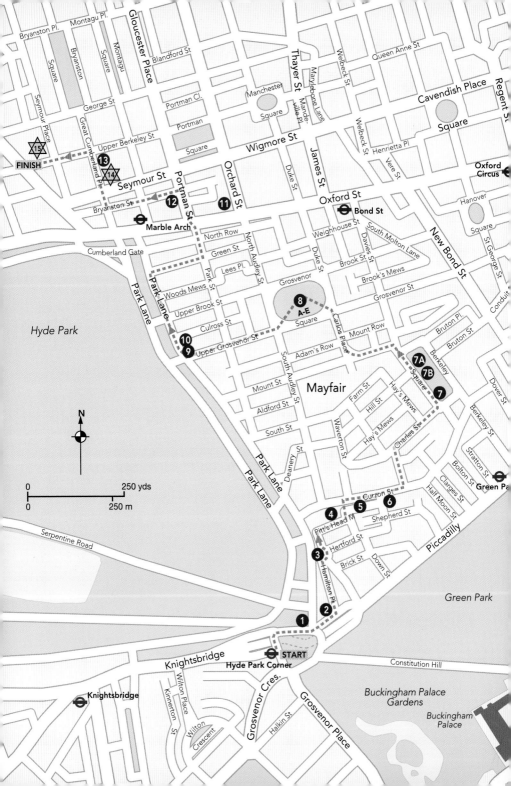

Bought in 1881 by **Leopold (Leo) de Rothschild**, this is a surviving London Rothschild mansion. Look up to your left and see the Rothschild symbol of five arrows engraved in the stone. Inside the woodwork is particularly ornate. Post-WWII it became an upmarket restaurant and dance club and is now a discreet club and casino. (See also p. 144.)

🚶 Continue and cross **Old Park Lane** and walk past the **Hilton Hotel** to your right. Turn right into **Pitt's Head Mews** and climb the short staircase to your left leading to a pedestrianized area, previously **Seamore Place**. ❹

32 Curzon Street.

No. 1 (demolished) was the home of **Alfred de Rothschild**, Bank of England director, respected banker, art collector and music expert. (See pp. 85, 142, 143 and 150.)

🚶 Leave this small square, turning right into **Curzon Street**. Stop outside **No. 19**. ❺

The plaque indicates **Benjamin Disraeli's** home, after his second term as prime minister ended in 1880. Alfred de Rothschild, one of his best friends, lived just around the corner and was able to be with Disraeli when he died on 19 April 1881. (See pp. 76–9.)

🚶 Continue to **No. 32** ❻ where a plaque indicates the home of **Sir Rufus Isaacs**.

Born the son of a Jewish Spitalfields market fruit trader, Isaacs (1860–1935) became a politician and diplomat, becoming US ambassador in 1918 and Lord Chief Justice and Viceroy of India between 1921 and 1926. Created first Marquis of Reading in 1914, his second wife, Stella, was ennobled in her own right, becoming Baroness Swanborough, for her charity work including the founding of the Women's Voluntary Service in 1938.

🚶 Continue along **Curzon Street**. To your right is **Shepherd Market**, a delightful enclave of narrow streets that is worth a short detour. Cross **Curzon Street**, turn left into **Queen Street** and right into **Charles Street**, reaching **Berkeley Square**. ❼

Laid out in the 1750s, it was a sought-after address but few residential premises remain. The plane trees, planted in 1789, are among the oldest in London and art fairs and parties are held in the gardens. The Rothschilds ordered refreshments from Gunter's, a café

Belisha Beacon in Berkeley Square.

and ice cream parlour, opened in the mid 18th century and by 1909, the square was home to several members of the Central Synagogue.

🚶 On the north side is **No. 25 ❼A**, now offices but once the London home of **Otto Schiff** (1875–1952).

An immigrant from Germany, he devoted his life to communal work, particularly the rescue, safety and rehabilitation of Jewish refugees during the two world wars. He became president of the Jews Temporary Shelter, assisted Belgian refugees during WWI and in 1933 established the Jewish Refugees Committee (JRC), which from 1938 was known as the German Jewish Aid Committee. In 1933 he established, with Anthony de Rothschild and Leonard Montefiore, the Central British Fund, providing funds for JRC activities, ensuring that no Jewish refugee would be a burden to the British state. Now known as World Jewish Relief, it continues to

assist Jews and other peoples in need. Jewish welfare homes in Hampstead and Golders Green are named in his honour.

🚶 Locate the **zebra crossing ❼B** on the west side of the square near the corner of **Hill Street**.

The black and white pole with the orange light on top is a Belisha beacon. It is named after **Leslie Hore-Belisha** (1893–1957) who, as an MP and Minister of Transport in the 1930s, revised the Highway Code and introduced driving tests and Belisha beacons. As Secretary of State for War in 1937, his popularity began to wane with the belief that his desire for war arose from his wish to protect the Jews in Europe. Despite implementing a modernization programme for the army, improving barracks, pay and promotions, he was suddenly dismissed. His post-war political career was variable, and today he is remembered mostly for these black-and-white-striped poles.

🚶 Leave **Berkeley Square**, turn left into **Mount Street** and immediately right into **Carlos Place**, passing the luxurious and discreet **Connaught Hotel**. On reaching **Grosvenor Square** walk into the public gardens. ❽

Named after Richard Grosvenor, who developed much of Mayfair during the 18th century, this is one of the largest squares in London. It has many American associations, being home to Eisenhower's WWII headquarters at No. 20 (see plaque) and from 1960, the American Embassy (due to move in 2016). Residents have included dukes and earls and several important Jewish personalities. Note that several sites have been redeveloped. Numbers given are those correct at time of residence.

No. 3 ❽A was the boyhood home of **Arthur Balfour** (1848–1930), MP and prime minister between 1902 and 1905. He was the signatory of the 'Balfour Declaration', a letter written to the 2nd Baron Rothschild, Walter, in November 1917, outlining the British government's support of a Jewish state in Palestine.

Samuel Lewis (1837–1901) lived at **No. 23 ❽B** between 1880–1900. Samuel made his fortune as a moneylender and endowed a charitable trust at his death, which provided social housing. The first Samuel Lewis block was built in 1910 on Liverpool Road, Islington, followed by others, including Whitechapel, Hackney and Stamford Hill. Since 2001 the housing trust has been known as the Southern Housing Group. He supported many local hospitals in Hove, his seaside home. In 1906 the Lewis Trust funded two lifeboats and in 2007 the Brighton and Hove Bus Company commemorated his philanthropy, naming the number 682 bus in his honour.

🚶 Samuel's wife, **Ada Lewis**, moved to **No. 16 ❽C**, living here with her second husband until 1906. At her death she left a substantial legacy towards the Jewish Maternity Hospital in Whitechapel (see p. 39).

No. 53 ❽D at 'Bentley Corner' to the south-east was one of the homes for **Joel Wolff Barnato** (1895–1948) and his friends. Joel was the son of Barney Barnato, the East End boy who migrated to South Africa and co-founded diamond firm De Beers. Barney died in mysterious circumstances and, Joel, aged two, inherited millions of pounds that he used to support and then buy the car company, Bentley. As one of the 'Bentley Boys' – young men who

93 Park Lane.

71

99 Park Lane.

A plaque indicates the marital home of **Benjamin Disraeli**. He lived here with Mary-Anne until her death in 1872, when her family regained ownership. (See pp. 76–9, 210–11.)

🚶 A couple of doors down at **No. 99** ⑩ a plaque indicates the home of **Moses Montefiore.**

This was his London home for 60 years. Following retirement his life revolved around communal leadership and philanthropy. (See pp. 22, 86 and 211–13.)

🚶 Continue on Park Lane and turn right into **Green Street**, then left into **Park Street**. Stop on the corner of **Oxford Street**. To your right in the distance, across the road you will see the Marble Arch branch of **Marks & Spencer** (M&S) ⑪.

Built in the 1930s, this is the flagship store, one of 600 M&S outlets in the UK at the time of writing. The business began in 1884 when Michael Marks, a Polish-Jewish immigrant, set up a stall in Kirkgate Market, Leeds, proclaiming 'Don't ask the price, it's a penny'. He teamed up with Tom Spencer in 1894 and Marks & Spencer was born. By the 1960s many British women were dressed from top-to-toe by M&S and, today, it still dominates the retail market.

🚶 Cross **Oxford Street** and continue into **Portman Street** until you reach **Bryanston Street**. Turn left. ⑫

In 1860 the foundation stone for the branch synagogue of Bevis Marks was laid in this street, following a breakaway by those committed to the modernization of Jewish worship. Some members later joined the Reform community, which ultimately moved to Seymour Place. See pp. 74–5 and 164.

drove and raced the cars – Joel was successful, winning the Le Mans 24 Hour race three consecutive times in 1928, 1929 and 1930.

At **No. 41** ⑧E resided **Sir Ernest Cassel** (1852–1921). Born to a German-Jewish banking family, he arrived in London aged 16. Later working for Bischoffheim & Co., he also made a fortune through personal investment. His friends included Churchill and King Edward VII, hence his nickname 'Windsor Cassel'. He married in 1878 and converted to Catholicism after his wife's death, fulfilling her dying wish. His fortune was spent on horses and charity, donating over £2 million in his lifetime.

🚶 Leave **Grosvenor Square** at **Upper Grosvenor Street** and stop on the corner of **Park Lane** at **No 93.** ⑨

Western Marble Arch Synagogue.

🚶 Turn right into **Great Cumberland Place**. Cross **Seymour Street** and stop at the small garden with the statue of **Raoul Wallenberg**. ⓭

The statue commemorates Wallenberg's efforts during WWII to save Jewish Hungarian lives. See p. 127.

🚶 Opposite, on the crescent is **Western Marble Arch Synagogue** ⓮.

(*32 Great Cumberland Place, W1H 7TN;* ☎ *020 7723 9333; www.marblearch.org.uk; for services see pp. 164–5.*) The building dates from 1961 and the name from 1986 when two communities merged, Marble Arch and the Western. In 1991 it became an independent synagogue, under the auspices of the United Synagogue.

Marble Arch Synagogue was founded in 1957 as a member of the United Synagogue and successor to the Duke's Place Synagogue that had been destroyed during WWII (see p. 20).

The independent **Western Synagogue** has had a nomadic existence since its foundation in

1761, when a group of maverick Jews moved westwards, against the wishes of Duke's Place Synagogue. Their first home was in Soho followed by Denmark Court, off the Strand. An inter-community dispute in 1810 resulted in a breakaway community established in Dean Street, ultimately ending up at St Alban Place, off Haymarket in 1826. Congregants included Samuel Montagu and Hannah Rothschild, Lady Rosebery. In 1909, the two communities reunited as the Western, moving to Alfred Place, off Tottenham Court Road in 1918 where it was bombed during WWII (see p. 101). In the 1950s its new premises were in Crawford Place.

When the **West End Great Synagogue** vacated Dean Street in 1996, it did not close but relocated here for services and communal events. See pp. 66 and 164–5.

🚶 Turn left into **Upper Berkeley Street** and stop opposite the building with the two pepper-pot towers, **West London Synagogue** (see pp. 74–5). ⓯

🚶 The tour ends here, 5 minutes from Marble Arch tube station.

WEST LONDON SYNAGOGUE

33 Seymour Place, W1H 5AU (postal address)/34 Upper Berkeley Street, W1H 5QE (entrance for services); ☎ *020 7723 4404; www.wls.org.uk; tube: Marble Arch (Central) – 10 mins; open by arrangement only; see p. 164 for details of services.*

Originally the Reform community had been a joint initiative, in the early 1840s, between the Sephardi and Ashkenazi communities who were disillusioned with the established synagogues, in particular sermons being in Hebrew, the length of services and lack of decorum. The congregation's first synagogue opened in 1841 in Burton Street.

Built in an ornate Byzantine style by Davis and Emanuel in 1870, the West London Synagogue is the flagship synagogue for the British Reform movement. The relatively plain exterior does not prepare you for the interior. The vast domed ceiling is lined with gilded mosaics and the bronzed ladies' gallery, unusual in a Reform synagogue, has an open lattice design often seen in mosques. It complements the ornate design of the choir and screen above the freestanding Ark with its open lattice doors, again unusual in a synagogue. There was a traditional central Bimah until 1897 when the community shifted to a more Reform style, integrating the Bimah and pulpit in front of the Ark.

An innovation was the organ and this remains the only British synagogue with an integrated pipe organ.

Hugo Gryn, the rabbi here from 1964 to 1996, the year he died, was described by Rabbi Friedlander as 'probably the most beloved rabbi in Great Britain' (see p. 152).

In 2011, Baroness Neuberger (see p. 91) became the Senior Rabbi after 22 years away from the pulpit.

DISRAELI'S LONDON

Benjamin Disraeli (1804–81), politician, prime minister, novelist and socialite is probably the most famous Jewish-born Briton. The number of plaques and memorials around London dedicated to him indicate the continuing fascination with his life and career. Many buildings associated with his life still exist and enable you to follow in his footsteps. To visit all of the sites would be lengthy as one walk but public transport enables you to get easily from place to place and en route you will also see other key London attractions. Use the map on pp. 118–19 to plan your journey.

Early Years

Begin at 22 Theobalds Road, Holborn ❶ (formerly No. 6 Kings Row) (see

Benjamin Disraeli by Sir John Everett Millais, 1881, National Portrait Gallery.

plaque), where he was born on 21 December 1804. His parents, Isaac D'Israeli and Maria Basevi, were both members of eminent Sephardi families. Maria's brother was George Basevi, a noted Victorian architect.

Benjamin's brothers, James and Ralph, were sent to public schools but he was educated privately, including at Dame Roper's Academy, Colebrooke Row, Islington. ❷ The building still stands.

The family worshipped at Bevis Marks Synagogue. ❸ They were not observant but in 1817 Benjamin's parents wanted to arrange his bar mitzvah. Due to a previous disagreement with the synagogue, the bar mitzvah did not take place and D'Israeli took his family to the church of St Andrew Holborn ❹, where, on 31 July 1817, the children were baptized.

A church has been here for over 1,000 years but the current building was designed by Sir Christopher Wren in the 1680s. Other associations include the tomb of Thomas Coram who established the Foundling Hospital in 1739 and William Marsden who founded, nearby in Gray's Inn Road in 1827, what is now the Royal Free Hospital, Hampstead.

Isaac D'Israeli, also in 1817, moved the family home to No. 6 Bloomsbury Square ❺. Bloomsbury was an attractive area to those in cultural, academic and literary circles and the plaque on the house honours his achievements as an author. His 1789 *Curiosities of Literature* ran to 13 editions. You will see a mezzuzah on the right-hand doorpost. This provides a clue to the current occupant as No. 6 is now the headquarters of the Board of Deputies of British Jews. Established in 1760 by the Sephardi community, it was later joined by the Ashkenazi community and has remained the umbrella organization for British Jewry.

Young Benjamin found Bloomsbury dull. He craved the world of society and politics but his father had other ideas and Benjamin was articled between 1821 and 1824 to the City law firm of Swain, Stevens, Maples, Pearse & Hunt at No. 6 Frederick's Place (see plaque) ❻, a delightful 1770s cul-de-sac designed by the Adam brothers.

Political Career

Benjamin spent time concocting investment ideas and after writing his first novel, *Vivien Grey*, in 1826 he embarked on a year of travel. On returning, he took rooms in the West End and began his campaign to enter Parliament. ❼ He had, by then, adopted 'Disraeli' as his

6 Bloomsbury Square.

6 Frederick's Place.

Disraeli, Parliament Square looking towards Big Ben.

Jewish MP, taking his oath on the Old Testament.

A statue of Disraeli by Mario Raggi is in Parliament Square ❽, opposite the Palace of Westminster. Unveiled in 1883, primroses, allegedly Disraeli's favourite flower, were sent from all over the UK to adorn it. He was Chancellor of the Exchequer three times and prime minister twice, in 1868 and between 1874 and 1880. Much important social legislation was passed during his tenure to improve housing, education and the workplace and led to him being much loved by the populace. Nearby in Westminster Abbey ❾ is a statue of Disraeli by Sir Joseph Boehm. It is situated in the Statesmen's Aisle next to his political rival, William Gladstone. The abbey authorities thoughtfully placed a statue of Peter Warren MP between them. A maquette of this memorial can be seen in the National Portrait Gallery ❿ (Room 25) together with a portrait by Millais, painted just before Disraeli died.

Family and Friends

He married the widow, Mary-Anne Wyndham-Lewis (née Evans) in August 1839 at the church at St George's, Hanover Square ⓫, built 1721–24. Handel had been a regular worshipper here and the weddings of George Eliot, John Galsworthy and John Buchan were also held in this church. The Disraeli marital home at No. 93 Park Lane, Mayfair ⓬, belonged to Mary-Anne and they lived there until her death in 1872.

Disraeli always had financial pressures and many people unkindly believed he married for money but he and Mary-Anne

surname. In 1837, after four attempts, he was elected MP for Maidstone. He was able to take his seat on the oath of the true faith of a Christian as he was no longer Jewish. It was not until 1858 that Lionel de Rothschild became the first

*Mary-Anne Evans, Mrs Benjamin Disraeli,*1840 by R. A. Chalon, Hughenden Manor, The Disraeli Collection (National Trust).

19 Curzon Street.

were a devoted couple. He also had friends in the highest social circles including Queen Victoria, who ennobled him in 1876 as Earl of Beaconsfield. When prime minister, his home was No. 10 Downing Street, off Whitehall **⑬**, the official residence for the office since 1742.

On leaving in 1880 he lodged with friends and in hotels but then bought No. 19 Curzon Street, Mayfair (see plaque) **⑭**, around the corner from his friend Alfred de Rothschild. The lease was short but Disraeli believed it sufficient to take him to the 'elysian fields'. He died there on 19 April 1881. His body was taken from the house at night to avoid crowds massing outside.

The Jewish community was somewhat ambivalent towards Disraeli. Uncomfortable because of his Christianity but proud because he climbed to the height of political power, never denied his Jewish heritage and was instrumental in removing civil disabilities to Jews and other minorities. He was buried by the church of St Michael and All Angels at Hughenden Manor (see pp. 210–11).

You can see some of these sites mentioned in this feature on the **Old Jewish East End** (see pp. 18–32), **Mayfair and the West End** (pp. 67–73) and **Jewish City** (pp. 80–88) walking tours.

JEWISH CITY – A WALK OF JEWISH FIRSTS

Set against the backdrop of the City of London this walk highlights the stories of Jewish emancipation and those who broke down the barriers of discrimination in England. Featured here are not only the first synagogues post-Resettlement but also the first Jewish-born prime minister, MP, Lord Mayor and lord.

▶ **START:** St Paul's tube, Cheapside exit (Central)

▶ **FINISH:** Near Aldgate, 5 minutes from Aldgate tube (Circle, Metropolitan)

▶ **DISTANCE:** 2.1km (1⅓ miles)

▶ **DURATION:** 1½ hours

▶ **REFRESHMENTS: Haz** (*9 Cutler Street, E1 7DJ;* ☎ *020 7929 7923; www.haz restaurant.co.uk*) Affordable, tasty Turkish cuisine; **Old Tea Warehouse** (*4–8 Creechurch Lane, EC3A 5AY;* ☎ *020 7621 1913; www.oldteawarehouse.co.uk*) Delightful pub situated within a warehouse courtyard; Or one of the better chain cafés and sandwich bars such as **Pret A Manger** and **EAT**

NOTE: At weekends many of the cafés in the City are closed. The area around St Paul's is the most lively.

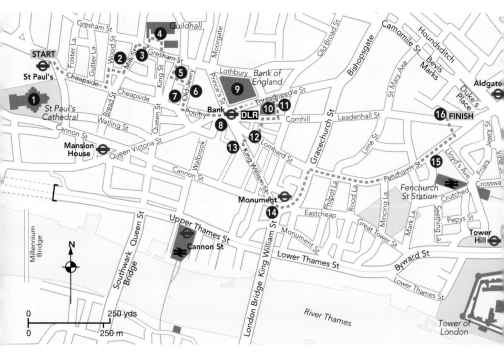

🚶 Start your walk at street level out- side St Paul's tube station, **Cheapside exit**. Walk down **Cheapside** and stop when you see the dome of **St Paul's Cathedral**. ❶

Built between 1675 and 1711 by Sir Christopher Wren, this is the church for the people of London. Big as it is today, the previous church destroyed by the Great Fire of 1666 (henceforth, the Great Fire) was nearly 183m (600ft) long and 152m (500ft) high. You can imagine the concern of Londoners in 1656 when they heard the Jews were to be readmitted into England and allowed two places of worship, one of which was St Paul's Cathedral. The rumour was not true but it indicated the worries of the local population.

In medieval London, **Cheapside** was the key shopping area and the names of the streets, including Honey Lane, Bread Street and Milk Street, are reminders of specialized markets. Today, it is once again a pre-eminent shopping street with New Change shopping mall having opened in 2010. This was also the centre for the medieval Jewish community in London.

🚶 Turn left into **Wood Street**, turn right into a pedestrianized passage and turn left on to **Milk Street**. ❷

At one time nearly all the houses on the left- hand side were owned by Jewish families. In and around the street were synagogues, schools and other community organizations. To the north-west of where you are standing, just outside the city walls at St Giles Cripplegate was the Jewish cemetery, the only one in England until 1177.

There was no ghetto in London but by the time of the Expulsion in 1290, it is agreed

MEDIEVAL MIKVAH

In 2001, the Museum of London Archaeology Service (MOLAS) undertook an archaeological dig at the southern end of Milk Street. Previous excavations in 1976 had confirmed that this was the site of a house owned by the Jewish Crespin family. In 1251 Christians acquired the house and much of the basement was filled in. MOLAS uncovered the basement and found a semi-circular well 1.2m (4ft) deep and 1.2m (4ft) across. There was a short stone staircase leading down. It was recognized as a private Mikvah, a Jewish ritual bath. With so few relics surviving from medieval Jewish London, the Mikvah was carefully dismantled to be re-erected. It is now prominently displayed in the Jewish Museum (see pp. 111–16).

Medieval Mikvah reconstructed at the Jewish Museum.

Guildhall Yard.

that there might have been only around 1,000 Jews in London, the community already having diminished due to discrimination and forced conversion.

🚶 Continue down **Milk Street** and stop on the corner of **Gresham Street** (see p. 81). ❸

🚶 Cross **Gresham street** and walk into **Guildhall Yard** ❹, passing the church of **St Lawrence Jewry** to your right.

Rebuilt by Christopher Wren in 1677 following the Great Fire, the church was rebuilt in the 1950s following the Blitz of WWII. Its name commemorates the medieval Jewish community who lived within the parish.

🚶 Opposite is **Guildhall**. Stand in the middle of the yard and look around.

It is from this area that the City of London has been governed for over 800 years. The first permanent brick building behind the

decorated porch dates from 1411, and has survived the Great Fire, Victorian redevelopment and two world wars. To your left, looking like a brandy glass, is the 1970s Court of Aldermen, with other offices behind. To your right is the Guildhall Art Gallery established in 1885. The gallery suffered bomb damage in WWII and did not open again until 1999 following rebuilding. It houses a collection of art pertaining to the history of London and its population. Guildhall as a whole is the headquarters of the Corporation of the City of London. It plays host to civic ceremonies, including the election of the Lord Mayor and his assistants, the two sheriffs. Originally the yard was the site of a Roman amphitheatre, outlined by the granite circle at ground level.

Guildhall was, until the Royal Courts of Justice were built, also a court of law. **Rodrigo Lopez** (*c*.1525–94), physician to Queen Elizabeth I, was tried here. Lopez, a Portuguese Jew, came to London in 1559 during the period of the Expulsion. He became doctor to Robert Dudley and Francis Walsingham, favourites of the queen, and subsequently became her physician in 1589. But his indiscretions led him to be accused of poisoning the queen and, while many doubted his guilt, he was tried, found guilty and executed at Tower Hill.

🚶 Leave **Guildhall Yard** by the eastern end of the church, turn left and cross **Gresham Street**. Turn right into **Ironmonger Lane**. Stop outside the churchyard on the corner of **St Olaf's Court**. ❺

Ironmonger Lane takes its name from the trade carried out in the street. The church tower is all that remains of St Olaf Jewry, another church name relating to the Jewish population. The church was demolished in 1892 and rebuilt in Stoke Newington in North London but the tower was saved. Also in the street were a synagogue and the Great School of the Jews (Magna Schola Juearum).

Old Jewry.

🚶 Turn left into the alleyway leading to **Old Jewry**. ❻

Opposite is a plaque indicating the site nearby of the **Great Synagogue**, on the corner of Gresham Street. It was closed in 1272 and given to the French Friars of Penitence.

🚶 Turn right and right again into **Fredericks Place**, a 1770s cul-de-sac designed by the Adam brothers.

A plaque on No. 6 ❼ indicates the workplace of Benjamin Disraeli between 1821 and 1824 (see pp. 76–9, 210–11).

🚶 Retrace your steps, turn right and then left on to **Poultry**. Across the street is the pink and grey granite building, **Number One Poultry**. The rooftop

Mansion House.

garden provides views over the City and is worth a detour. Continue and stop opposite **Mansion House ❽**, the building fronted with columns and a triangular pediment.

Built in 1753, it is the official residence for the Lord Mayor of the City of London. Lord Mayors have been appointed since 1189 and elected annually since 1215. The first Jewish Lord Mayor was David Salomons, in 1855 (see pp. 156 and 207–09).

Subsequently, at the time of writing, there have been nine other Jewish Lord Mayors including Marcus Samuel (Viscount Bearsted), founder of the Shell Oil Company and Peter Levene, chairman of Lloyd's of London, the insurance market.

🚶 Cross **Princes Street**, then cross **Threadneedle Street** reaching **Bank junction** and climb the few steps alongside the equestrian statue of the Duke of Wellington. Stand by the war memorial. To your left is the **Bank of England ❾**, established in 1694.

Royal Exchange and Bank of England.

The current ground level, almost windowless and doorless, was designed in 1788 by Sir John Soane. The current upper levels and unseen basements date from the 1930s. The bank began here in the home of the first governor and gradually bought up the full island site including what was the site of the London home of **Aaron of Lincoln** (unknown–1186).

A leading banker in the 1100s, Aaron's stone house in Lincoln is believed to be the oldest private residence surviving in England. With clients in 25 counties, including the Archbishop of Canterbury and nine Cistercian abbeys, he was exceptionally wealthy, worth by today's standards over

Sir David Salomons, *c.*1840.

£20 billion. When he died, as a Jew, all his property and outstanding loans were due to the Crown. Debts owed to him were colossal and the special office set up to collect them, known as Aaron's Exchequer, took over 20 years to do so.

By the 1720s, of 168 stockholders in the Bank of England just six were Jewish and it was not until 1868 that the bank appointed the first Jewish director, **Alfred de Rothschild**. Alfred was a noted socialite, art connoisseur and music lover but he also had a business brain, being re-elected for 21 years as a director of the bank. See also pp. 69 and 142.

🚶 Turn to see the **Royal Exchange ➓**, the building with the colonnaded frontage with triangular pediment above.

It was built in 1844 as the third exchange on this site. The first was erected in 1566, on the initiative of Sir Thomas Gresham, as a place for merchants to trade and for people to meet and shop. Currently, it is again open to the public. Do go inside. It has recently been renovated to include offices, luxury shops (also along the outside) and a Conran café and restaurant.

Areas of the exchange were delineated by type of goods traded and by ethnicity of brokers. It subsequently specialized in bills of exchange and foreign exchange and was an early home to

Paul Julius Reuter.

financial institutions such as Lloyd's of London, the Stock Exchange and LIFFE.

In 1697, of 100 licensed brokers only 12 were allowed to be Jewish. The south-east corner was known as Jews' Walk. Samson Gideon and David Ricardo, both Jewish brokers who renounced their Judaism, made their fortunes here.

In the second exchange, **Nathan Mayer Rothschild** and **Moses Montefiore** are perhaps the two most famous Jewish brokers. They became brothers-in-law, marrying sisters Hannah and Judith Barent-Cohen respectively, lived together nearby in St Swithin's Lane and worked together establishing the Alliance Insurance Company. Nathan was nicknamed 'the Pillar of the Exchange' and contemporary etchings depict him standing in Jews' Walk. See also pp. 141–6.

Take a look at the murals on the first floor, depicting 24 events in the history of the City. One is by the Jewish artist Solomon J. Solomon. See p. 135.

🚶 If the exchange is closed walk around the exterior and turn into the pedestrianized walkway. Otherwise, exit through the other end to see the herm (a bust where the plinth merges into the neck of the subject) of **Paul Julius Reuter** (1816–99). ⓫

Born in Kassel, Germany, as Israel Beer Josaphat, Reuter moved to London in 1845, changed his name and converted to Christianity. Having revolutionized the transmission of news using pigeon post, he set up a system of correspondents in key cities using electric cable. His first offices were established in 1851 at Royal Exchange Buildings and the company NM Rothschild was the first commercial client. Reuters ultimately became the pre-eminent global information news service, only recently being taken over by Thomson in 2008.

At Capel Court, now demolished but on the site of the large office block visible across Threadneedle Street, was the boxing academy established by Daniel Mendoza (see p. 51).

🚶 Cross **Cornhill**, previously the site of the corn market, and walk through **Change Alley** to **Lombard Street**. ⑫

When the Jews were expelled in 1290 their network of moneylending also disappeared so bankers from Lombardy, north Italy, arrived in London and set up their *banques* in this area, hence Lombard Street. The hanging signs, dating from the time when buildings did not have numbers, make this one of the City's most attractive streets.

🚶 Walk through **Post Office Court**, cross **King William Street** and stop at the top of **St Swithin's Lane**. ⑬

In 1809 **Nathan Mayer Rothschild** made his home and set up his business in New Court, a gated courtyard. Today, over 200 years later, the site is still the headquarters of NM Rothschild, the global financial services company (see also p. 141).

🚶 Retrace your steps. Turn right and walk down **King William Street**. Turn left. Stop between the two subway entrances to Monument tube station and look towards London Bridge. The office block with the overhanging first floor was the office of **SG Warburg** ⑭, a global investment bank, during the late 20th century.

Siegmund Warburg (1902–82), from a wealthy German banking family, arrived in

London in 1934. In 1946 he teamed up with another refugee, Henry Grunwald, and established merchant bank SG Warburg. It overturned conventions, being responsible for the first hostile takeover in 1958 between Tube Investments and British Aluminium and in 1963 the bank initiated the first Eurobond, issued for the Italian company, Eurostrade. Today, London trades 70 per cent of the world's Eurobond market.

🚶 Turn left into **Gracechurch Street** and turn right into **Fenchurch Street**. Many of the businesses in this area are related to insurance. To your left, beyond the offices, you will see the glass and steel outline of Lloyd's of London. Stop at St Katherine's Passage. Another glass and steel building with blue and yellow lifts is **Lloyd's Register**. ⑮ This company assesses and grades the seafaring condition of ships.

The building displays the trademark glass and colourful designs of **Lord (Richard) Rogers of Riverside** (b.1933). Born Richard Geiringer in Florence to a cultured family with Jewish heritage, he was six when they fled Italy in 1939. His first prominent commission was the Centre Pompidou, better known as the Beaubourg Centre, in Paris, followed shortly by Lloyd's of London in 1986. Another Rogers trademark is evident in these two buildings and also here – lifts and other utilities on the exterior allowing for uncluttered interiors. He was chair of the Urban Task Force and nicknamed 'Architect to London' despite outspoken views on London's new architecture.

The alleyway was also the site of the **Hambro Synagogue**, the second Ashkenazi synagogue following the Resettlement. In 1704 after a disagreement at Duke's Place

Lloyd's Register.

Synagogue, Marcus Hambro established a private synagogue at his home in Fenchurch Street, as Bevis Marks and Duke's Place would not allow a third public place of Jewish worship in the City. After a period in India, Hambro re-established his house of worship in 1726 but as a public synagogue. Never a large community and often in need of funds, it left Fenchurch Street in 1893 eventually moving to Adler Street in 1899. It closed in 1936 when remaining members, ironically, joined Duke's Place.

🚶 Continue down **Fenchurch Street**. Turn left into **Hart Horn Alley**. Turn left on to **Leadenhall Street**. Stop outside the **London Metal Exchange**, opposite the church of **St Katherine Cree**, a pre-fire church that survived 1666. ⓰

In 1763, the third post-Resettlement Ashkenazi synagogue, **New Synagogue** (see also p. 200), was established, housed in the Bricklayers' Hall where the basement used to be a wine cellar. Hence the rhyme 'The spirits above are spirits divine, the spirits below are made of wine'. It moved to St Helen's, Bishopsgate, in 1838 where an ornate cathedral-like building was designed by David Mocatta, of the prominent Sephardi bullion-trading family. In 1915 it moved to Egerton Road, Stamford Hill.

🚶 The tour ends here. Turn around and turn left at Aldgate High Street to reach Aldgate tube station.

MITTEL EUROPE IN NW3 WALK

Walking through the leafy suburb of Hampstead you will discover stories of the German and Austrian refugees of the interwar years who did not go east but settled in NW3, including Sigmund Freud with his daughter Anna and architect Erno Goldfinger. By the beginning of WWII, nearly a third of the residents were immigrants and German was the lingua franca of the area.

▶ **START:** Swiss Cottage tube, Eton Avenue exit (Jubilee)

▶ **FINISH:** 2 Willow Road, 10 minutes from Hampstead tube (Northern)

▶ **DISTANCE:** 2.75km (1¾ miles)

▶ **DURATION:** Around 1 hour (allow longer if you wish to include a visit to the Freud Museum and/or No. 2 Willow Road)

▶ REFRESHMENTS: **Freemasons Arms** (*32 Downshire Hill, NW3 1NT;* ☎ *020 7433 6811; www.freemasonsarms.co.uk*) A spacious pub with restaurant and garden; **Burgh House** (*New End Square, NW3 1LT;* ☎ *020 7431 0144; www.burghhouse. org.uk*) Houses the Hampstead Museum and a friendly café; One of the many excellent coffee shops in and around Hampstead High Street such as **Gail's** or **Louis'**

🚶 Leave Swiss Cottage tube station via the Eton Avenue exit. Look to your right towards the **Central School of Speech and Drama**. ❶

This was previously the Embassy Theatre, famous for repertory and concerts post-WWI. In May 1945, the first public meeting of the Association of Jewish Refugees (AJR) was held here. Over 800 people attended and another 200 were turned away. A second meeting in October 1945 was as popular. The AJR, founded in 1941, provided practical advice and assistance on housing, employment and integration into British society. It still exists today, serving elderly refugees, Holocaust survivors and their descendants.

🚶 Turn right into **Fitzjohn's Avenue**. Cross the road, walk down the wide steps and turn right until you reach

Eriki Restaurant at **No. 4 Northways Parade**. ❷

The refugees soon established their own shops, cafés and restaurants with Finchley Road the centre of this new 'Mittel Europe'. Despite Anglicizing their names, they continued to communicate in their native tongues. At the Cosmo restaurant on this site you could eat schnitzel with red cabbage well into the late 20th century. It was beautifully portrayed as the Willow Tea Room in the novel *The Morning Gift* by Eva Ibbotson. The author had been a child refugee from Vienna and she remembers Belsize Park, today a sought-after residential area, being 'rather shabby'.

🚶 Retrace your steps. Turn left into Fitzjohn's Avenue. Stop opposite the Tavistock Clinic ❸, where you will see a statue of a seated figure on the corner. See p. 91.

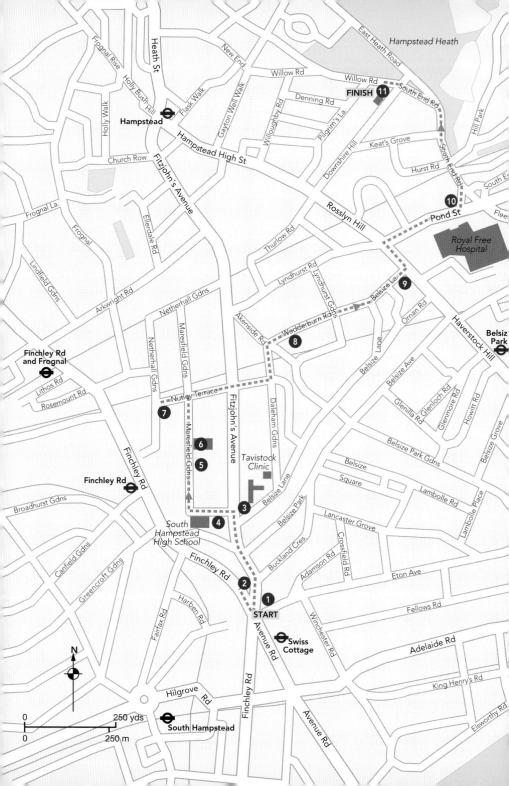

FREUD SCULPTURE

This is the psychoanalyst, Sigmund Freud, sculpted by Oscar Nemon (1906–85) in 1931 to commemorate Freud's 75th birthday. Freud had always refused to have a likeness made and it was only due to the tenacity of his protégé, Paul Federn, a friend of Nemon, that he eventually agreed. Nemon made several preliminary portraits in a variety of media, continuing to sculpt Freud after they both moved to England. An early woodcarving can be seen in the Freud Museum (see pp. 92–3) and a later head was eventually used on this seated statue. See also pp. 135–6.

The Tavistock Clinic was founded in 1920, where its research made significant progress to understand the traumatic effects of trench warfare and the effects of shell shock during WWI. It moved here in 1967 and remains pre-eminent in psychotherapy and family relationships.

Melanie Klein (1882–1960), the Austrian-born psychoanalyst who pioneered therapy work with children, was invited to London in 1926. She worked at the Tavistock Clinic but her theories clashed with those of Anna Freud causing a split in the profession, which survives today. She was the first continental European to be a member of the British Psychoanalytic Society.

🚶 Turn left into **Maresfield Gardens and stop outside South Hampstead High School. ④**

Established in 1876 by the Girls' Public Day School Trust, its geographic situation resulted in a high proportion of Jewish students, particularly from the 1930s. Julia Schwab (b.1950) was head girl here in the 1960s. Her father, the son of pre-WWI German-Jewish immigrants, married a young German-Jewish refugee who had arrived in 1937. In 1977, as **Julia Neuberger**, she became the first female rabbi in the UK to have a community of her own, the South London Liberal Synagogue. Ennobled Baroness Neuberger of Primrose Hill in 2004, her work currently concentrates on the voluntary sector. The Schwab Trust supports and educates young refugees and asylum seekers.

South Hampstead High School.

91

Above: Freud Museum. Right: Freud's study.

Lyndsey Rubin also born in 1950 became a successful songwriter in the 1970s as **Lyndsey de Paul**. She composed many top 10 hits here and abroad, including the poignant teenage ballad 'Won't Somebody Dance With Me'.

Other alumni include the actresses Miriam Karlin and Helena Bonham-Carter.

🚶 Maresfield Gardens bears to the right. Continue and stop outside No. 16, the **Anna Freud Centre**. ❺

Anna Freud (1895–1982), Sigmund's youngest child, became an eminent child psychologist. Originally collaborating with her father she then forged her own career in Vienna, specializing in child development. Her work continued in London from 1938, being also her father's key carer. The centre was established in 1947 as the Hampstead Child Therapy Course, and the Hampstead Clinic opened in 1952.

They later merged, and following her death the clinic was named in her memory.

By the 1930s, large houses such as these had been subdivided into bedsits, becoming homes for the refugees.

🚶 Continue walking and stop outside No. 20, the **Freud Museum**. ❻ Plaques indicate this was the home of both Anna and her father, Sigmund Freud.

(*20 Maresfield Gardens, NW3 5SX;* ☎ *020 7435 2002; www.freud.org.uk; tube: Finchley Road (Jubilee, Metropolitan); open Wed–Sun 12pm–5pm; adm. fee.*) **Sigmund Freud** (1856–1939) is best known for his theories on the subconscious, dreams and sexual desire. Austrian-born, he was the eldest of eight children and the favourite of his parents. Rejecting hypnosis as a form of therapy, he formulated what became the 'talking cure',

whereby patients could release dreams and phobias. His work was much feted, but being Jewish, life became gradually more intolerable in Vienna and in 1938 he and his family, with much practical help from supporters, escaped to London. This house had been purchased in readiness by his son, Ernst, who had left Europe in 1933. Freud did not live in freedom for long, dying just after WWII began.

The house is now a museum, where visitors discover the many facets of Freud, his work, his family and his love of travel and culture.

🚶 Turn left into Nutley Terrace and stop at the junction with **Netherhall Gardens**. Stop outside **No. 14, Otto Schiff House**. ❼

This Jewish Care home, established for Jewish survivors from WWII but now open to other Jewish people, is named after the man who

devoted his life to providing facilities to new refugees in Britain. See p. 70.

🚶 Retrace your steps. Cross Maresfield Gardens and stop on the corner of **Fitzjohn's Avenue**.

Fitzjohn's Avenue was built rapidly between 1876 and 1886 with large homes for aspiring professionals. The house on the corner was the home of Dr William Gull, physician to Queen Victoria. By 1918 most of the houses had been converted to flats and boarding houses and by the end of WWII this was bedsit land.

🚶 Cross the road and turn into **Nutley Terrace**. Turn left into **Daleham Gardens** and turn right into **Wedderburn Road**. Stop outside **No. 13**. ❽

In 1941, Anna Freud established the **Children's Rest Centre** here, to provide a safe haven for

children who had suffered trauma during the Blitz. Later known as the Hampstead War Nurseries, they provided respite for hundreds of children and the opportunity to research the effects of stress upon young people.

🚶 Continue down **Wedderburn Road** and stop on the corner of **Rosslyn Hill**. ❾ Look to your right down the hill towards Belsize Park.

View of the exterior of 2 Willow Road at night.

By 1945 many residents resented the refugees, believing they inhabited homes required for returning soldiers. Two women, Sylvia Gosse and Margaret Crabtree, gathered a list of 2,000 names and presented their **'Hampstead Petition'** to the local authorities with demands for the refugees to be returned home. There was considerable opposition and the petition was quietly dropped. Not long after, in 1953, Hampstead elected **Emanuel Snowman** as its first Jewish mayor. His acceptance speech spoke for his fellow Jewish community when he said: '*When I walk along the highways and byways of Hampstead I have the feeling of treading sacred soil. It is because I remember with the deepest gratitude the welcome Hampstead gave to some of my brethren ...*'

🚶 Turn left and cross **Rosslyn Hill** in front of newly restored St Stephen's Church built in 1869. Turn right into **Pond Street**, walk down the hill with the Royal Free Hospital on your right. Stop at the junction with **South End Green**. ❿

On the corner, a plaque commemorates the **bookshop** where novelist and journalist George Orwell worked for six months in the mid-1930s. He worked in shifts with Jon Kimche, a Swiss Jew who arrived in England aged 12, and later became a socialist and successful journalist. In 1936, the shop was immortalized in Orwell's short essay, 'Bookshop Memories'.

🚶 Turn left and walk along **South End Road**, past the parade of shops. Hampstead Heath is to your right. Cross **Downshire Hill**, bearing left into **Willow Road**. Stop at **No. 2**. ⓫

(*2 Willow Road, NW3 1TH;* ☎ *01494 755 570; www.nationaltrust.org.uk; tube: Hampstead (Northern) – 10 mins; Overground: Hampstead Heath – 3 mins; open Mar–Oct Thur–Sun, weekends in Nov; opening times subject to change, check website; adm. fee.*) Hungarian born **Erno Goldfinger** (1902–87) studied architecture in Paris. He and his young family moved to London, living in Highgate in flats designed by another Hungarian émigré, Berthold Lubetkin. In 1939, Erno designed this family home, one of only two post-WWII domestic buildings he built. It is modernist in style, with large windows, and coordinating fixtures and fittings. His public housing was controversial, including Balfron and Trellick towers, in East and West London respectively, but his work is being reappraised with Trellick Tower now a listed building. His temper was legendary and the writer, Ian Fleming, vented his displeasure with him by naming a villain in his James Bond books, Goldfinger.

🚶 The tour ends here, a few minutes from the eateries and shops of Hampstead High Street and South End Green.

HIDDEN JEWISH LONDON

Leave Central London, Jewish suburbia and the City behind and you will find that Jewish connections abound in London when you are least expecting them. Hidden Jewish London is a selection of our favourites. See where Vidal Sassoon, the Swinging Sixties hairdresser, went to school and where the first president and first prime minister of Israel lived when resident in London. By taking a tube journey you can discover a synagogue from a Jewish hospital for 'Incurables' that has been painstakingly recreated in a chapel converted for synagogue use and the kitchens of a Rothschild mansion where lavish parties were prepared.

This chapter takes you out of Central London to discover places with Jewish connections but also introduces you to places that will give you a greater understanding of the varied Jewish life and personalities in London since the 19th century. Rothschild hospitality was legendary but Philip Sassoon rivalled them at Trent Park and while Portobello Road is famous for its antiques market, a stone's throw away you will stumble across the disused synagogue for the lower-middle class Jewish community of Notting Hill. A visit to Holland Park and its wonderful gardens is but a few minutes walk from facilities for today's Sephardi community and to complement a visit to the national art galleries, a visit to Dorich House on the edge of Richmond Park to see the work of Dora Gordine will prove a perfect day out.

Sukkat Shalom, Bimah (see pp. 108–09).

NOTTING HILL AND BAYSWATER

The move beyond the West End started in earnest in the mid 19th century when wealthy communal leaders acquired spacious homes in Bayswater. Poor, but Orthodox immigrants later formed a small, vibrant community in Notting Hill. Memories remain of both and provide an opportunity to discover a couple of under-visited London neighbourhoods.

BAYSWATER JEWISH SCHOOL

111–117 Lancaster Road, W11 1QT; tube: Ladbroke Grove (Circle, Hammersmith & City) – 3 mins. ❶

The school was established in 1866 in Chichester Place by Bayswater Synagogue, for 20 children of 'poorer brethren'. It moved in 1867 to Paddington and was renamed Bayswater Jewish School. In 1879, it moved to 179 Harrow Road, and in 1930 to Lancaster Road, North Kensington. From 1938, donations by the Wolfson family, owners of Great Universal Stores, ensured its survival, with a new name, the Solomon Wolfson School. Post-

WWII student numbers dropped and, in 1981, the school moved to the suburb of Kenton and was renamed Michael Sobell Sinai School. The original Lancaster Road school building is now used by the Terrence Higgins Trust.

BAYSWATER SYNAGOGUE (DEMOLISHED)

It was consecrated in 1863 as a branch of the Duke's Place and New Synagogues for their West London members for whom an 8km (5 mile) walk to services was proving unsatisfactory.

Beginning as a purpose-built synagogue at Chichester Place, near Harrow Road, it was

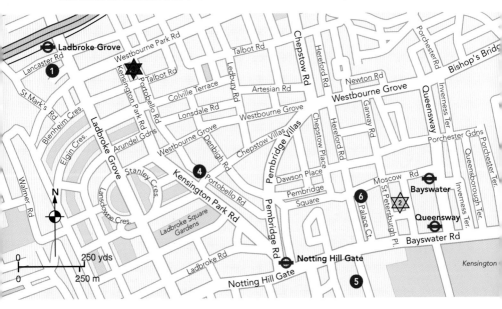

one of the five original members of the United Synagogue. Among its rabbis was Hermann Adler, who after 27 years in service at Bayswater became Chief Rabbi in 1891, following his father, Nathan Adler.

In the mid-1960s, the building was demolished to allow the construction of the Westway and the community moved to Ashworth Road before its last home in Andover Place, Maida Vale. Membership reached over 400 male seat holders by the 1960s but rapidly declined to about 190 by 1970.

The synagogue closed in 1984. Before demolition the premises were used for a Jewish school and the Saatchi Synagogue.

NEW WEST END SYNAGOGUE

St Petersburgh Place, W2 4JT; ☎ 020 7229 2631; www.newwestend.org.uk; tube: Bayswater (Circle, District), Queensway (Central) – 7 mins from either; to visit, contact synagogue; voluntary donation appreciated; see p. 164 for details of services. ❷

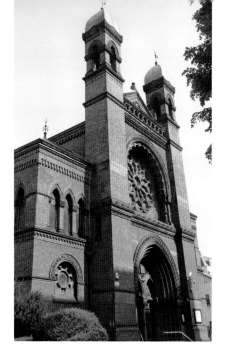

New West End Synagogue.

This Grade I listed building was consecrated in 1879. The red brick exterior topped with two towers and with a large rose stained-glass window to the front hides one of the most ornate synagogue interiors in London. By the 1860s, the central West End had branches of the City synagogues and the Reform movement was gaining members. Further west in Bayswater, a synagogue for the Orthodox Jewish community was also needed. To reflect their lifestyle, no expense was spared on the design.

Inside, the style is oriental, with alabaster and marble veneer from Europe added in 1895, all in a warm colour scheme of green, cream and gold. Unusually for a synagogue, along the front of the gallery there are inscriptions of extracts from Psalms, chosen by Simeon Singer, rabbinical leader from 1879 until his death in 1906. In 1890 he compiled a standard service text, the Authorised Daily Prayer Book, commonly known as the Singer's Prayer Book. Its successors are still used today.

The stained glass dates from the early 20th century, with the eastern rose window executed in 1937 by Erwin Bossanyi, an Hungarian émigré, in memory of Emma, Lady Rothschild, widow of the 1st Lord Rothschild.

The community was considered the 'aristocracy' of Anglo-Jewry. Worshippers included the Montagus, Herbert Samuel, Rufus Isaacs, Walter Rothschild (2nd Lord) and the Sieff family of Marks & Spencer.

It was Dr Louis Jacobs, arriving in 1953, who really shook the foundations of this community when he left in 1960 and was not permitted by the then Chief Rabbi to return in 1964. Many of his supporters resigned their memberships to join him at his new community in St. John's Wood. See p. 193.

The late 20th century saw membership and activities dwindle but as other local synagogues closed, their members joined and the community has revived, under the active leadership of Rabbi Geoffrey Shisler, here since 2000.

The Herbert Samuel Hall was built in 1957 and named after Viscount Samuel, the first Jewish cabinet minister and British High Commissioner in Palestine.

NOTTING HILL SYNAGOGUE

206 Kensington Park Road, W11 1NR; tube: Ladbroke Grove (Circle, Hammersmith & City) – 5 mins. ❸

During the late 19th century, a few minutes' walk from the splendid mansions of Anglo-Jewish aristocracy, a small community of 30 Jewish families developed in the streets off Portobello Road. Making livings as tailors, trimming merchants and market-stall traders they lived in flats within substantial houses. The existing Bayswater and New West End synagogues, established in 1863 and 1879 respectively, were considered too grand and too 'English' by these families and in 1897 they commenced services in a private home on Lancaster Road. Soon after, members of the New West End proposed and funded a new synagogue for them. A church meeting hall on Kensington Park Road was purchased and consecrated in 1900 as the Notting Hill Synagogue, a member of the Federation.

It established several youth clubs, including the Notting Hill Jewish Lads' Club and Beatrice

Club for Jewish Girls, a highly regarded cheder and a Talmud Torah. This blue and white building, now a Montessori school, remained for more than 100 years the synagogue for the local Orthodox community. The congregation increased steadily with around 600 families by the 1920s.

The community always remained lower middle class and the synagogue struggled to survive following WWII when many members moved to Cricklewood and Willesden. After a short renaissance in the 1980s, economics dictated its closure in 2000.

PORTOBELLO ROAD MARKET

Portobello Road runs from near Notting Hill Gate to Lancaster Road; tube: Notting Hill Gate (Circle, District), Ladbroke Grove (Circle, Hammersmith & City) – 10 mins; note: Antiques Market (www.portobelloroad.co.uk) Sat only; shops & other market stalls open daily. ❹

The original market sold fresh produce. The antiques market arrived in the 1960s. Jewish market-stall holders predominated during the first half of the 20th century.

Notting Hill Synagogue
(currently a Montessori school).

IN THE FOOTSTEPS OF LILY MONTAGU

The **Hon. Lilian (Lily) Montagu** (1873–1963) was a social worker, co-founder of what is now Liberal Judaism and a pioneer for women playing an equal role in Judaism. (Map references refer to page 96.)

Lily was the sixth of ten children born to the wealthy banker and MP, Samuel Montagu (later Baron Swaythling). Despite her privileged background, Lily lived a simple life. She walked almost everywhere, only accepting lifts in her sister's Rolls Royce when she became infirm.

Her childhood home was in **Kensington Palace Gardens ❺**, one of London's richest streets. Politicians such as Gladstone, famous intellectuals and leaders of the Jewish community were frequent visitors.

She was brought up in a strictly Orthodox household. Her family belonged to the **New West End Synagogue** in St Petersburgh Place where, aged 17, Lily ran successful Shabbat services in English.

Social Work

Lily also became involved in social work at an early age. With her sister Marian, her lifelong companion, Lily ran evening classes and 'happy Sunday afternoons' in rooms in Devonshire Street for Jewish girls working in the millinery and tailoring industries around **Soho**. Cheap accommodation had attracted many of the late 19th-century Jewish immigrants fleeing persecution in Eastern Europe.

In 1893 Lily, Marian and their cousin Beatrice Franklin founded the **West Central Jewish Girls' Club** 'to bring brightness and refinement to the lives of Jewish working girls'. From two rooms at **71 Dean Street** in Soho, the club expanded and moved to **8 Frith Street**, and then, in 1896, to **8a Dean Street**. The club grew into a nationally recognized institution and, by the time of Lily's death, it had over a thousand members. She was adored by club members who referred to her as 'Miss Lily'.

Lily was involved in the **National Union of Women Workers** and the **Women's Industrial Council**, which campaigned to improve the working conditions of the girls with whom she worked. These two bodies were located at **8 Dean Street** and were later absorbed into the National Association of Girls Clubs (now Youth Clubs UK), which Lily helped to found.

Lily Montagu.

Liberal Jewish Synagogue, St. John's Wood.

Liberal Judaism

Lily's involvement in the setting up of the Jewish Religion Union (JRU) led to a family rift. The forerunner of what is now Liberal Judaism, the JRU organized Saturday afternoon services for people who could not attend Shabbat morning services because they worked a five-and-a-half-day week. The first services were held in the **Wharncliffe Rooms** in the **Great Central Hotel, Marylebone Road** (now the Landmark Hotel).

The JRU went on to found The Liberal Jewish Synagogue (LJS) initially located in a former Baptist chapel in **Hill Street**, near Baker Street station (now the site of **Rossmore Court**). In 1918, Lily was invited to preach the sermon at the synagogue, one of the first women in the country to occupy a pulpit.

In the same year, Lily and Marian set up the West Central Settlement at **31/32 Alfred Place**, off Tottenham Court Road, to provide a range of services and activities for the Girls' Club. In 1926, Lily became the lay minister of the congregation she had

established at the Settlement in 1916, the West Central Section of the JRU (later the West Central Liberal Synagogue).

By 1925, the LJS had outgrown its premises in Hill Street and an impressive new synagogue was erected at **28 St. John's Wood Road**, where Lily played a leading role. Lily Montagu was one of the first to witness the extensive damage caused by a bomb that fell on the night of 1 November 1940. The synagogue was restored and re-consecrated in 1951. A new wing added in 1963 was designated the Lily Montagu Wing.

Lily at Work, Rest and Play

The new LJS was situated opposite the **Grace Gates** at **Lord's Cricket Ground**. Lily, Marian and their older sister, Henrietta Franklin (a well-known educationalist), were enthusiastic cricket fans and regularly attended matches at Lord's. The three sisters are described as sitting in a row wearing 'long coats and large hats looking like something from a bygone era'.

In 1926, Lily helped found and eventually became president of the World Union for Progressive Judaism. Its offices were located in her home at **Red Lodge, 51 Palace Court, Bayswater ❻**, where Lily lived with Marian and their close friend Constance Lewis. They held regular Friday night 'at homes', which were noted for a welcoming atmosphere but also for the austerity of the food and the chilliness of the surroundings.

Lily had a lifelong interest in the welfare of children, and, in 1942 she and Marian set up the **Maude Nathan Home for Little Children** at **72 Crystal Palace Park Road,** Sydenham. Lily and Marian travelled most Sunday afternoons to the

Above: Lily and Marian Montagu with
Constance Lewis when young women.
Right: Red Lodge, Palace Court.

home on the top deck of a bus eating
their sandwiches.

The West Central Settlement at Alfred
Place was bombed in April 1941 with the
loss of 27 lives. After several temporary
homes, the Settlement eventually moved to
its current site on the corner of **Whitfield
and Maple streets**, where it subsequently
became the headquarters for the Union of
Liberal and Progressive Synagogues (later
Liberal Judaism) and named the Montagu
Centre. Lily played a leading role in the setting up of many of the congregations that
today form the Liberal movement.

Lily was buried alongside her father in
the family grave at **Edmonton Federation
Cemetery**.

Pam Fox, author of A Place To Call My Jewish
Home: Memories of The Liberal Jewish
Synagogue 1911–2011. *(See also p. 192.)*

HOLLAND PARK AND MAIDA VALE

The Sephardi community predominates in these two upmarket residential areas. Maida Vale, with its proximity to Regent's Canal, is nicknamed 'Little Venice' and Holland Park with its ruined mansion and beautiful gardens was home in Victorian times to eminent artists.

THE SPANISH AND PORTUGUESE SEPHARDI SYNAGOGUE – HOLLAND PARK

8 St James's Gardens, Holland Park, W11 4RB; ☎ *020 7603 7961; www.hollandparksynagogue. com; tube: Shepherds Bush (Central) – 10 mins; for services see p. 164.*

The Holland Park Sephardi Community was from Greece and Turkey, many from Salonika where a high percentage of the population were Jewish. Some had come to the area for the Anglo-French Exhibition held at the new White City complex in 1908. Following this exhibition, more families joined the community from the East End of London and others arrived from the then declining Turkish Empire, with a further influx at the start of WWI when young men emigrated to avoid the draft into the Turkish Army.

By 1914 some 700 families had settled in the area and were holding their own services with a view to having their own synagogue. This took a further 14 years as this was a poor community, but was eventually opened in 1928 following the purchase of a piece of land in St. James's Gardens in 1924. The synagogue is named after a major benefactor, Sassoon David Sassoon, and his name is in Hebrew above an entrance. The dark wood furniture is reminiscent of Bevis Marks and the dome provides oriental and Moorish influence. The stained glass, depicting David's Harp, the Horn of Plenty and fruits of the Holy Land are particularly beautiful.

Holland Park Synagogue.

LAUDERDALE ROAD SYNAGOGUE

2 Ashworth Road, W9 1JY; ☎ *020 7289 2573;*
www.lauderdaleroadsynagogue.org; tube: Maida
Vale (Bakerloo) – 7 mins; visits by prior arrangement
only; for services see p. 192.

The history and development of
Lauderdale Road Synagogue is also the
story of the move of the Sephardi community to West London. Until the mid 19th
century there was only one London
Sephardi synagogue, Bevis Marks, and
residents in the West End had to walk
across London to worship. In 1840 both
Sephardi and Ashkenazi residents began
to consider opening a synagogue in Central
London. In 1842 the West London Synagogue
was opened in Burton Street, but eventually Bevis Marks recognized the need for a
branch of its own. In 1860, a synagogue
was built in Bryanston Street, near Marble
Arch. With a synagogue in the West End it
was decided to demolish Bevis Marks but
an 'anti-demolition' campaign saved it. By
the late 1880s, the Sephardi community
was growing and concentrated around
Clifton Road, Maida Vale and the decision

was made to build a new large synagogue.
The synagogue opened in 1896 and next
door was The Orphanage (see p. 104).

The building is Grade II listed with a
Byzantine exterior design, with dome and
cupola dominating the skyline. The
imposing Ehal replaced the modest original, which was presented to the Home
and Hospital for Jewish Incurables.
Inside it is light and spacious and,
although dating from the 1890s, has
always been lit by electricity.

Above: Lauderdale Road Synagogue.
Below: Interior of Lauderdale Road Synagogue.

LAUDERDALE ROAD SYNAGOGUE HALL (PREVIOUSLY THE ORPHANAGE)

The Orphanage was built at the same time as the synagogue and on closing in 1940 was converted into a centre for communal activities. **Vidalico (Vidal) Sassoon** (b.1928), the hairdresser, lived here as a boy for seven years. His mother was born in London but his father originated from Salonika. Their early family life with the Saloniki community was in Shepherds Bush where Vidal was born. His father abandoned the family and later, aged five, Vidal was sent to the Sephardi Orphanage. He was apprenticed to a hairdressing salon on the Whitechapel Road, became a member of the 43 Group, fighting Fascism in London and fought for Israel in 1948. His first salon opened in the mid 1960s. His geometric haircuts for fashion luminaries including Mary Quant and Twiggy made him one of the most famous hairdressers in the world.

MONTEFIORE COLLEGE

2 Ashworth Road, W9 1JY; www.montefiore endowment.org.uk.
Originating as the Judith, Lady Montefiore Theological College in Ramsgate, it remains funded by the Endowment as the Montefiore College, training Sephardi rabbis and judges of Jewish law. See also p. 213.

JEWISH RESIDENTS

David Ben Gurion (1886–1973) (*75 Warrington Crescent, W9 1EH; tube: Warwick Avenue (Bakerloo) – 3 mins.*) Russian-born, he moved to Palestine as a young man. He became the first prime minister of Israel in 1948. He lived briefly in London.

Michael Winner (b.1935) Film director and restaurant critic, he currently lives in Melbury Road, Holland Park. His parents, members of Notting Hill Synagogue, made a comfortable living from the family emporia. His home contains an excellent collection of illustrations, which he is bequeathing, with his mansion, to the nation.

Chaim Weizmann (1874–1952) (*67 Addison Road, W14 8JL; station: Olympia (tube (District), Overground) – 5 mins.*) The first president of Israel lived in London between 1916 and 1919. Russian-born, he became a scientist and committed Zionist and migrated to England in 1904 as a research chemist. His government work during WWI introduced him to the establishment and through them Weizmann became a Zionist spokesman culminating in the 1917 Balfour Declaration. He subsequently moved to Israel.

Right: Chaim Weizmann lived here.

SEPHARDI COMMUNITY

The UK Sephardi community currently accounts for about 3.5 per cent of total UK synagogue membership. It maintains a Sephardi kashrut supervisory board and cemeteries. Bevis Marks and Lauderdale Road are the largest synagogues but the number of congregations has grown following migrations from India in the 1940s, Egypt in the 1950s, Iran in the 1970s and in recent years from France, Morocco and Uzbekistan. Smaller synagogues have since been established including Wembley, Hendon and Stamford Hill and services are also held within large Ashkenazi synagogues such as St. John's Wood.

OFF THE BEATEN TRACK

To visit places of Jewish interest off the beaten track, four destinations have been selected, one at each compass point. All are easily reached by public transport and each gives a different insight into London's Jewish heritage: country estates owned by Anglo-Jewish aristocracy, an artist's studio and one combining Christian, Jewish and medical heritage.

NORTH: TRENT PARK

Cockfosters Road, Enfield, EN4 0PS; ☎ *020 8441 7833; www.enfield.gov.uk; tube: Cockfosters (Piccadilly) – a few mins walk to entrance; open daily, times vary, check website; notes: Swiss Lodge Visitor Centre provides advice on walks & wildlife; café open from 11am all year round, picnic tables provided; Sassoon's other country home, Port Lympne, part of Kent Safari Park & Zoo, www.aspinallfoundation.org/portlympne.*

Trent Park was the home of two members of the Sassoon family, who were known as 'the Rothschilds of the East'. In the 14th century, the estate was a hunting ground for King Henry IV. In 1777, King George III leased the site to his favourite doctor, Doctor Jebb, who had saved the life of the king's brother. The estate was sold in 1908 to Sir Edward Sassoon, MP for Hythe, and married to a Rothschild. On his death in 1912, Trent Park passed to his son, Philip Sassoon (1888–1939) who became MP for Hythe a few weeks later. A respected art collector and trustee of the National Gallery, the Tate and the Wallace collections, Sassoon rejected the business world to pursue a life of arts, politics and hospitality.

In 1923 he commissioned Philip Tilden to redevelop the estate. The house was transformed into the essence of an English country home complete with private runway and golf course. Sassoon's reputation as a host was legendary and guests included Charlie Chaplin, Winston Churchill and George Bernard Shaw. He died suddenly in 1939 and his ashes were scattered over the park. During WWII Trent Park was used as a prison for captured German generals and officers. They were treated well, but microphones were hidden around the house. In 1951 the estate became part of Trent Park College, now Middlesex University. Trent Park opened to the public in 1973, providing a 167ha (413 acre) country park, farmland, golf and equestrian centre. Original landscaping by Humphrey Repton, prior to Sassoon's ownership, remains with a water garden, lakes and an avenue of lime trees.

Visitors can view the exterior of the house (Middlesex University property) and explore the grounds, in which several nature trails have been laid.

SOUTH: DORICH HOUSE MUSEUM

67 Kingston Vale, SW15 3RN; ☎ *020 8417 5515; www.dorichhousemuseum.org.uk; tube: Putney Bridge (District), then Bus 85; Overground: Kingston, then Bus 85/K3 from Cromwell Road bus station; open selected days only, check website; adm. fee; booking in advance advised; guided tours offered on open days.*

Dorich House was built in 1936 as the studio, gallery and home of the sculptor Dora Gordine (1895–1991) and her husband, the Hon. Richard Hare, a professor in Russian literature. Restored by Kingston University in the 1990s it is a wonderful example of modernist design in which visitors can

discover not only the warmth of the art deco interior but also the largest display of work by Dora together with Richard's collection of icons and artefacts from Imperial Russia.

Above: Dorich House.

Below: Dora Gordine sculpting *Arabian Princess, c.*1948.

Born 'Dora Gordin', she was born in Latvia to Russian-Jewish parents. Studying in Paris, she added an 'e' to her surname and met eminent sculptors including Maillol. Her first piece to win critical acclaim, *Head of a Chinese Philosopher* from 1926, is on display. Prestigious commissions followed including one in the late 1920s for City Hall, Singapore. By 1938, some considered her the finest female sculptor in the world. She was inspired by the human form and, following her marriage, she sculpted many society figures including actresses Dorothy Tutin and Dame Edith Evans and the dancer Beryl Grey. Public commissions included sculptures for Holloway Prison's mother and baby unit, Esso oil refinery and the Royal Marsden Hospital.

EAST: SUKKAT SHALOM REFORM SYNAGOGUE

1 Victory Road, Wanstead, E11 1UL; ☎ *020 8530 3345; www.sukkatshalom.org.uk; tube: Snaresbrook (Central) – 10 mins; open by appt; voluntary donation appreciated.*

In the suburb of Wanstead you can find two pieces of hospital history in the Sukkat Shalom Synagogue. It is housed in a disused chapel dating from the 1860s Merchant Seaman's Orphan Asylum, built for children of destitute seamen. It outgrew its original premises in East London and moved to Wanstead, with room for 250 children, and this Venetian-Gothic chapel was built next door. The orphanage was converted into Wanstead Hospital and when the hospital closed in 1994, the chapel was redundant.

The current congregation was established in 1980 as a branch of the South West Essex Reform Synagogue. After 15 years in Buckhurst Hill, and with a membership of over 300 adults, the community reopened here in 2000 as Sukkat Shalom (Shelter of Peace) Reform Synagogue.

The building had been purchased with help from the Heritage Lottery Fund. The interior features preserved woodwork with intricate designs of flora and fauna, ram's horns and Ionic columns, an allusion to the Temple of Solomon. The joinery and stained-glass windows were transported from the Jewish Home and Hospital at Tottenham, North London, which closed in 1995. The hospital had originally opened in 1889 in Hackney as the Home and Hospital for Jewish Incurables. It moved in 1903 to a three-storey red-brick building on Tottenham High Road designed to house 80. In 1914 an extension and synagogue were completed, but despite further additions in the 1960s, the home closed.

Right: Sukkat Shalom Reform Synagogue.
Inset: *Synagogue at the Home and Hospital for Jewish Incurables* by Beverley-Jane Stewart.

WEST: GUNNERSBURY PARK MUSEUM

Gunnersbury Park, Popes Lane, W3 8LQ;
☎ *020 8992 1612; tube: Acton Town*
(Piccadilly/District); bus: E3 from station; open
Apr–Oct daily 11am–5pm, Nov–Mar daily
11am–4pm; see also p. 144.

In 1835 Gunnersbury became the first Rothschild country house when Nathan Mayer Rothschild bought the Large Mansion, built in 1802, and its adjoining park. He died a year later, in 1836, before moving in. Subsequently, Leopold, Nathan's grandson, acquired the adjoining Small Mansion with its grounds in 1889, and Gunnersbury remained in Rothschild hands until 1925. The Rothschilds extended Gunnersbury from 30ha (75 acres) to 75ha (186 acres) of landscaped grounds. Their elegant parties were legendary, with often more than 500 guests in attendance.

Gunnersbury Park Museum.

Local residents would queue along the streets to view the procession of carriages arriving. Menus would run to 16 courses and there were two French chefs permanently employed. The marriage of Alphonse de Rothschild to his cousin Leonora in 1857 took place here in the presence of the Chief Rabbi.

Large kitchens were essential for such entertaining and they have been renovated to look as they would have in the Rothschilds' time. Leopold died in 1917 and subsequently the site was sold for public use. The public park opened in 1926 and the house, as a museum, in 1929. Do not miss the Rothschild chariots, on display in the former Pink Saloon. Painted in the family colours of blue and gold, there was one for every type of journey – town or country, home or abroad.

JEWISH MUSEUM

Established in 1932 in Woburn House, Bloomsbury, the collection concentrated on the development of British Jewry and displayed Judaica from the time of the Resettlement onwards. In 1995 it moved to the current Albert Street site. In the same year it merged with the Finchley-based London Museum of Jewish Life, which concentrated on social history, particularly the Jewish East End.

Raymond Burton House, 129–131 Albert Street, Camden Town, NW1 7NB; ☎ *020 7284 7384; www.jewishmuseum.org.uk; tube: Camden Town (Northern) – 3 mins; open Sat–Thur 10am–5pm, Fri 10am–2pm; adm £7.50, conc. £6.50, children £3.50, Museum Friends free (check website for group tickets & other concessions).*

In March 2010, following the purchase of a former piano factory next door and a £10 million two-year Heritage Lottery funded-project, the museum fulfilled a longstanding aim and reopened on one site. The new building has four permanent galleries and a changing exhibitions gallery, kosher café and museum shop.

The displays, many interactive, celebrate Jewish life and cultural diversity and explore Jewish heritage as part of the wider story of Britain. Volunteer staff are delighted to answer questions and explain exhibits. There is free entry to the Welcome Gallery; access to the upper galleries is by paid admission. There is an imaginative cultural events programme, the ticket price usually includes access to the museum.

GROUND FLOOR: WELCOME GALLERY

The Welcome Gallery also includes the ticket desk, museum shop and kosher café. On entering, you will see and hear a multimedia installation featuring 10 Jewish people living in London today. These short films demonstrate the diversity of the Jewish community and include a Jews' Free School student, a fourth-generation smoked-salmon smoker, a taxi driver and an Indian-born Orthodox grandmother who has completed more than 20 marathons.

As you continue up the steps on your left you will see the **Bakers' Union Banner**, a wonderful survival of radical Jewish politics. It publicizes the campaign to encourage shoppers to buy only Union bread, meaning that it had been produced in a bakery that guaranteed fair conditions for workers.

Ahead is the reconstructed 13th-century medieval Mikvah, discovered in 2001 during excavations in the City of London (see p. 81).

RAYMOND BURTON

Raymond Burton House is named after the son of Montagu Burton, founder of the menswear retail firm. Raymond Burton purchased the original Camden site for the museum in the late 1980s.

Entrance corridor, Jewish Museum.

JEWISH MUSEUM TOP 10

1 Bakers' Union Banner
2 Medieval Mikvah
3 Italian synagogue Ark
4 Lindo Chanukah lamp
5 Kandler Torah scroll case
6 Daniel Mendoza jug
7 East End
8 Holocaust Gallery
9 Yiddish theatre karaoke
10 Children's activity packs (ask at the ticket desk)

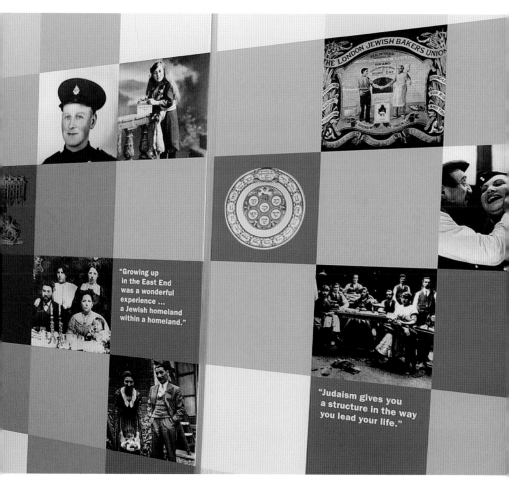

"Growing up in the East End was a wonderful experience ... a Jewish homeland within a homeland."

"Judaism gives you a structure in the way you lead your life."

FIRST FLOOR: JUDAISM – A LIVING FAITH

The Judaica collection has been designated by the British government as being of 'Outstanding Importance to the National Heritage' and is one of the finest in the world. As you enter there is a desk with an open Torah scroll, displayed with items used to read it, for example the silver pointers. In the distance you can see an Ark, giving the impression of entering a synagogue. The Ark was one of the first exhibits, being acquired in 1932. Discovered as a steward's wardrobe in Chillingham Castle, Northumbria, it is in fact a wooden and richly decorated Ark from Italy, dating from the late 1600s or early 1700s.

The cabinets around the room display Judaica and personal articles linked to the Jewish year, providing an insight into Shabbat, festivals and synagogue worship. A table is set for Shabbat and accompanying films and recordings bring to life the celebrations, songs and prayers.

Other displays are an engaging introduction to life events within the Jewish community – birth, circumcision, bar mitzvah, marriage, death and mourning.

Exhibits from around the world show the common function of religious objects but also how design is strongly influenced by local styles. A delightful example is the German filigree and enamel spice box.

The oldest piece of English Judaica is the

Judaism: A living faith.

Chanukah lamp made in 1709 for Elias Lindo to commemorate his marriage. The Kandler travelling scroll case, made in 1766/67, belonged to Samuel Falk (see pp. 45, 140 and 155) and is named after the maker, Frederick Kandler. The clever design uses the pointer as the clasp.

SECOND FLOOR: HISTORY – A BRITISH STORY

This gallery shows Jewish history as part of British history and follows a broadly chronological approach.

The entrance display case prompts thoughts of origins and journeys. Inside is a beautiful bar mitzvah robe brought to Britain from Bukhara; the suitcase carried by Ken Ambrose, who arrived here as a refugee from Nazi Europe; and the OBE awarded to Helen Bamber, who assisted at Belsen following the liberation.

The map alongside shows the diverse geographic origins of the current British Jewish community, embedded with objects brought by immigrants.

Key themes to explore include:

Major Migrations – the first medieval settlers, the Expulsion, the Resettlement, the late 19th-century mass migration from Eastern Europe, 1930s refugees fleeing Nazi Europe and post-WWII migrations.

Jewish East End – this is a particularly rich collection seen through the evocation of an East End street, where you can visit an immigrant home, smell the chicken soup and hear tailors talk about their work.

Above: Daniel Mendoza jug c. 1800.
Left: *The King of Lampedusa* at the Grand Palais.

115

East End tailoring shop.

Yiddish Theatre – a permanent display relating to the theatres, actors and plays, with an opportunity to try karaoke in Yiddish.
20th-Century Issues – the British-Jewish experience is linked to major events of the 20th century including the two world wars, the rise of Fascism at home and abroad, the growth of the suburbs, refugees from Nazism and concludes with Zionism and new migrant communities.
Contemporary – an interactive display explores the contemporary issues facing the Jewish community.
Holocaust Gallery – see p. 121.

THIRD FLOOR: CHANGING EXHIBITIONS GALLERY

Exhibitions presented include 'Illumination – Hebrew Treasures from the Vatican and Major British Collections', 'Morocco' and 'Entertaining the Nation – Jewish Stars of Music, Stage and Screen'.

CAFE AND SHOP

The café is managed by Adafina (see p. 191). It serves chicken soup, smoked-salmon and salt-beef sandwiches, drinks and cakes (SKA). It is open during museum hours (except Sat). The Museum Shop sells a wide selection of Jewish-themed secular books, modern Judaica, jewellery and gifts.

HOLOCAUST MEMORIALS IN LONDON

Holocaust is the term given to the murder of six million European Jews, including one and a half million children, by the Nazis in WWII. Most were systematically murdered in death camps as part of the Final Solution.

Whilst Britain was not directly affected by the Nazis' persecution of the Jews, it became home for around 75,000 refugees from Nazi Europe before WWII, including 9,354 Kindertransport children, and many Holocaust survivors settled in Britain after WWII.

It is only in the last 30 years that Holocaust-related memorials have been established in London. These range in size from the comprehensive Holocaust Exhibition at the Imperial War Museum, to the smaller and more personal Holocaust exhibits at the Jewish Museum and the Czech Scrolls Museum, to the Holocaust Memorial Garden in Hyde Park. In addition there are public sculptures and plaques commemorating the Kindertransport and individuals such as Anne Frank and Raoul Wallenberg. Many other private Holocaust memorials can be found in London's synagogues.

As time goes on, more memorials are being erected, but this chapter concentrates on those in Central London. Map references refer to the map on pp. 118–119 unless otherwise stated.

HOLOCAUST MEMORIAL DAY

An international day of remembrance for the victims and survivors of the Holocaust and subsequent genocides takes place annually on 27 January, the anniversary of the day that the largest Nazi concentration camp, Auschwitz-Birkenau, was liberated in 1945. Holocaust Memorial Day has been commemorated in the UK since 2001, and was declared an international day by the United Nations in 2005. Hundreds of events of commemoration are held throughout the UK (*www.hmd.org.uk*).

British Holocaust survivor Leon Greenman's son Barney's shoes (see p. 121).

0 1 km 1 mile

N

tzjohns Ave
Chalk Farm Rd
Malden Rd
Kentish Town Rd
Adelaide Rd
Kilburn High Rd
Quex Rd
Belsize Rd
Finchley Rd
Avenue Rd
Camden High
Abbey Rd
Boundary Rd
Brondesbury Rd
Primrose Hill
28 2
Wellington Rd
Prince Albert Rd
Regent's Park
Albany St
Grove End Rd
Park Rd
Lisson Grove
Eu
Edgware Rd
Great Portland St
Portland Place
Marylebone Rd
Gloucester Place
Baker St
Cavendish Square
Praed St
Sussex Gardens
Edgware Rd
Wigmore St
New Bond St
Conduit St
Seymour St
Oxford St
Bayswater Rd
Park Lane
Hyde Park
Park Lane
Piccadilly
Green Park
Knightsbridge
Buckingham Palace
Brompton Rd
Sloane St
Belgrave Square
Grosvenor Place
Pont St
Sloane Eaton Gate King's Rd
Buckingham Palace Rd
Eccleston Bri
Fulham Rd
Sloane Square
King's Rd
Pimlico Rd
Warwick Way
Sydney St

Holocaust Memorials

1 Imperial War Museum
2 Jewish Museum
3 Czech Memorial Scrolls Museum
4 Children of the Kindertransport sculpture
   and Fur Das Kind sculpture –
   Liverpool Street Station
5 Kindertransport plaque – House of Commons
6 Holocaust Memorial Garden – Hyde Park
7 Raoul Wallenberg Memorial
8 Anne Frank bust, trees and plaque –
   British Library
9 Anne Frank tree and plaque –
   The Round House Pub
10 Sanctuary sculpture
11 Wiener Library
12 The Liberal Jewish Synagogue

Art and Artists

13 Ben Uri Gallery
14 King's Fund
15 London Transport
16 National Portrait Gallery
17 Royal Exchange
18 Royal Society of Medicine
19 Tate Britain
20 Tate Modern
21 Tavistock Clinic
22 Whitechapel Art Gallery
23 Zimbabwe House
24 Statue of Montgomery of Alamein, Whitehall

Judaica

25 Bevis Marks Synagogue
26 British Library
27 British Museum
28 Jewish Museum
29 Victoria and Albert Museum

Disraeli's London

1. No. 22 Theobalds Road, Holborn
2. Colebrooke Row, Islington
3. Bevis Marks Synagogue
4. St Andrew Holborn
5. No. 6 Bloomsbury Square
6. No. 6 Frederick's Place
7. Palace of Westminster
8. Parliament Square
9. Westminster Abbey
10. National Portrait Gallery
11. St George's, Hanover Square
12. No. 93 Park Lane
13. No. 10 Downing Street
14. No. 19 Curzon Street

N

Hyde Park

1 Holocaust Memorial Garden
2 Czech Memorial Scrolls Museum

Serpentine Road

The Serpentine

Rotten Row

South Carriage Drive

Knightsbridge   Knightsbridge

Rutland Gardens
Montpelier Square
Trevor Pl
Trevor St
Trevor Sq
Lancelot Pl
Raphael St
Basil St
Pavilion Rd
Harriet Walk
Lowndes Square

0   250 yds
0   250 m

HOLOCAUST EXHIBITION AT THE IMPERIAL WAR MUSEUM

Imperial War Museum, Lambeth Road, SE1 6HZ; ☎ 020 7416 5000; www.iwm.org.uk; tube: Lambeth North (Bakerloo) – 7 mins, from the station exit, cross the road and take the second left down Kennington Road to the traffic lights and turn left along the Lambeth Road, the Imperial War Museum is on the right; open daily 10am–6pm; exhibition not recommended for children under 14. ❶

Opened by Queen Elizabeth II in 2000, the entrance to the Holocaust Exhibition is located on the third floor, where events up until the start of WWII are covered. The exhibition continues on the second floor with the start of WWII leading to the Final Solution. The collection consists of films, recordings, photographs, original documents, artefacts, posters, personal possessions and survivors' testimonies. Key sections are described below.

The exhibition starts with life for the Jews before the rise of the Nazis, illustrated by family photos, films and survivors' testimonies. It continues with the rise of Adolf Hitler, with a section on anti-Semitism and the pursuit of purity, and includes a film about how the hatred of Jews arose featuring Julius Streicher, the editor of the Nazi newspaper, *Der Stürmer*, with original copies of that paper displayed.

The exhibition continues with the Nazi invasion of Poland and Russia, ghettos and then a large section on the Final Solution with films, photographs and personal items – saucepans, utensils, buttons and mugs – which were excavated from the Chelmno death camp. Exhibits include a funeral cart that was used to collect the dead in the Warsaw Ghetto and part of a deportation railcar.

One display explains that the British Signals Intelligence were able to decode radio messages from some German mobile killing units and so were immediately aware of the large-scale killings in Europe. However, this information had to be kept secret as otherwise the Germans would have known that their codes had been broken, which would have compromised the Allies' war strategy.

Poignantly, the text from the last letters of two deportees is shown – one had been thrown from a train en route to Auschwitz.

Alongside a large model showing the murder process at Auschwitz II-Birkenau, visitors can sit and listen to survivors' testimonies. More are heard as you walk around. Displays include camp prisoner uniforms and shoes belonging to victims of Majdanek concentration camp.

The exhibition continues with filmed testimonies from a British soldier who had taken part in the liberation of the camps and survivors talking about their liberation.

The last display shows filmed testimonies of 18 Holocaust survivors and a film of Auschwitz as it is today.

HOLOCAUST GALLERY, JEWISH MUSEUM

See Jewish Museum, p. 111, for listing. ❷
The gallery tells of the events of the Holocaust in a very personal way – through the narrative, photographs and personal possessions of a British Holocaust survivor, **Leon Greenman**. He survived six concentration camps, including Auschwitz.

Leon was born in East London in 1910 and married Else in 1935. They settled in Rotterdam to look after Else's grandmother and their son Barney was born there. The Nazis invaded the Netherlands in 1940 and Leon was arrested in 1942, spending the next three years in six concentration camps.

Leon's voice is heard telling his story as you walk around the exhibit. Amongst the objects on display are a postcard Leon wrote to his father in January 1944, a spoon Leon used in Buchenwald concentration camp and Leon's son Barney's shoes. Leon's wife and son did not survive.

In November 1945, Leon returned to

The Holocaust Gallery tells the story of British-born Auschwitz survivor Leon Greenman, and also features filmed testimony from four other survivors who settled in Britain after the war.

England. He spoke publicly about his experiences and the dangers of prejudice and racism until he died in 2008 aged 97. He never remarried.

The gallery also has a 22-minute film featuring testimonies from four other Holocaust survivors.

FUR DAS KIND SCULPTURE – FLOR KENT

Liverpool Street Station main concourse (located at entrance to Liverpool Street tube station); tube: Liverpool Street (Central, Circle, Hammersmith & City, Metropolitan). ❹

The Venezuelan artist **Flor Kent** (b.1961) was so moved by the Kindertransport story that she has created several memorials to commemorate it. Her sculpture *Fur Das Kind* (For The Child), which included a glass case filled with objects belonging to Kindertransport children, was unveiled at Liverpool Street Station in 2003 but had to be dismantled due to environmental conditions.

In May 2011 a second sculpture of two children and a suitcase, also called *Fur Das Kind*, was rededicated by **Sir Nicholas Winton** in the week of his 102nd birthday. Known as the British Schindler, he was the son of German-Jewish parents who had organized the rescue of 669 mostly Jewish children from German-occupied Czechoslovakia, arranged transport for them to Britain and found homes for them there. Flor Kent has created two other Kindertransport memorials located at railway stations in Vienna and Prague.

CZECH MEMORIAL SCROLLS MUSEUM

Third Floor, Kent House, Rutland Gardens,
Knightsbridge, SW7 1BX; ☎ *020 7584 3741;*
www.czechmemorialscrolltrust.org; tube:
Knightsbridge (Piccadilly) – 7 mins; open Tue &
Thur 10am–4pm, at other times by arrangement –
email: e.friedlander@virgin.net; donations welcome;
lift & disabled access. ❸ *(and* ❷ *on inset map*
on p. 119).

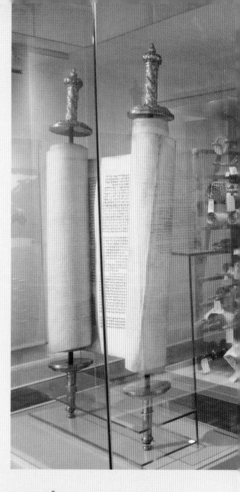

Following a renovation, the small but fascinating Czech Memorial Scrolls Museum reopened in **Kent House** in 2008. The building also houses **Westminster Synagogue**. The museum tells the story of the rescue of 1,564 Czech Torah scrolls in 1942, their purchase from the Czechoslovak communist state in 1964, their journey to London and subsequent repair and distribution.

In 1963 an American art dealer living in London, **Eric Estorick**, arranged for the purchase of the scrolls and 400 Torah binders from the Czechoslovak communist state. The purchase was funded by **Ralph Yablon**, a member of Westminster Synagogue, and was conditional on the scrolls being entrusted to Westminster Synagogue.

The scrolls and binders had originally been amongst 100,000 religious treasures, which in 1942 had been rescued from the provinces of Bohemia and Moravia for safekeeping at the Central Jewish Museum in Prague, pending the end of WWII. After WWII, the scrolls were transferred to a disused synagogue outside Prague, where they remained until their transfer to London in 1964.

Upon arrival in London, work commenced to establish whether the scrolls could be used. Coincidentally, a professional scribe, **David Brand**, had contacted Westminster Synagogue seeking work, completely unaware of the existence of the scrolls. He was subsequently employed in their restoration for the next 27 years. His work table and tools are on display.

One kosher scroll from Lostice is displayed as well as a **Wall of Scrolls** containing 150 unkosher scrolls that had been damaged through humidity, water or chewing by animals.

There is also a display of delicately patterned Torah binders, and on loan from the Prague Museum are a Torah shield, Torah pointer and finials (rimonim). Wall panels contain information about those

Wall of Scrolls.

from the Prague community who helped to save the scrolls, only one of whom survived WWII. There is a 10-minute presentation of photos of the Czech synagogues where the scrolls were used before WWII.

Over 1,400 scrolls have been transferred on permanent loan to synagogues and institutions around the world. Scrolls that could no longer be used for religious purposes serve as memorials to the communities from which they came, and can be found at the Royal Library at **Windsor Castle** and the **White House** (Washington DC, USA).

The museum was designed and built in Germany by the award-winning designer **Fritz Armbruster**. One of the museum's trustees, **Mrs Evelyn Friedlander**, states that this is an ongoing part of the act of reconciliation.

VISITOR REQUESTS

Visitors can arrange a personal tour of the museum by one of its knowledgeable trustees, Mrs Evelyn Friedlander. Westminster Synagogue (see p. 165) is also in Kent House and a visit can be requested.

CHILDREN OF THE KINDERTRANSPORT SCULPTURE – FRANK MEISLER

Hope Square, Liverpool Street Station, EC2M 7QH, Liverpool Street exit; tube: Liverpool Street (Central, Circle, Hammersmith & City, Metropolitan). ❹ As a result of the Kristallnacht pogroms in Austria and Germany on 9–10 November 1938, when nearly 100 Jews were murdered and 30,000 Jewish men were arrested and sent to concentration camps, a delegation of British Jewish leaders approached the then prime minister, Neville Chamberlain, to help the Jewish children in these countries.

On 21 November 1938, the British government agreed to allow a limited number of unaccompanied Jewish children aged under 17 to enter Britain on temporary travel documents on the understanding that a guarantee of £50 was provided for each child. The Central British Fund for World Jewish Relief provided the guarantee and other Jewish organizations raised funds for travel.

On 1 December 1938, the first transport left Berlin carrying 196 children from an orphanage that had been burned down by the Nazis during Kristallnacht. The last transport left Berlin on 31 August 1939. During this period, 9,354 children were rescued from Nazi Germany, Austria, Czechoslovakia and the Free City of Danzig.

These transports became known as the Kindertransport (Children's Transport). Their main route was by train to the Hook of Holland, boat to Harwich and then by train to London's Liverpool Street Station.

The internationally renowned sculptor, **Frank Meisler**, was commissioned to create a sculpture in honour of the Kindertransport and their arrival at

Liverpool Street Station, and as a tribute to Britain for taking in the children.

The bronze group sculpture was unveiled by Prince Charles in September 2006. It is 2.3m (7½ft) high and depicts a group of five children with their suitcases on railway tracks. The sculpture sits on a plinth surrounded by 16 milestones, each stating the name of a city from which the Kindertransports departed. The plaque on the wall of **Hope Square** was dedicated in 2006 to the Children of the Kindertransport. The plaque states: '*Hope Square dedicated to the Children of the Kindertransport who found hope and safety in Britain through the gateway of Liverpool Street Station*'.

Frank Meisler was one of the Kindertransport children. He had left his hometown of Gdansk (then known as the Free City of Danzig) with 14 other children and arrived in London two days before the outbreak of the war. Meisler was met at Liverpool Street station by two aunts who lived in London, but most of the children had no family in Britain, and were either placed with foster parents, in hostels or on farms. Eighty per cent of the Kindertransport children's parents perished in the Holocaust, including Frank Meisler's parents who died at Auschwitz.

Meisler now lives and works in the Artists' Quarter in Jaffa, Israel. He has also sculpted two other Kindertransport-related groups: one in Berlin, unveiled in 2008; and the other unveiled in 2009 at the main railway station in Gdansk.

Children of the Kindertransport sculpture.

KINDERTRANSPORT PLAQUE AT THE HOUSE OF COMMONS

Located opposite Admission Order Office, off Central Lobby at House of Commons, Palace of Westminster, St Margaret Street, SW1A 2PW (visitors' entrance in St Margaret's Street); tube: Westminster (Circle, District, Jubilee) – 5 mins; www.parliament.uk/visiting/; UK residents should contact their MP for permit to visit Palace of Westminster; overseas visitors *can tour Palace of Westminster during summer recess in Aug & Sept, pre-booking recommended.* ❺

This plaque was erected in the **House of Commons** in gratitude to the UK government and people for permitting the Kindertransports. It was unveiled to coincide with the 60th Kindertransport reunion in June 1999.

HOLOCAUST MEMORIAL GARDEN, HYDE PARK

The Dell, Rotten Row, Hyde Park, W2; tube: Knightsbridge (Piccadilly, Sloane Street exit) – 10 mins; from the Sloane Street exit, turn right along Knightsbridge, cross the road and take the first exit on the left, Albert Gate, to reach Hyde Park. Whilst the garden is marked on the map at the park entrance, there are no signs indicating the garden from the main footpath *and it is quite hard to find. Follow the main footpath that leads to the Serpentine. Opposite the Dell bridge, walk to the right across the grass for about 20 seconds and you will arrive at the garden.* ❻ *(and* ❶ *on inset map on p. 119).*

The **Holocaust Memorial Garden** was inaugurated in 1983, 38 years after the end of WWII, and was Britain's first public memorial dedicated solely to the victims of the Holocaust. The garden contains four large boulders set on raked gravel, surrounded by silver birch trees. The largest boulder contains the following inscription in English and Hebrew: '*For thee I weep, streams of tears flow from my eyes because of the destruction of my people (Lamentations)*'.

An annual remembrance ceremony takes place at the garden each **Yom Hashoah** (Holocaust Remembrance Day), usually in April.

Holocaust Memorial Garden.

RAOUL WALLENBERG MEMORIAL

*Located opposite
Western Marble Arch
Synagogue, 32 Great
Cumberland Place, W1H
7TN; tube: Marble Arch
(Central) – 5 mins.* ❼
Raoul Wallenberg was
a Swedish diplomat who
worked in Budapest
from August 1944 as
first secretary to the
neutral Swedish
Legation. He saved the
lives of over 100,000
Hungarian Jews by
issuing them with
protective passports and
providing safe houses.
The Soviets arrested
Raoul Wallenberg in
1945, suspecting him of
being an American spy. It
is believed he was
executed by them.

Unveiled by Queen
Elizabeth II in February
1997, the memorial,
created by the
renowned sculptor
Philip Jackson, was
commissioned by the
Wallenberg Appeal
Committee and shows
Raoul Wallenberg
wearing a trench coat and concealing several
passports in his hand. He is standing against a
wall. The rear of the wall is draped with the
false passport documents he issued to the
Hungarian Jews. There are inscriptions around

Raoul Wallenberg memorial.

the base and on the east and west sides of
the memorial which movingly tell Raoul
Wallenberg's story.

ANNE FRANK BUST, TREES AND PLAQUES

BRITISH LIBRARY

96 Euston Road, NW1 2DB; ☎ *0843 2081144;*
www.bl.uk; tube: Kings Cross/St Pancras
(Circle, Hammersmith & City, Metropolitan,
Northern, Piccadilly, Victoria) – 5 mins; open
Mon, Wed–Fri 9.30am–6pm, Tue
9.30am–8pm, Sat 9.30am–5pm, Sun
11am–5pm. ❽

Anne Frank is famous for her diary, written
whilst in hiding from the Nazis in an
Amsterdam attic. Anne and her family were
discovered and arrested by the Nazis and
Anne died from typhus in the Bergen-Belsen
concentration camp in 1945.

There is a life-sized bust of Anne Frank
entitled *A Triumph of Spirit* on the lower ground
floor adjacent to the lifts. It was sculpted by
Doreen Kern and unveiled on 12 June 1999 to
mark the 70th anniversary of Anne's birth.

In 1998 the **Anne Frank Educational Trust**
instigated a tree-planting project to dedicate
trees in Anne's name to commemorate her
death and all children killed in wars and
through persecution. The first tree was planted
in the piazza outside the British Library. There
is a plaque by the tree with an excerpt from
Anne Frank's diary. Since then more than 500
trees have been planted across Britain.

The tree and plaque are positioned at the
Euston Road end of the piazza outside the
library. You should walk into the planet
sculpture circle, and turn left – just above is
the tree and plaque.

On 23 August 2010, the chestnut tree
outside the attic in Amsterdam from which
Anne Frank took much comfort, and which
inspired this project, collapsed due to very
strong winds.

THE ROUND HOUSE PUB

Tree & plaque at corner of Garrick Street &
New Row, WC2; tube: Leicester Square
(Northern, Piccadilly) – 5 mins. ❾

The Anne Frank Educational Trust also planted
a tree to commemorate its 10th anniversary
on 22 October 2001, in front of a plaque
dedicated by the actor, **Sir Ben Kingsley**. The
plaque on the wall of The Round House pub
at 1 Garrick Street states that the site is to
serve as an inspiration to work together
towards a better world free of bigotry.

Sculpture of Anne Frank, British Library.

SANCTUARY – A SCULPTURE BY NAOMI BLAKE

Located in front of St Botolph-without-Aldgate, Aldgate High Street, EC3N 1AB; tube: Aldgate (Circle, Metropolitan) – 1 min. ⑩
The sculpture was unveiled in 1985. Made of fibreglass and painted to resemble bronze, it is a plain featureless figure sitting hunched under a large drooping leaf. The inscription on the front of the base reads 'To all victims of oppression'. (See also p. 18.)

Naomi Blake was born in Czechoslovakia and as a child survived Auschwitz. Much of her work reflects sorrow but also hope for the future. Other works include *Renew Our Days*, which can be seen in the garden of **New North London Synagogue**, Finchley (see p. 179); and *Against the Odds* at **New London Synagogue** (see p. 193).

INSTITUTE OF CONTEMPORARY HISTORY AND WIENER LIBRARY

29 Russell Square, WC1B 5DP; ☎ *020 7636 7247; www.wienerlibrary.co.uk; tube: Russell Square (Piccadilly) – 5 mins; open Mon–Fri 10am–5.30pm; proof of address & photo ID required for first visit.* ⑪
The library is the world's oldest institution devoted to the study of the Holocaust and the Nazi era, and is Britain's most extensive archive on this period. It contains 70,000 books, 17,000 photographs, 2 million press cuttings, eyewitness testimonies, videos, periodicals and other source materials, and is open to the public.

The library was originally established in 1933 in Amsterdam by **Dr Alfred Wiener** to inform Jewish communities around the world about Nazi persecution of the Jews. It relocated to London in 1939 and became a research institution and public library. After the war the library provided original documents and eyewitness accounts to the UN War Crimes Commission for use in the Nuremberg and Eichmann trials.

The library moved to premises in Russell Square in 2011 so that its collection could be housed in climate-controlled conditions.

THE LIBERAL JEWISH SYNAGOGUE HOLOCAUST MEMORIAL

See The Liberal Jewish Synagogue, p. 192; memorial in front foyer of building on wall between two entrance doors and is located on an axis with Ark and Ner Tamid (eternal flame). ⓬ Unveiled on 10 November 1996 on the 58th anniversary of **Kristallnacht**, this memorial was created by the renowned Jewish

Holocaust Memorial.

sculptor, **Anish Kapoor** (see p. 137). The memorial is made from a slab of black Kilkenny limestone hollowed out to create a void. There is an inscription: 'We have vowed to remember'.

ART AND ARTISTS

London provides a varied backdrop to works produced by Jewish artists. They can be found in the Ben Uri Gallery (The London Jewish Museum of Art), which surveys the work of Jewish artists within the artistic context; national collections such as Tate Modern, Tate Britain and the National Portrait Gallery; and organizational premises including the Royal Exchange and Royal Society of Medicine. Sculptures are also found in public parks and churchyards.

Early Jewish artists to gain wide public popularity included Solomon J. Solomon and Simeon Solomon, both in the late 19th century. The early 20th century saw talented artists from the East End being funded by the Jewish Education Aid Society to attend art school and having fled Nazi Europe in the 1930s, several refugees subsequently forged successful careers as artists.

Map references refer to the map on pp. 118–119.

NATIONAL PORTRAIT GALLERY

St Martin's Place, WC2H 0HE; ☎ *020 7306 0055; www.npg.org.uk; tube: Charing Cross (Bakerloo, Northern); open daily 10am–6pm, Thur & Fri until 9pm; note that works on display can change.* ⓰

Founded in 1856 as a collection to represent history, not art, the National Portrait Gallery (NPG) is a perfect way to experience not only works by Jewish artists, but also Jewish personalities who have shaped the community since the Resettlement.

In Room 19 is the earliest known Jewish sitter **David Ricardo** (1772–1823), an MP and economist who married a Quaker and was disowned by his family.

The bronze statuettes of **Ludwig Mond** (1839–1909) and his son **Robert Ludwig Mond** (1867–1938) are in Room 27 (Science and Industry) and commemorate their gas and chemical companies, which became ICI in 1926. Much of Ludwig's art collection was left to the

Sir Nikolaus Pevsner by Hans Schwarz, 1969.

Above: *Lew Grade, Baron Grade* by Ruskin Spear, exhibited 1988.
Right: *Man in a Chair* by Lucian Freud, 1989.

National Gallery, and Robert left a collection of Egyptian artefacts to the British Museum.

A portrait of **Benjamin Disraeli** (1804–81) by the great Victorian artist John Everett Millais and a plaster model of the Westminster Abbey memorial by Joseph Boehm (see p. 78) are both displayed in Room 25. Nearby is a portrait of **Arthur Balfour** (1848–1930), author of a letter of 1917 known as the Balfour Declaration, which stated British policy towards a Jewish homeland in Palestine.

Within different rooms are examples of bronze sculpted heads by American-Jewish artist **Sir Jacob Epstein** (1880–1959) (see p. 136), including depictions of the artist Augustus John and novelist Joseph Conrad.

EARLY 20th CENTURY GALLERY

This gallery includes works by Jewish artists from the East End and those who arrived in the 1930s. The portrait of Julian Huxley is by **Mark Gertler** (1891–1939). **Nikolaus Pevsner** (1902–83), the architectural historian, was painted by **Hans Schwarz** (1922–2003). Both escaped Nazi Europe in the 1930s and were interned, and both went on to have successful careers in the UK. The bust of Winston Churchill was sculpted by **Oscar Nemon** (see pp. 135–6) and a plaster bust of noted pathologist Dorothy Stuart Russell is by **Ismond Rosen** (1924–96) (see p. 135).

1960s TO 1990s AND CONTEMPORARY GALLERIES

The 1960s to 1990s Gallery displays a range of Jewish personalities. Look for the portraits of impresario and TV mogul **Lord (Lew) Grade** (1906–98), the German banker **Sir Siegmund Warburg** (1902–82) who transformed the corporate finance industry post-WWII and a self-portrait by **Leon Kossoff** (b.1926). *Man in a Chair* by **Lucian Freud** (1922–2011) depicts financier and philanthropist **4th Baron (Jacob) Rothschild** (b.1936) (see pp 142 and 145). Freud, the grandson of psychoanalyst Sigmund Freud, was brought to the UK from Berlin as a boy in 1933.

The Contemporary Gallery includes **Sir Sigmund Sternberg** (b.1921), proponent of Christian-Jewish understanding and **Harold Pinter** (1930–2008), the playwright.

BEN URI GALLERY

The London Jewish Museum of Art, 108A Boundary Road, off Abbey Road, NW8 0RH; ☎ *020 7604 3991; www.benuri.org.uk; tube: St. John's Wood (Jubilee) – 10 mins; open Sun–Fri; gallery is seeking to relocate, call or check website before visiting for current location & opening hours.* ⑬

Founded at Whitechapel's Gradels Restaurant in July 1915 by a Russian immigrant Jewish artist Lazar Berson (1882–1954), Ben Uri is Europe's only dedicated Jewish museum of art. After occupying various locations in the East End, Ben Uri moved to Central London in 1925. After a period in Great Russell Street it moved to Portman Square, then Berner Street, before finally occupying the top floor of the West End Great Synagogue in Dean Street, Soho until 1996.

Since 2002 the museum has been located in St. John's Wood, presenting a changing menu of temporary international exhibitions. Ben Uri is planning a return to the heart of Central London.

Ben Uri works in partnership with national and international museums presenting surveys of Jewish and non-Jewish artists within an artistic rather than religious context. Its internationally renowned collection of over 1,000 works includes rare and important bodies of work by Solomon, Auerbach, Bomberg, Epstein and Gertler, contemporary art and new media, as well as new acquisitions including the recently discovered and acquired 1945 *Crucifixion 'Apocalypse en Lilas'* by Chagall.

WHITECHAPEL BOYS

In 2002 Ben Uri initiated a series of exhibitions titled 'The Whitechapel Boys', a title which has since become synonymous for the artists Bomberg, Gertler, Rosenberg, Wolmark, Kramer and Meninsky, amongst others. The most famous today is **David Bomberg** (1890–1957), who, born in Birmingham, grew up in the East End. He studied at the Slade from 1911–15 and was deeply engaged with Ben Uri throughout his life. A founding member of the London Group, he practised Vorticism, experimented with Cubism and Futurism, moved from figurative to abstract in 1919 and pre- and post-WWII concentrated on landscapes, often working, and eventually living in, Spain. He became a respected art teacher; Frank Auerbach and Leon Kossoff were among his pupils. His exclusion of the human form made his work unfashionable and he died neglected, both commercially and critically. Following a major reappraisal, Bomberg is now recognized as one of the country's great masters and his early Whitechapel works (held almost entirely by Tate and Ben Uri) and Spanish landscapes are greatly sought after.

TATE MODERN

Bankside, SE1 9TG; ☎ *020 7887 8888;*
www.tate.org.uk/modern/; tube: Southwark
(Jubilee) – 5 mins; open Sun–Thur 10am–6pm,
Fri & Sat 10am–8pm. ❷⓿
Housed in a converted power station and
opened in 2000, the building is worth a visit in its
own right. The collection 'States of Flux' contains
the largest selection of Jewish artists' works
including *Vision of Ezekiel,* inspired by the Biblical
text and *Study for Sappers at Work,* a WWI work,
both by **David Bomberg** (see p. 133). *Portrait of a*
Girl by **Amedeo Modigliani** (1884–1920), an
Italian who lived in France, is an example of the
simplistic and elongated portraiture that became
his trademark. A bohemian who abused drink and
drugs, he died penniless, aged 36. The sculpture
Head is by Modigliani's friend **Jacques Lipchitz**
(1891–1973). Born Chaim Jacob Lipchitz in
Lithuania, he came to prominence in Paris but
during WWII fled to the USA.

In the 'Material Gestures' collection, *Ishi's Light*
by **Anish Kapoor** (see p. 137) is an egg-shaped
dark interior containing a column of light.

WHITECHAPEL ART GALLERY

77–82 Whitechapel High Street, E1 7QX;
☎ *020 7522 7888; www.whitechapelgallery.*
org/; tube: Aldgate East (District, Metropolitan);
open Tue, Wed, Fri, Sat, Sun 11am–6pm, Thur
11am–9pm, closed Mon. ❷❷
There is no permanent display in the gallery,
but regularly changing exhibitions. The archive
includes extensive records relating to the artists
associated with the gallery, many of whom also
met at the Whitechapel Library next door, now
part of the gallery. See also pp. 48–9 and 133.

TATE BRITAIN

Millbank, SW1P 4RG; ☎ *020 7887 8888;*
www.tate.org.uk/britain/; tube: Pimlico
(Victoria) – 5 mins; open daily 10am–6pm. ❶❾
The *Merry-Go-Round* painted by **Mark**
Gertler (see also pp. 32, 48, 151) in 1916
during WWI is fiercely anti-war, merging the
fun of the fair with the mechanization of the
military. Gertler declared himself a
conscientious objector together with
another Whitechapel Boy, John Rodker. Their
contemporaries, Isaac Rosenberg and David
Bomberg, went to fight at the Front.

Several **Jacob Epstein** sculptures are
displayed, including the vast *Jacob and the*
Angel hewn from alabaster in 1940 and *Torso*
in Metal from the *'Rock Drill'.* A **Lucian Freud**
portrait *Man in a Chair* depicts industrial
magnate and art collector Baron Thyssen. The
same title is used for a portrait in the
National Portrait Gallery (see p. 132).

The Merry-Go-Round by Mark Gertler, 1916.

OUT AND ABOUT

There are many opportunities to spot works by Jewish artists as you travel around London. Detailed below are a few favourites.

ROYAL EXCHANGE

Bank Junction, EC3V 3LR; www.theroyal exchange.com; tube: Bank (Central, Northern, DLR); open Mon–Fri. Murals are visible from first floor bar. See also pp. 85–6. ⓱
The third exchange was opened in 1844 by Queen Victoria. Later, a mural was commissioned representing 24 key events in the history of the City. One depicts King Charles I at the Guildhall, demanding the five members of parliament. It is by **Solomon J. Solomon** (1860–1927), an artist of the Pre-Raphaelite school, much influenced by Frederic Leighton. He was in demand for society portraits, was a noted book illustrator and during WWI was instrumental in developing camouflage for netting and tanks.

The Kiss by Ismond Rosen.

ROYAL SOCIETY OF MEDICINE

1 Wimpole Street, W1G 0AE; ☎ 020 7290 2900; www.rsm.ac.uk; tube: Oxford Circus (Bakerloo, Central, Victoria); open Mon–Fri; arrange in advance to view works; this is very close to King's Fund (see p. 136). ⓲
Three works by **Ismond Rosen** are displayed that illustrate his ability to work with different mediums: a bronze bust of **John Hunter,** the surgeon; a marble sculpture *The Kiss* (also seen from outside through the window); and the stainless steel *Civilization*. Rosen, a South African, was both an eminent psychoanalyst and a talented artist. As a teenager he was unable to decide between the two careers so chose both. He specialized

in delinquency and childhood behaviour, working for a time with Anna Freud (see pp. 92–3). His standard work *Sexual Deviation* has *The Kiss* on its cover. (See also p. 132).

TAVISTOCK CLINIC

120 Belsize Lane (corner of Fitzjohn's Avenue), NW3 5BA; tube: Swiss Cottage (Jubilee). ㉑
The seated statue of **Sigmund Freud** (1856–1939), not far from the Freud Museum (see pp. 91 and 92–3) was sculpted in 1931 by **Oscar Nemon** (1906–85), a Croatian who lived in Paris and Brussels before fleeing Europe in 1938. With supportive patrons, Nemon was already a favoured sculptor, with commissions including the Belgian royal family. He visited Freud in Hampstead, but

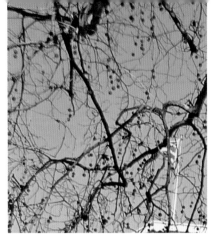

made his home in Oxford where his commissions subsequently included Queen Elizabeth II, Margaret Thatcher and, his unfinished last work, Diana, Princess of Wales.

When **Winston Churchill** (1874–1965) wanted to commence sculpting, it was Nemon to whom he turned for assistance. Nemon sculpted more than a dozen likenesses of Churchill, one of which is in the Guildhall. Another is in the lobby of the Palace of Westminster and nearby, on Whitehall, is his statue of WWII military leader **Montgomery of Alamein** (1887–1976). ㉔

Top: *Monty of Alamein* by Oscar Nemon, Whitehall.
Right: Nemon with his bust of Winston Churchill and Churchill's bust of Nemon, the only sculputre Churchill produced.

WORKS BY JACOB EPSTEIN

Outside of galleries, Jacob Epstein has work on public display throughout Central London including:
Day and Night – his controversial nude statues unveiled in 1928, adorn the exterior of London Transport's headquarters (*55 Broadway, SW1H 0BD* ⑮).
The Ages of Man – these nude figures, male and female, caused a sensation in 1908 when sculpted for the British Medical Association headquarters (*Zimbabwe House, Strand, WC2R 0JR* ㉓).
Madonna and Child – unveiled in 1953 on the archway to a convent, this sculpture adorns the archway leading to the King's Fund, a charity dedicated to how the health system in England can be improved (*Nos 11–13 Cavendish Square, W1G 0AN* ⑭).

Day and Night by Jacob Epstein, London Transport headquarters.

DORICH HOUSE

Built in the 1930s for artist and sculptor Dora Gordine (1895–1991) and her husband Richard, it is now a museum (see pp. 106–07).

WORKS BY ANISH KAPOOR

Anish Kapoor (b.1954), born in India to a Jewish mother and Hindu father, moved to London in 1973. Outside of galleries his work is often monumental in size but temporary, such as *Marsyas* at Tate Modern (2002) and *Turning the World Upside Down* in Kensington Gardens (2010). Permanent works on view include the *Shoah Memorial* commissioned by the Liberal Jewish Synagogue (see p. 130). At the time of writing, his designs have been accepted for the *ArcelorMittal Orbit* sculpture for the 2012 Olympic Park.

WORKS BY NAOMI BLAKE

Sculptures by **Naomi Blake**, a Holocaust survivor, can be seen throughout London (see pp. 18, 62, 129 and 193), including in synagogue grounds, garden squares and the Friends House at Euston. The sculpture at Friends House honours Bertha Bracey (1893–1989), who gave practical leadership to Quakers in quietly rescuing and re-settling thousands of Nazi victims and lone children between 1922 and 1938.

KINDERTRANSPORT MEMORIALS

There are two Kindertransport memorials at Liverpool Street station (see pp. 124–5).

The sculpture by Naomi Blake at Friends House, Euston.

JUDAICA IN LONDON

Following the Resettlement, the Jewish community soon commissioned silverware for use in synagogues and private homes. Outside of individual synagogues there are several opportunities in London to view both early and contemporary Judaica.

British Museum

Great Russell Street, WC1B 3DG; ☎ *020 7323 8299; www.britishmuseum.org; tube: Holborn (Central, Piccadilly) – 5 mins, Tottenham Court Road (Central, Northern) – 5 mins; open daily 10am–5.30pm, Fri until 8.30pm.* ㉗

The collection of Judaica dates from the opening of the museum in 1759, when Solomon da Costa donated 180 Hebrew books and manuscripts, now in the British Library. The following are worth seeking out.

Room 40 – Medieval Europe Includes a section reflecting Jewish life, including a 13th-century coin hoard from Colchester, probably deposited by a

Jewish financier; a seal which belonged to Rabbi Samson of Coursy in France, a famous Talmudic commentator; and a brass astrolabe from Spain produced in about 1350 during the period of co-existence between Jewish, Muslim and Christian scholars. The Chalcis Treasure, from the former Venetian colony in Greece, includes two mounts decorated with Hebrew inscriptions, indicating the Jewish communities in Venice and its colonies.

Room 45 – The Waddesdon Bequest
Ferdinand de Rothschild's collection bequeathed to the British Museum includes gold and silverwork, ceramics and firearms. The Pressburg Cup c.1600 features a Hebrew inscription, added in 1740, recording its use by the Jewish community of Pressburg (Bratislava). Two gold Jewish wedding rings, 18th or 19th century, are also displayed. One is beautifully enamelled in blue, green and turquoise and the other, inscribed inside with 'Mazel Tov', depicts the story of Adam and Eve. See pp. 214–16 for more on Waddesdon.

Much of the British Museum's Judaica collection is not on display, but may be viewed on the museum's website. Notable objects include a wedding ring dated 1699 which belonged to a couple who were members of Bevis Marks Synagogue; silver items from Plymouth synagogue, the oldest surviving Ashkenazi synagogue in the UK; and a beautiful embroidered Torah binder dated 1750.

Astrolabe, British Museum.

Jewish marriage ring, V&A.

Victoria and Albert Museum

Cromwell Road SW7 2RL; ☎ *020 7942 2000;*
www.vam.ac.uk; tube: South Kensington (Circle,
District, Piccadilly) – 5 mins; open daily
10am–5.45pm, Fri until 10pm. ㉙

The collection at the V&A is vast and contains approximately 100 exquisite examples of items used by the Jewish faith. The display in the **Sacred Silver Gallery, Rooms 83 and 84** on the second floor, includes Havdalah spice boxes, decorations for Torah scrolls, wedding rings, one Seder plate and Kiddush cups representing Jewish worship, lifecycle and festival celebration. Do seek out the following items.

In 1855 a small 13th-century spice box from Spain was the first piece of Jewish art to be bought by the V&A. At the time of purchase it was believed to be a Christian reliquary.

There is a golden marriage ring from 18th- or 19th-century Germany, which includes a model of a small house representing the new home for the couple. The design is complex but is made with no breaks, a prerequisite of any Jewish marriage ring.

A contemporary miniature set of silver rimonim, breastplate and silver pointer designed for a Torah scroll were made by Gerald Benney (b.1930), a non-Jewish silversmith whose work is also found in several synagogues.

The **Gilbert Collection** was bequeathed to the nation in 1996 by Sir Arthur Gilbert (1913–2001), the son of Polish-Jewish immigrants. It is one of the world's great decorative art collections and includes silver, mosaics, enamelled portrait miniatures, gold boxes and Judaica of the finest quality. Highlights include a set of late 18th-century Dutch silver rimonim that belonged to the Sassoon family.

Pieces from the collection of Sir Moses Montefiore and his synagogue in Ramsgate (see pp. 211–13) on loan from The Montefiore Endowment include one set of silver mid-18th-century rimonim.

British Library

See p. 128 for details; Hebrew material not on display can be viewed and consulted in Asian and African Studies Reading Room, 3rd floor; admission to Reading Room is by valid reader's pass only, contact Ilana Tahan, M.Phil. OBE, ilana.tahan@bl.uk, ☎ *020 7412 7646.* ㉖

The British Library was originally housed in the British Museum and the founding collections, from Sir Hans Sloane, Sir John Cotton and Robert Harley, all included historic Hebrew manuscripts. Today, the library holds about 80,000 printed books, over 3,000 manuscripts and about 10,000 fragments deriving from the Cairo Genizah. The Hebrew

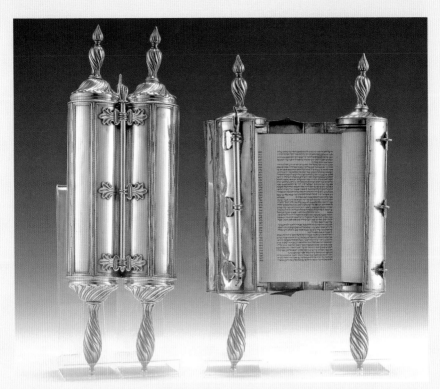

Kandler Scrolls, 1766–7, Jewish Museum. Previously owned by Samuel Falk (see p. 45).

collection of manuscripts and printed books forms part of the Asian and African Studies Department of the library. A small selection of illuminated Hebrew manuscripts are on permanent display in the 'Sacred Treasures' section of the John Ritblat Gallery, also known as the Treasures Gallery.

Do not miss the **Golden Haggadah**. Dating from *c.*1320, it was made in Barcelona and is famous for the 14 full-page miniatures of tooled gold leaf depicting scenes from Genesis and Exodus. The first known owner was an Italian and very likely the manuscript was taken to Italy when the Jews were expelled from Spain in 1492. The British Museum acquired it in 1865 as part of the Almanzi collection. The 'Turning the Pages' interactive display allows you to view each page as though reading the original book.

Another treasure featured on the 'Turning the Pages' interactive display is the **Lisbon Bible**, a beautifully illuminated Hebrew Bible created in Portugal in 1482. It was acquired by the British Museum in 1882.

Jewish Museum
See pp. 111–16 for details. **28**

Bevis Marks Synagogue
See pp. 22–3 for details. **25**

Selected pieces from their collection are displayed.

THE ROTHSCHILDS IN LONDON

The Rothschild name conjures up a vivid image of a wealthy Jewish family but there was also communal and civic duty, philanthropy and love of arts and heritage. In London you can discover sites related to their business, entertaining, charity and worship.

It all began in 1798 when Mayer Amschel Rothschild (1744–1812) in Frankfurt despatched his son, Nathan Mayer (1777–1836), to live in England. His four brothers also established business houses in other European cities following their father's death. This increased the Rothschild business presence but also ensured a strong network of family cooperation. Nathan Mayer originally went to Manchester as a textile merchant but soon moved to the capital and so the story of the Rothschilds in London begins.

BUSINESS LIFE

ROYAL EXCHANGE

The current Royal Exchange is the third on this site. Nathan Mayer was a broker in the second exchange and was a master of the two main financial businesses – foreign exchange and bills of exchange – conducted there by the early 19th century (see pp. 85–6).

NEW COURT, ST SWITHIN'S LANE

NM Rothschild, St Swithin's Lane, EC4P 4DU; ☎ 020 7280 5000; www.rothschild.com; no access to NM Rothschild without prior arrangement.

No. 2 New Court, within a gated courtyard, was Nathan Mayer's home and office between 1809 and 1825. He lived there with his wife, Hannah, who he married in 1806. Hannah's sister Judith married Moses Montefiore in 1812, and they lived next door at **No. 4**.

Nearly 200 years later the family bank is still independent and operating from the same site but within a new building occupied from 2011. The company emblem is five arrows, often depicted being held by a

A Pillar of the Exchange,
by Thomas Jones, 1829.

clenched fist, representing the combined union of the original five brothers.

In more recent years the 3rd Baron, Victor, headed the company for part of the

New Court c.1809.

Rothschild, St Swithin's Lane.

20th century but did not take an active role in the banking business. On his retirement in 1976 his cousin, Evelyn de Rothschild, took over as chairman. Victor's son and heir, Jacob (b.1936), now 4th Baron Rothschild, who worked at the bank, relocated with the Rothschild Investment Trust (RIT) to St James's in the West End.

BANK OF ENGLAND

Nathan Mayer's grandson, Alfred de Rothschild, became the first Jewish director of the Bank of England in 1868 remaining until 1889 (see p. 85).

SPENCER HOUSE

27 St James's Place, SW1A 1NR; ☎ *020 7499 8620; www.spencerhouse.co.uk; tube: Green Park (Jubilee, Piccadilly, Victoria) – 5 mins; open to public Sun (not Jan & Aug) 10.30am–5.45pm (last tour at 4.45pm), booking advised; adm. fee.*
Using RIT as his springboard, Jacob Rothschild (now Lord Rothschild) established an

extensive and innovative wealth-management business in St James's, often working with major financiers including Sir Mark Weinberg and Sir James Goldsmith.

In 1985, RIT Capital Partners acquired the lease of Spencer House, situated opposite Jacob Rothschild's company offices. Built between 1756 and 1766 as a private palace for the first Earl Spencer, it is the only remaining aristocratic town house in central London to remain intact. Latterly converted to commercial use, the extensive renovation

Spencer House, west facade.

programme restored the rooms to their original grandeur and the building is now offices with state rooms open to the public for tours and private entertaining. At No. 14 St James's Place, you will see the emblem of the five arrows.

HOME LIFE

Early homes of Nathan Mayer included those at New Court, Great St Helen's in the City, an estate in Stamford Hill and in 1825 he acquired the lease of **107 Piccadilly**, now the site of the Park Lane Hotel. He died suddenly in 1836, when in Frankfurt for the marriage of his son Lionel. Various family members were, by then, neighbours on Piccadilly, giving the stretch of road opposite Green Park the nickname 'Rothschild Row'. One son, Mayer, moved into No. 107, while Lionel built **148 Piccadilly**, where Park Lane is today beside Apsley House.

Modelled on the Palazzo Farnese in Rome, No. 148's relatively modest exterior hid a magnificent interior with marbled halls and eight staircases. Entertaining was lavish, including the marriage of their daughter Evelina to Ferdinand de Rothschild, and a regular guest was the Prince of Wales, later Edward VII. Regular meetings for charitable initiatives supported by Lionel's wife Charlotte were also held there.

Nearby at **No. 143** lived Ferdinand, and his sister, Alice, lived next door at **No. 142**.

Benjamin Disraeli described Alfred's home at **1 Seamore Place**, as 'the most charming house in London, the magnificence of its decorations and furniture equalled by good taste'. Alfred was dapper, slim and blue-eyed, with elaborate whiskers changing with the fashion. His parties, here and at his country estate of Halton, were extravagant. He used his diamond-encrusted ivory baton to conduct his private orchestra and famous opera singers of the day would entertain his guests.

Alfred did not marry, but his illegitimate daughter, Almina, married George Herbert, 8th Earl of Carnarvon, who funded the expedition of Howard Carter to Egypt, during which Tutankhamun's tomb was discovered in 1922.

Above: Alfred de Rothschild at Halton House.
Left: Lionel de Rothschild, *c*.1870.

5 Hamilton Place.

One Rothschild mansion remains, **5 Hamilton Place**, the home of Leopold, son of Lionel. A successful racehorse owner and breeder, Leo's spontaneous natural good humour made him a favourite of all he met.

Bought by Leopold in 1881, it was designed by William Rogers, who also designed Alfred's extravaganza at Halton. Built in the 17th-century French style, the interior woodwork for the staircase and library are in walnut and mahogany, which was carved by 40 Italian artisans employed for two years. It is now an exclusive club, Les Ambassadeurs (see p. 67).

Hannah, the wife of Nathan Mayer, encouraged her family to embrace the lifestyle of the English aristocracy and soon all had country estates. The first, and nearest to London, was **Gunnersbury**, bought in 1835 by Nathan Mayer and later home to Leo (see p. 110). Otherwise they were mostly around Aylesbury, an area dubbed 'Rothschildshire'; Nathaniel lived at Tring, Mayer at Mentmore, Anthony at Aston Clinton, Leo at Ascott, Alfred at Halton and Ferdinand at **Waddesdon** (see pp. 214–16).

CIVIC LIFE

In 1858 Lionel de Rothschild, representing the City of London, became the first Jewish MP to take his seat at the Palace of Westminster without the obligation of the oath on the true faith of a Christian.

In 1885 his son, Nathaniel Rothschild, became the first Jewish lord and, on vacating his parliamentary seat for Aylesbury, he was succeeded by his cousin Ferdinand as MP. Mayer sat as MP for Hythe from 1859. His son-in-law, Lord Rosebery, became prime minister in 1894.

Lionel de Rothschild introduced in the House of Commons, 26 July 1858, painted by Henry Barraud, 1872.

Navarino Mansions, Dalston.

CHARITABLE AND HERITAGE LIFE

Hannah, wife of Nathan Mayer, began supporting the **Jews' Free School** in Bell Lane in the 1820s. Subsequent Rothschild funding included 'suits and boots', spectacles and scholarships. The Rothschild ladies taught, provided books and attended prize-givings. There was a Rothschild on the board of governors until the 1960s. See also p. 25.

The ladies also regularly visited the 'Jewish East End' to serve at the Soup Kitchen, support youth clubs and act as visitors for the Benevolent Loan Society.

More recently, **Lord Jacob Rothschild** was chair of the trustees at the National Gallery between 1985 and 1991. His name is latinized within an inscription around the cornice of the Central Hall. He was chair of the **National Heritage Memorial Fund** and **National Heritage Lottery Fund** in the 1990s, actively involved with the restoration of **Somerset House** and was responsible for the restoration of **Spencer House** (see pp.142–3). He is chair of the Rothschild Foundation (Europe), the family charitable trust.

The **Evelina Children's Hospital**, now part of Guy's and St Thomas's NHS Foundation Trust, was originally endowed by Ferdinand de Rothschild in 1869 in memory of his wife who died in childbirth. Built in poverty-

Ferdinand and Evelina de Rothschild mausoleum, West Ham Cemetery.

stricken Southwark, it moved to Guy's Hospital in 1976 and reopened at St Thomas's in 2004.

Nathaniel, Lord Rothschild, established the **Four Per Cent Industrial Dwellings Company** in 1885 providing affordable housing for the working poor. Early blocks have been demolished (see p. 26) but **Stepney Green Dwellings** (now Court) of 1896 survives (see p. 55), together with **Evelina Mansions**, Camberwell (1900); **Navarino Mansions**, Dalston (1905); and **Mocatta House**, Whitechapel (1905, see p. 36).

JEWISH LIFE

Lionel laid the foundation stone at **Central Synagogue, Great Portland Street** (see pp. 163–4) and Ferdinand and Leopold both held communal positions there. Nathan was a warden at **Duke's Place Synagogue**. His son Lionel was then president and served on the Council of the **United Synagogue** where his brother Anthony was president. Lionel was also a member of the Board of Deputies, and although elected president preferred not to serve.

For information on where members of the family were laid to rest see pp. 150 and 156.

JEWISH LONDONERS – WHERE THEY LIVED

Many well-known Jewish Londoners' birthplaces, homes and work are commemorated throughout the city. Many of them are mentioned in the walking tours and other chapters. However, here are a few other people who are commemorated but are not featured elsewhere in the book.

Harold Abrahams (1899–1978); *home: Hodford Lodge, 2 Hodford Road, NW11 8NP; tube: Golders Green (Northern).*

He lived in Golders Green between 1923 and 1930, the years of his greatest athletic successes. His 100 metres Olympic gold medal win in 1924 was immortalized in the 1981 film *Chariots of Fire.*

Jack 'Kid' Berg (1909–91); *birthplace (demolished): Noble Court, Cable Street, E1 8HS; Overground: Shadwell.*
Nicknamed the 'Whitechapel Windmill', he was world junior welterweight and world lightweight champion in the 1930s.

Ernst Chain (1906–1979); *home: 9 North View, Wimbledon Common, SW19 4UJ; tube: Wimbledon (District).*
Won Nobel Prize for Medicine in 1945. Chain left Germany in 1933 and worked with Howard Florey, continuing the research into penicillin begun by Alexander Fleming.

Lord Delfont (1909–94); *workplace: Coventry Street, W1D 6AS; tube: Piccadilly Circus (Bakerloo, Piccadilly), Leicester Square (Northern, Piccadilly).*
Born Boris (Barnet) Winogradsky in Ukraine, his career as an impresario dominated London theatre and entertainment from the 1950s. His

Plaque on Harold Abrahams's home.

theatres included Talk of the Town and the London Palladium. A plaque celebrating his career is on another theatre, the Prince of Wales.

Dame Myra Hess (1890–1965); *home: 48 Wildwood Road, Hampstead Garden Suburb, NW11 6UP; tube: Golders Green (Northern).*
Classical pianist remembered for organizing over 1,700 lunchtime music concerts at the National Gallery during WWII.

David Gestetner (1854–1939): *home; 124 Highbury New Park, Islington, N5 2DR; tube: Arsenal (Piccadilly); Overground: Canonbury.*
Hungarian born, in 1881 he invented the Cyclostyle, a form of stencil copying that

Home of Myra Hess.

MARCEL
DE SCHUTZENAU

33, Markhouse Avenue,
WALTHAMSTOW.

David Gestetner outside his home.

enabled documents to be copied quickly. It was a predecessor of the modern photocopier. He lived here for 41 years from 1898.

Sid James (1913–76); *home: 35 Gunnersbury Avenue, W5 3XD; tube: Ealing Common (District, Piccadilly).*
Born Solomon Joel Cohen in South Africa, he became one of Britain's best-loved TV and film comic actors, starring in 19 of the Carry On films. His home between 1956 and 1963 is commemorated.

Oscar Kokoschka (1886–1980); *home: Eyre Court, Finchley Road, NW8 9TU; tube: St. John's Wood (Jubilee).*
A successful artist, he fled Nazi Europe in 1938, his intense works having been designated degenerate. He made his home in St. John's Wood, close to other émigrés, but in 1947 moved to Switzerland where he died.

Minnie Lansbury (1889–1922); *memorial clock: Electric House, Bow Road, E3 2BL; tube: Bow Road (District, Hammersmith & City).*
Born off Brick Lane, she married Edgar, son of Labour politician George Lansbury. A communist and suffragette, she became the first woman councillor for Poplar in 1919. After a spell in prison during the 1921 councillors' rate revolt her health never recovered and she died aged 32.

Minnie Lansbury Memorial Clock.

Ted 'Kid' Lewis (1893–1970); *place of death: Nightingale House, Nightingale Lane, SW12 8NB; Overground: Wandsworth Common.*
British, European and world champion in a range of weights from feather to middle. His last home was Nightingale House, a Jewish nursing home. It was established in 1894 in the East End and moved to Clapham in 1908.

Simon Marks (1888–1964); *home: 35 Frognal, NW3 6YD; tube: Finchley Road (Jubilee, Metropolitan).*
The son of Michael Marks, co-founder of Marks & Spencer, lived here between 1920 and 1931. Taking over the helm of the company in 1916 he steered M&S to be the foremost store brand in the UK, guaranteeing quality clothing and food at affordable prices. He was enobled as Lord Marks of Broughton in 1961.

Abe Saperstein (1902–66); *childhood home: Rothschild Arch, Wentworth Street, E1; tube: Aldgate East (District, Hammersmith & City).*
Aged seven he left Charlotte de Rothschild Dwellings (see p. 26) when his family moved to the USA. In Chicago he coached a team of basketball players, renaming them the Harlem Globetrotters. He returned to the East End to unveil a plaque in his honour but it disappeared when the Dwellings were demolished.

Siegfried Sassoon (1886–1967); *homes: 23 Campden Hill Square, W8 7JY; tube: Holland Park (Central). 54 Tufton Street, SW1P 3RA; tube: Westminster (Circle, District, Jubilee).*
Born to a Jewish father and a Catholic mother, Sassoon became a poet, writer and courageous WWI soldier who famously refused to return to the Front. His friendship with poet Wilfred Owen was transformed into a book and film, *Regeneration*, and a play, *Not about Heroes*. They are two of the WWI poets commemorated in Westminster Abbey.

Peter Sellers (1925–80); *childhood home: 10 Muswell Hill Road, N6 5UG; tube: Highgate (Northern).*
Born to a Protestant father and a Jewish mother who descended from the Mendozas (see p. 51). A talented mimic, his career as a comedian and film actor, famously as Inspector Clouseau, was cut short with his untimely death at the age of 55.

Peter Sellers's childhood home.

JEWISH LONDONERS – WHERE THEY LIE

The first recorded cemetery for medieval Jewry was situated near Moorgate, and until 1177 was the only one in England. No other Jewish burial grounds were evident in London until the Resettlement of 1656 when both the Sephardi and Ashkenazi communities opened cemeteries in Mile End. By the late 19th century new cemeteries were established, mainly in North London suburbs. Currently, there are over 30 Jewish cemeteries in Greater London, providing for all religious levels. The cemeteries are easily reached by public transport and provide an opportunity to identify Jewish personalities who led the community and shaped politics, art, finance and industry.

OPEN CEMETERIES

These cemeteries are open to visit daily except Saturdays and Jewish festivals. It is advisable to confirm opening times before starting your journey.

WILLESDEN CEMETERY

Beaconsfield Road & Glebe Road (entrance), NW10 2JE; ☎ *020 8950 7767; www.theus. org.uk; open: daily (except Sat) 9am–5pm, early closing on Fri & in winter, check website; tube: Dollis Hill (Jubilee) – 8 mins.*

The United Synagogue, founded in 1870, established its first cemetery in 1873 in Willesden, then still a rural suburb. As you enter, the earliest burials are to your left. The cemetery has since been enlarged several times. The first burial was the MP **Samuel Moses** (1775–1873), the tombstone complete with his full address, a practice no longer followed. Nearby is Pre-Raphaelite artist **Simeon Solomon** (1840–1905), born in the East End. After a short, successful career, he died in a workhouse.

The cemetery is most noted for the burials of the 'Cousinhood', a network of Anglo-Jewish aristocracy. Following the main central path you will locate several prominent graves.

In one Rothschild family enclosure lie **Nathaniel Mayer Rothschild** (1840–1915), ennobled as the first Jewish peer in 1885, and his wife **Emma**.

His parents **Lionel de Rothschild** (1808–79), the first Jewish MP in 1858, and **Charlotte**, his brothers **Alfred** (1842–1918), banker, art collector and music expert, and **Leopold** (1845–1917), whose great passion was horse racing, lie alongside.

Lionel's brothers, **Mayer** (1818–74), the first Jewish member of the Jockey Club, and **Anthony** (1810–76), first president of the United Synagogue, have their own enclosure. Their daughters, **Hannah, Lady Rosebery, Annie** and **Constance, Lady Battersea** all married non-Jewish politicians but are buried alongside their parents.

Nearby are **Dorothy** (1895–1988) and **James de Rothschild** (1878-1957), who bequeathed Waddesdon to the National Trust in 1957 (see pp. 214–16 and also pp. 141–6).

Willesden Cemetery.

Other noteworthy burials include: The **Waley-Cohen** and **Samuel** families including **Marcus Samuel** (1853–1927), 1st Viscount Bearsted, a banker and founder of the Shell Oil Company. The Samuels were related to Samuel Montagu MP.

Harris Lebus (1852–1907), the son of 1840s German immigrants, ran the family furniture business, relocating from Shoreditch to Tottenham, North London in 1904. It became the largest furniture manufacturer in the UK.

Sir Israel Gollancz (1863–1930), eminent literary academic and son of the Central Synagogue chazan, he has an unusual roughly hewn tombstone.

Mark Gertler (1891–1939), the East End artist (see pp. 32 and 133).

Sir Jack Cohen (1898–1979), founder of supermarket chain Tesco (see p. 42).

You will also find graves of four successive Chief Rabbis: the father and son **Nathan** (1803–90) and **Hermann Adler** (1839–1911); **J. H. Hertz** (1872–1946); and **Israel Brodie** (1895–1979). Alongside is **Simeon Singer** (1848–1906), whose 1890 translation of the authorized Orthodox Jewish prayer book is still used today.

Nathaniel (Nathan) Mayer, 1st Lord
Rothschild and his wife, Emma Louise.

HOOP LANE – REFORM
AND SEPHARDI

Hoop Lane, NW11 7NJ; ☎ *020 8455 2569;
open daily (except Sat) 9am–5pm; early
closing on Fri & in winter; tube: Golders Green
(Northern) – 10 mins.*
In 1894 West London Reform Synagogue
purchased a site in suburban Golders Green.
The area was as yet undeveloped, with the
tube station not being built until 1907. In

1896 part was sold to the Spanish and
Portuguese community who planned to close
their Mile End cemetery. In 1902 the
crematorium opened opposite, hence the
juxtaposition of three different burial grounds.

As you enter the complex, to your left are
the Reform Synagogue burials. Looking
straight ahead, you will see the tombstones
of **Rabbi Dr Albert Friedlander** (1927–2004),
of Westminster Synagogue (see p. 165) and
Rabbi Hugo Gryn (see below).

Further left are:

Rabbi Leo Baeck (1873–1956), a German
rabbi who survived Theresienstadt, he became
president of the Reform Synagogue
movement in Britain. In 1956 a centre for
Progressive Jewish learning was renamed Leo
Baeck College in his honour.

Sir Basil Henriques (1890–1961), founder
of the Oxford and St George's Settlement
(see p. 45).

The entertainment world is represented by
Jack Rosenthal (1931–2004), playwright and
husband of comedienne Maureen Lipman; and
Jacqueline du Pré (1945–87), the cellist who
converted to Judaism to marry Daniel

MORAL MAVEN

Rabbi Hugo Gryn (1930–96) was a Reform rabbi beloved
and respected throughout Anglo-Jewry and beyond.
Czechoslovakian born, he survived Auschwitz and devoted
his life to promoting peace and humanity. Encouraged by
Leo Baeck and Lily Montagu to become a rabbi, Gryn gained
his semicha in the USA but made his career in the UK. He
was rabbi at the West London Reform Synagogue for over 30
years, but his influential work for interfaith dialogue, ethical
ideals, Progressive Judaism, refugees and his humane BBC
radio broadcasts brought him a loyal global audience.

Grave of Rabbi Hugo Gryn, Hoop Lane.

DNA DISCOVERY

Rosalind Franklin (1920–58) was born into an established Ashkenazi family. Her father, Ellis Franklin, worked at the family bank Keyser's and was active in Jewish communal affairs. She pursued further education and a career in biophysics and chemistry against her father's wishes and was invited to research at King's College, London. There, she worked on isolating the double helix of DNA using X-rays. Her notebooks of 1953 contained important discoveries and, unbeknown to her, her colleague Maurice Wilkins shared her findings with James Watson and Francis Crick in Cambridge who subsequently concluded the evidence for DNA. They and Wilkins shared the Nobel Prize for Medicine in 1962 but Franklin's contributions to the discovery are often overlooked. Franklin died of cancer aged just 38, and her work was only fully recognized posthumously. Her depiction is included in the stained-glass window of King's College Chapel, which commemorates the college's scientific research.

King's College Chapel, Strand, Science Faculty window with depiction of Rosalind Franklin in lower right-hand corner.

Barenboim. She died tragically young from multiple sclerosis.

Right of the ohel are the Sephardi burials, easily distinguished as the tombstones are flat. It includes **Nathan Saatchi** (1907–2000), a textile merchant who left Iraq in 1946. His sons Charles and Maurice founded the Saatchi & Saatchi advertising agency in 1970.

Across the road is the crematorium where you can find a memorial to, among others, **Mark Bolan** (born Feld) (1947–77), the 1970s popstar with group T. Rex, who was killed in a car crash aged 29.

EAST HAM

Marlow Road, East Ham, E6 3QG; tube: East Ham (District, Hammersmith & City) – 15 mins. Opened in 1919 by the United Synagogue, the first burial was a WWI naval casualty, Able Seaman **John Kelly**, born Isaac Jacob Shadbrisky. Also here are Gerson Mendeloff, who as **Ted 'Kid' Lewis** (1893–1970) was world welterweight boxing champion in 1915 and **Isidore Berliner** (1869–1925), who established the London Jewish Hospital (see p. 53).

CLOSED CEMETERIES

These cemeteries are closed to burials and to the public but will open for visitors on request. Tours are also available with Go London Tours (*www.golondontours.com*).

SEPHARDI: VELHO (OLD) CEMETERY

Queen Mary College, Mile End Road, E1 4NS; call the Spanish & Portuguese Synagogue office to arrange a visit ☎ 020 7289 2573; www.sandp.org.

Situated behind the Lying-In Hospital on Mile End Road and opened in 1657, this is the oldest Jewish cemetery in Britain following the Resettlement. Plague victims of 1665 were buried here. It was extended, but closed in 1735. All that remains are hundreds of plain, flat tombstones lying in a grassy field. The inscriptions are mostly unreadable but the boundary wall at the north side has a restored plaque from 1684. Antonio Carvajal, who supported Cromwell, and Simon de Caceres, a signatory of the Resettlement petition, were signatories to the lease. Alvaro da Costa and Fernando Mendes, doctor to Catherine of Braganza, wife of Charles II, were both buried here. These families often married each other and the Mendes da Costa name survives to this day.

SEPHARDI: NUEVO (NEW) CEMETERY

See p. 51 for details.

Opened near to the Velho Cemetery in 1733, the land purchased in 1724 by da Costa and Mendes was leased out until required. Notable burials included **Samson Gideon** (1699–1762), the financier and **Daniel Mendoza**, the boxer. The last burial was in 1918 and the cemetery officially closed in 1936. Only a fraction of the original site remains. In 1974 Queen Mary College acquired a large portion and 7,500 graves were reinterred at Brentwood, Essex. Samson Gideon and religious leaders were reinterred at Hoop Lane, Golders Green (see pp. 152–3).

Velho Cemetery.

Nuevo Cemetery.

Family names on graves remaining include Montefiore and Sassoon.

ASHKENAZI: ALDERNEY ROAD JEWISH CEMETERY

Alderney Road, E1; ☎ *020 8950 7767; www.theus.org.uk; call to arrange visit.*
From the pavement all you can see is a tall brick wall. A small doorway leads to the oldest existing Ashkenazi cemetery in Britain, established in 1696 by the Great Synagogue, Duke's Place and funded by Benjamin Levy, one of the synagogue founders. Until its existence Ashkenazi Jews were buried in the Sephardi Cemetery. Land adjoining the Velho was bought and extended in 1749 before closing in 1852. Important burials include **Chief Rabbi David Tevele Schiff** (unknown–1791) and **Samuel Falk** (unknown–1782). (See pp. 45, 114 and 140). Some tombstone inscriptions, unusually, include a skull and crossbones and cherubs.

ASHKENAZI: BANCROFT ROAD

Bancroft Road, E1; ☎ *020 7543 5400; www.bod.org.uk; call to arrange visit.*
Opened in 1810 by the independent Maiden Lane Synagogue, Covent Garden, the last interment was in 1923. It is in a poor state of repair but is clearly visible through the railings.

Alderney Road Cemetery.

Above left: Back to back tombstones, Brady Street Cemetery. Above right: Brady Street Cemetery.

ASHKENAZI: BRADY STREET JEWISH CEMETERY

Brady Street, E1; ☎ *020 8950 7767; www.theus.org.uk; call to arrange visit.*
This was opened in 1761 for the New Synagogue, which was established in the same year. Over 3,000 tombstones still stand, with a variety of emblems providing a fascinating insight into the early London Jewish community. Some inscriptions are in Hebrew, some in English. Some provide the deceased's address, others their town of origin. Depictions of musical instruments, fish and books indicate occupations. Some stones are back to back, dating from when an additional layer of soil was added in the 19th century due to lack of space.

Burials include brothers **Abraham** (1756–1810) and **Benjamin** (1755–1808) **Goldschmid**, wealthy money brokers, who both committed suicide. **Miriam Levy** (1801–1850), a social worker, has a tombstone decorated with a relief of her face, rarely seen in a Jewish cemetery. The most notable burials are those of **Nathan**

Mayer Rothschild (1777–1836), founder of the eponymous banking business and the English Rothschild dynasty, and his wife **Hannah**. Alongside is a red granite chest tomb for **Victor, 3rd Baron Rothschild** (1910–1990). The cemetery had been closed to new burials in 1858 but Victor put arrangements in place so that he could be buried alongside his ancestors. See also pp. 141–6.

WEST HAM

Buckingham Road, E15; ☎ *020 8950 7767; www.theus.org.uk; call to arrange visit.*
The cemetery was opened in 1856 by the New Synagogue to replace Brady Street and closed in 2002. The marble Renaissance-style rotunda was built for **Ferdinand de Rothschild** (1839–98), creator of Waddesdon, and his wife **Evelina** (1839–66), daughter of Lionel, who died in childbirth just over a year into her marriage (see pp. 214–16). Also buried here is **Sir David Salomons** (1797–1873), first Jewish Lord Mayor of London (see pp. 84 and 207–09).

JEWISH LONDON TODAY

This book features those parts of the city which readers keen to experience Jewish London are most likely to visit; be it to stay, eat, shop, pray or explore. Consequently, this chapter focuses on North-west London, where there is a large Jewish population and a wide range of kosher facilities; and Central and East London, where most visitors are likely to stay, or explore.

The majority of the city's Jewish population live in the North-west, where most of London's kosher restaurants, cafés and shops are located, especially in Golders Green, Temple Fortune, Hendon and Edgware, all of which also have large orthodox communities. The area became especially popular with the Jewish community after WWI, as a result of their desire to move from the East End to the suburbs. The Jewish presence increased both before and following WWII with the influx of refugees from Central and Eastern Europe. Since then the area has retained a relatively large proportion of Jewish residents. The ultra-orthodox community of Stamford Hill is also included. Apologies to London's other Jewish communities where lack of space has dictated their absence.

CAFES, RESTAURANTS, SHOPS AND HOTELS

The majority of kosher cafés, restaurants and shops are located in North-west London, predominantly in the main Jewish areas of Golders Green, Temple Fortune, Hendon and Edgware. We have also included 'kosher-style' and vegetarian eateries, particularly in areas lacking kosher facilities. Space allows us to list just a selection of our favourites, catering to all budgets and dietary needs.

The listings in these sections are alphabetical and state, where appropriate and available, the name, address, telephone number, website, café and restaurant opening hours, nearest tube station and approximate walking time from the station, the supervising kashrut authority (see p. 8) and where credit cards are not accepted. An indication of price is given for eateries and hotels. If there is an area map, the map reference is given.

Fish lovers may be interested to know that the following commonly found fish in London's restaurants are kosher: anchovy, bass, black cod, bream, brill, carp, cod, haddock, hake, halibut, herring, mackerel, mullet, perch, plaice, red snapper, salmon, sardine, sole, trout, tuna, whitebait and whiting.

Kosher establishments that are open on Fridays will usually close at least one hour before Shabbat, and if open Saturday night, will reopen one hour after Shabbat at the earliest.

For each café and restaurant, an indication of the price of a main course is shown as follows:
£ – under £10
££ – £10–20
£££ – Over £20

TOP 4 KOSHER CAFES AND SNACK BARS

Isola Bella (Westfield) (see p. 159)
Pita (West Hampstead) (see p. 195)
Pizaza (Hendon) (see p. 182)
Taboon (Golders Green) (see p. 168)

TOP 4 KOSHER RESTAURANTS

Aviv (Edgware) (see p. 186)
Bevis Marks (Aldgate) (see p. 198)
Kaifeng (Hendon) (see p. 180)
Met Su Yan (Golders Green) (see p. 166)

There is a wide range of accommodation in London with a few kosher hotels located in North-west London and one in Stamford Hill. We have listed hotels convenient for synagogues and kosher facilities. For non-kosher hotels, there is information on their ease of use for the Shabbat observant, covering electronic entrances, electric door keys and, where provided, the heating of food.

Visitors can arrange for kosher meals to be delivered to their hotels from Adafina (see p. 191) and Hermolis (☎ *020 8810 4321; www.hermolis.com*).

For each hotel an indication of the price of a double room without breakfast (unless otherwise stated) is shown as follows:
£ – Under £100
££ – £100–200
£££ – Over £200

SYNAGOGUES

For each area, a range of local synagogues are listed. Information provided includes religious affiliation (see p. 9), visitor welcoming, kiddush provision, Shabbat hospitality,

website (most have their own websites with service times and general information), tube station and distance from the station.

Synagogues are security conscious. As such, it is advisable to call in advance of Shabbat before visiting. Many of the listed shuls will also provide Shabbat hospitality and welcome advance notice if this is required, usually by the Thursday before the relevant Shabbat.

ERUVIM AND MIKVAOT

Information is provided in each area where appropriate.

TRAVEL INFORMATION

Whilst the listings show the nearest tube station, bus details are not usually listed, but the area maps indicate bus stops. Full information about bus and tube travel is provided by Transport for London (*www.tfl.gov.uk*).

Western Marble Arch Synagogue, stained-glass window.

CENTRAL LONDON

Central London stretches eastwards from Holland Park via Knightsbridge and Marble Arch to the West End. Easy access to London's premier tourist sites, Theatreland and shopping districts makes this the area of choice for many Jewish visitors.

Our listings include the small number of kosher and several unsupervised eateries, mostly vegetarian. Map references refer to pp. 160–61.

KOSHER CAFES AND RESTAURANTS

ISOLA BELLA

Dairy café within Westfield London Shopping Centre ££

First Floor, The Village (opposite House of Fraser), Westfield London Shopping Centre, Ariel Way, W12 7SL; ☎ 020 8740 6611; www.isolabella.co.uk; tube: Shepherd's Bush (Central) – 5 mins; open Sun–Thur 9am–11pm, Fri 9am–1 hr before Shabbat, Sat 1 hr after Shabbat–11pm; LBD; branch in Golders Green. ❶

An island of calm amidst a busy shopping mall, this is a pleasant, well-designed mid-priced café offering an extensive menu of breakfast items and all-day dishes including soups, pizzas, pasta, salads, Thai specialities and a mouth-watering selection of cakes and desserts. Portions are large – an individual serving is perfect for sharing.

JEWISH MUSEUM CAFE

Meat café £ ❷

The Jewish Museum is in Camden Town, just north of Central London (see p. 116).

REUBENS

Meat deli/restaurant ££/£££

79 Baker Street, W1U 6RG; ☎ 020 7486 0035;

tube: Baker Street (Bakerloo, Circle, Jubilee, Metropolitan) – 8 mins; open Sun–Thur 11.30am–4pm & 5.30pm–10pm, Fri 11.30am–2 hrs before Shabbat; SKA; no credit cards in deli. ❸

Established in 1973, this is just 10 minutes' walk from Oxford Street. The ground floor deli-diner for quick bites and takeaways provides traditional favourites such as chicken soup with matzah balls, gefilte fish, and great salt-beef sandwiches that were listed as one of the Evening Standard's 10 best sandwiches in London in 2011. A restaurant in the basement offers a more formal menu. Portions are more than generous.

UNSUPERVISED CAFES AND RESTAURANTS

FOOD FOR THOUGHT

Vegetarian £

31 Neal Street, WC2H 9PR; ☎ 020 7836 0239; www.foodforthought-london.co.uk; tube: Covent Garden (Piccadilly) – 4 mins; open Mon–Sat 12pm–8.30pm, Sun 12pm–5.30pm; no credit cards. ❹

Established in 1974, this cheap and cheerful basement café serves a daily changing menu of delicious and wholesome vegetarian cuisine. Ideal for a quick bite, or takeaway, the queues for food are testament to its popularity. The café is small, so be prepared to share a table.

GABYS

Middle Eastern £

30 Charing Cross Road, WC2H 0DB; ☎ 020 7836 4233; tube: Leicester Square (Northern, Piccadilly) – 1 min; open Mon–Sat 11am–12am, Sun 12pm–10pm; no credit cards. ❺

Conveniently located by Leicester Square tube station, this busy long-established falafel bar and café is perfect for a quick meal in Theatreland. Falafel in pitta and salt-beef sandwiches are traditional favourites. There is a good salad bar and various vegetarian options.

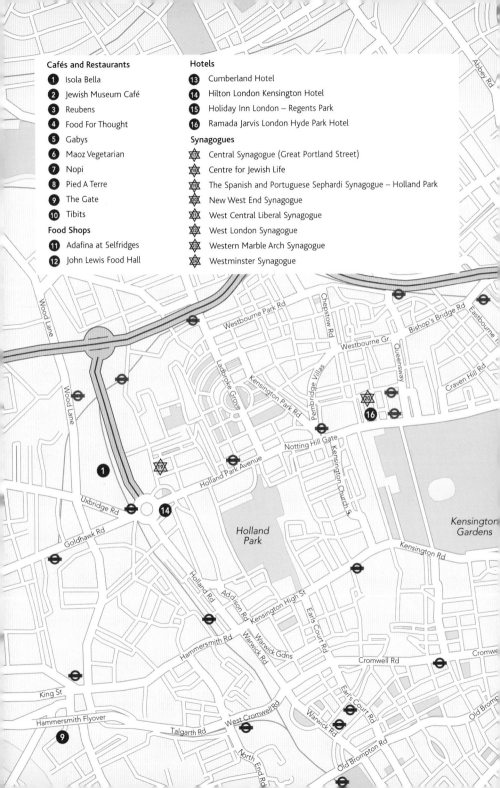

Cafés and Restaurants

1. Isola Bella
2. Jewish Museum Café
3. Reubens
4. Food For Thought
5. Gabys
6. Maoz Vegetarian
7. Nopi
8. Pied A Terre
9. The Gate
10. Tibits

Food Shops

11. Adafina at Selfridges
12. John Lewis Food Hall

Hotels

13. Cumberland Hotel
14. Hilton London Kensington Hotel
15. Holiday Inn London – Regents Park
16. Ramada Jarvis London Hyde Park Hotel

Synagogues

✡ Central Synagogue (Great Portland Street)
✡ Centre for Jewish Life
✡ The Spanish and Portuguese Sephardi Synagogue – Holland Park
✡ New West End Synagogue
✡ West Central Liberal Synagogue
✡ West London Synagogue
✡ Western Marble Arch Synagogue
✡ Westminster Synagogue

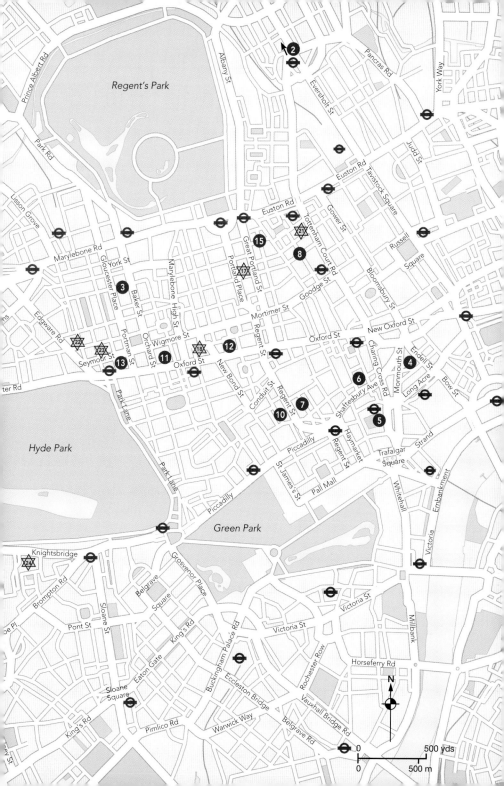

MAOZ VEGETARIAN

Falafel bar £

43 Old Compton Street, W1D 6HG; ☎ 020 7851 1586; www.maozusa.com; tube: Leicester Square (Northern, Piccadilly) – 10 mins; open Mon–Wed 11am–1am, Thur 11am–1.30am, Fri–Sat 11am– 2.30am, Sun 11am–12am; no credit/debit cards. ❻

A branch of the popular Dutch falafel bar chain that is very handily located in the heart of Soho, Maoz is ideal for a meal that is quick, cheap, filling and tasty. The short menu features falafel in pitta with hummus, a self-service salad bar and chips. Eat in or take away.

NOPI

Mediterranean/Middle Eastern/Asian brasserie ££/£££

21/22 Warwick Street, W1B 5NE; ☎ 020 7494 9584; www.nopi-restaurant.com; tube: Oxford Circus (Bakerloo, Central, Victoria) – 11 mins; open Mon–Fri 8am–2.45pm & 5.30pm–11.30pm, Sat 9am–11.30pm, Sun 10am–4pm. ❼

The most recent addition to the Israeli chef Yotam Ottolenghi's excellent restaurant chain named after its location north of Piccadilly Circus, this all-day dining venue serves sharing-size portions of delicious original cuisine in an informal environment.

PIED A TERRE

Haute cuisine £££

34 Charlotte Street, W1T 2NH; ☎ 020 7636 1178; www.pied-a-terre.co.uk; tube: Goodge Street (Northern) – 7 mins; open Mon–Fri 12.15pm– 2.30pm & 6pm–11pm, Sat 6pm–11pm. ❽

For a special treat, this Michelin-starred restaurant within a cosy and relaxed Fitzrovia townhouse serves an exquisite vegetarian tasting menu for £85 – including six savoury courses, cheese, two desserts and coffee with petits fours.

THE GATE

Vegetarian ££

51 Queen Caroline Street, Hammersmith, W6 9QL; ☎ 020 8748 6932; www.thegate.tv; tube: Hammersmith (District, Metropolitan, Piccadilly) –

5 mins; open Mon–Fri 12pm–3pm & 6pm–10.30pm, Sat 6pm–11pm. ❾

Located outside the Central London area, but easy to travel to, this excellent vegetarian restaurant, opened in 1989, is worthy of mention. The delicious food reflects the heritage of the founders, two Indo-Iraqi Jewish brothers. The reasonably priced meals are generous and service is friendly. Eat in the first-floor former artists' studio, or, in summer, outside on the terrace.

TIBITS

Vegetarian £/££

12–14 Heddon Street (off Regent Street), W1B 4DA; ☎ 020 7758 4110; www.tibits.co.uk; tube: Oxford Circus (Bakerloo, Central, Victoria) – 10 mins; open Mon–Sat 9am–12am, Sun 11.30am–10.30pm. ❿

This London branch of the Swiss chain is just off one of London's premier shopping streets. Help yourself to fast, fresh and tasty vegetarian food, including hot daily specials and over 30 homemade salads. Your meal is priced depending on its weight. Eat in or take away.

KOSHER FOOD SHOPS

ADAFINA AT SELFRIDGES

400 Oxford Street, W1A 1AB; ☎ 0800 123400; www.selfridges.com; tube: Bond Street (Central, Jubilee) – 5 mins; open Mon–Sat 9.30am–10pm (Sat 9pm), Sun 11.30am–6pm; LBD/SKA. ⓫

Adafina, the St. John's Wood kosher traiteur (see p. 191), has a counter within the Food Hall and stocks a good selection of pre-cooked dishes including fried fish, chicken and salads. A separate chilled cabinet stocks sandwiches and salads, and lasagne and meatballs ready to heat.

There are kosher challot and bread in the Food Hall's bakery section and kosher goods, wine and candles on the grocery shelves.

OTHER SOURCES OF KOSHER FOOD

JOHN LEWIS FOOD HALL

300 Oxford Street, W1A 1EX; ☎ 020 7629 7711; www.johnlewis.com; tube: Oxford Circus (Bakerloo,

Central, Victoria) – 5 mins; open Mon–Sat 9.30am–8pm (Thur –9pm), Sun 11.30am–6pm. **⑫**

John Lewis sells kosher bread and challot in its bakery section, Adafina kosher sandwiches and bagels in the chilled counters, kosher wines and a basic range of other kosher groceries.

SUPERMARKETS

A limited kosher range, including sandwiches, can be found at several Central London supermarkets including Tesco, Waitrose and Sainsbury's (various locations).

NON-FOOD SHOPS

JEWISH MUSEUM SHOP

Camden Town (see p. 116). **❷**

You'll find here a wide variety of Jewish themed books and gifts.

HOTELS

Shabbat facilities – with advance notice, the following hotels will arrange for guests' bedroom doors to be opened as keys are electronic, and staff will open the main entrance door where this is electronic. Rooms on lower floors should be requested.

CUMBERLAND HOTEL

££

Great Cumberland Place, W1C 1LZ; ☎ *0871 376 9014; www.guoman.com; tube: Marble Arch (Central) – 2 mins.* **⑬**

With Oxford Street and the Western Marble Arch Synagogue nearby, this modern four-star luxury hotel has over 1,000 en suite bedrooms.

HILTON LONDON KENSINGTON HOTEL

££

179–199 Holland Park Avenue, W11 4UL; ☎ *020 7603 3355; www.hilton.co.uk; tube: Shepherds Bush (Central) – 5 mins.* **⑭**

Five minutes' walk from Holland Park Synagogue and Westfield Shopping Centre, this

modern hotel has 601 en suite bedrooms. There is a manual entrance that can be opened by exception on Shabbat. Guests are asked to request a first-floor room as Shabbat access is via the fire stairs with assistance from a porter.

HOLIDAY INN LONDON – REGENTS PARK

£/££

Carburton Street, W1W 5EE; ☎ *0871 942 9111; www.holidayinn.com; tube: Great Portland Street (Circle, Metropolitan) – 5 mins.* **⑮**

Ten minutes' walk from Oxford Street and five minutes' walk to the Central Synagogue, this is a modern four-star hotel with 325 en suite bedrooms. The hotel can order kosher meals for guests on 48 hours' prior notice, and they will also heat guests own kosher meals. Rates are discounted by at least 20 per cent when booked on the hotel's website at least 21 days in advance.

RAMADA JARVIS LONDON HYDE PARK HOTEL

££

150 Bayswater Road, W2 4RT; ☎ *0844 815 9048; www.ramadajarvis.co.uk/hydepark; tube: Queensway (Central) – 5 mins.* **⑯**

Opposite Hyde Park and close to the New West End Synagogue, this is a modern four-star hotel with 213 en suite bedrooms. There is a standard door at the rear of the hotel that can be used by Orthodox guests. Kosher meals can be heated for guests.

SYNAGOGUES

CENTRAL SYNAGOGUE

(known as Great Portland Street)

36 Hallam Street, W1W 6NW; ☎ *020 7580 1355; www.centralsynagogue.org.uk; tube: Great Portland Street (Circle, Metropolitan) – 5 mins.* **⑰**

Established on its present site in 1870, it was one of the original five synagogues that formed the United Synagogue, also in 1870. It was destroyed in 1941 during WWII and rebuilt in 1958.

Members of the Welcoming Committee greet visitors on Shabbat and can introduce them to someone to sit with. Shabbat Shacharit starts at 9.15am and around 100 members attend. There is a weekly kiddush. Shabbat hospitality can be provided with prior notice. There are also daily services.

CENTRE FOR JEWISH LIFE

Media House, 4 Stratford Place, W1C 1AT; ☎ *020 7495 6089; www.thecjl.org; tube: Bond Street (Central, Jubilee) – 1 min.* ⓲

Close to Bond Street tube station on Oxford Street, the Centre for Jewish Life hosts Mincha at 1.15pm, Monday–Thursday. It also has a library covering a wide variety of subjects, open from 9.30am–5pm Monday–Thursday. Wi-Fi access and laptops available. Occasional Friday-night dinners are held – check website for details.

THE SPANISH AND PORTUGUESE SEPHARDI SYNAGOGUE – HOLLAND PARK

St James's Gardens, Holland Park, W11 4RB; ☎ *020 7603 7961; www.hollandparksynagogue. com; tube: Shepherds Bush (Central) – 10 mins.* ⓳

This Sephardi synagogue holds services conducted in the traditional Spanish and Portuguese liturgy, mainly in Hebrew with some Ladino. Visitors are welcome to attend Shabbat services, but are encouraged to call the synagogue beforehand. Shabbat Shacharit is at 8.45am and around 30–40 members attend. There is a weekly kiddush. See also p. 102 .

NEW WEST END SYNAGOGUE

(also known as St Petersburgh Place)

St Petersburgh Place, Bayswater, W2 4JT; ☎ *020 7229 2631; www.newwestend.org.uk; tube: Queensway (Central) – 7 mins; office open Mon–Thur 8am–4pm, Fri 8am–2pm, Sun 10am–12pm.* ⓴

This United Synagogue is one of the oldest and most beautiful in London (see pp. 97–8). Visitors should contact the synagogue before planning to attend a service. The community is friendly and visitors are welcomed at the door by shul members. Shabbat Shacharit starts at 9.15am and around 100 people attend. There is a weekly kiddush.

WEST CENTRAL LIBERAL SYNAGOGUE

The Montagu Centre, 21 Maple Street, W1T 4BE; ☎ *020 7636 7627; www.wcls.org.uk; tube: Warren Street (Northern, Victoria) – 5 mins.* ㉑

This community was originally founded in 1916 by Lily Montagu (see pp. 99–101). Today it is an inclusive, diverse and friendly community that uniquely holds its Shabbat services at 3pm, with men and women encouraged to play equal roles in the service. Talks on subjects of Jewish interest follow the service.

WEST LONDON SYNAGOGUE

33 Seymour Place, W1H 5AU (entrance for services is around corner in 34 Upper Berkeley Street); ☎ *020 7723 4404; www.wls.org.uk; tube: Marble Arch (Central) – 10 mins.* ㉒

This is one of the largest and most beautiful Reform synagogues in the country (see pp. 74–5), with a membership of 1,700 families.

Friday-night services are at 6pm, with fortnightly Shabbat Shira (Shabbat of Song) services, which are informal participatory services with singing accompanied by musicians. Around 50 attend Shabbat Shacharit at 11am.

WESTERN MARBLE ARCH SYNAGOGUE

(known as Marble Arch)

32 Great Cumberland Place, W1H 7TN; ☎ *020 7723 9333; www.marblearch.org.uk; email: office@marblearch.org.uk; tube: Marble Arch (Central) – 5 mins.* ㉓

This Modern Orthodox independent synagogue in association with the United Synagogue is the product of a merger, in 1991, of the Western Synagogue and the Marble Arch Synagogue. It is housed in the latter's large and impressive premises consecrated in 1961, which feature beautiful stained glass.

Visitors are welcomed on Shabbat, and the main Shacharit service starts at 9.15am and attracts around 200 people; more for simchas. There is an excellent weekly kiddush. Shabbat hospitality can be provided with prior notice.

A separate Shabbat service known as the Chevra Minyan, for young members, takes place

Above left: Stained-glass window, Western Marble Arch Synagogue. Above right: Synagogue Ark, Westminster Synagogue.

fortnightly in the adjacent Mintz Bet Hamidrash. It begins at 10am and they have their own separate kiddush. It is part of the West End Great Synagogue service. This community, founded originally in 1880 (see p. 73) still functions with about 10–12 regulars who are glad to welcome the young people to their community.

Daily Shacharit followed by breakfast, and Mincha and Ma'ariv take place in the adjacent Mintz Bet Hamidrash.

WESTMINSTER SYNAGOGUE

First Floor, Kent House, Rutland Gardens, Knightsbridge, SW7 1BX; ☎ *020 7584 3953; www.westminstersynagogue.org; email: secretary@westminstersynagogue.org; tube: Knightsbridge (Piccadilly) – 8 mins; office open Mon–Fri; lift & disabled access.* ㉔ *(and* ❷ *on inset map on p. 119)*

This independent Reform synagogue is located in Kent House, a beautiful Victorian townhouse. It was built in 1870 and was at one time owned by Sir Saxton Noble and Lady Noble, the granddaughter of Isambard Kingdom Brunel, the

famous British engineer. The Nobles left Kent House in 1940 when it was used as wartime offices. It was acquired by Westminster Synagogue in 1960.

Consecrated in 1963, the synagogue is located on the first floor in the former ballroom. The Ark is particularly unusual having been created from the fireplace. It contains one of the Czech Torah scrolls on permanent loan from the museum on the third floor of Kent House (see pp. 122–3).

The Reinhart Library on the ground floor contains signed prints of Marc Chagall's 12 stained-glass windows at the Hadassah University Medical Center's synagogue in Jerusalem.

The community are very welcoming to visitors, who should call the synagogue office to inform them of their proposed attendance. There are services on Friday night, and Shabbat morning at 11am with a female chazan accompanied by an organ. There is a weekly kiddush.

ERUV

There is no eruv in Central London.

NORTH-WEST: GOLDERS GREEN

The heart of modern Jewish London is in Golders Green, just 8km (5 miles) north of the centre. Golders Green Road is 'the' place in London to find kosher bagels, kugel, falafel and shawarma, together with bookshops, Judaica stores and kosher supermarkets.

In recent years the established Jewish community has been joined by thousands of Israelis; some of the 50,000 estimated to be in the UK. Their presence has contributed to the cosmopolitan atmosphere and pavement-café lifestyle.

With the many synagogues, outreach projects and the young community, this is an area of almost constant hustle and bustle. Friday mornings it is at its busiest, with families preparing for Shabbat. Once night falls, Golders Green becomes quiet and tranquil until Shabbat is over on Saturday night when the queues for bagels begin outside Carmelli Bakeries.

Unless otherwise stated, the cafés, restaurants and shops are within 5–10 minutes' walk of Golders Green tube station. The others are within walking distance of Brent Cross tube station. Both stations are on the Northern line. Several buses go along Golders Green Road – bus stops are shown on the map.

KOSHER CAFES AND RESTAURANTS

During the past 25 years the number of kosher establishments in Golders Green has proliferated, fuelled, in part, by the influx of Israelis to London. Bloom's, the long-established restaurant founded in 1920 in Whitechapel, closed in 2010, but those remaining offer a diverse array of food styles including Israeli, Chinese, Indian, Italian and deli-style. The following is a selection of the cuisines available.

LA FIESTA

Steakhouse/grill ££

235 Golders Green Road, NW11 9ES; ☎ *020 8458 0444; tube: Brent Cross – 10 mins; open Mon–Thur 12pm–3pm & 6pm–10.30pm, Sun 6pm–10.30pm; LBD.* ❶

Popular with carnivores, this informal Argentinian steakhouse serves excellent chargrilled entrecôte steaks of various weights with crisp, chunky chips.

MATTANCHERRY

Indian/meat ££

109a Golders Green Road, NW11 8HR; ☎ *020 8209 3060; www.mattancherry.co.uk; open Mon–Thur 12pm–3pm & 6pm–11pm, Sun 12pm–11pm, 30 mins after Shabbat in winter; Kedassia.* ❷

This welcoming comfortable restaurant has an extensive menu of traditional Indian dishes including tandoori specialities, and a variety of curries. It's known for friendly service and good-value set meals. There is a takeaway service too.

MET SU YAN

Pan-oriental/meat ££

134 Golders Green Road, NW11 8HB; ☎ *020 8458 8088; www.metsuyan.co.uk; open Sun–Thur 12pm–3pm & 6pm–11pm, after Shabbat from Oct–Apr; KF ; reservations advisable.* ❸

In Hebrew, 'metsuyan' means 'excellent', which is entirely appropriate for one of the best kosher dining experiences in London. With simple but stylish decor, it serves a tempting Japanese and Chinese menu. Recommended dishes include the imperial hors d'oeuvres, the crispy aromatic duck with pancakes and sushi. Portions are generous and service is polite and attentive. The set lunch menu is good value.

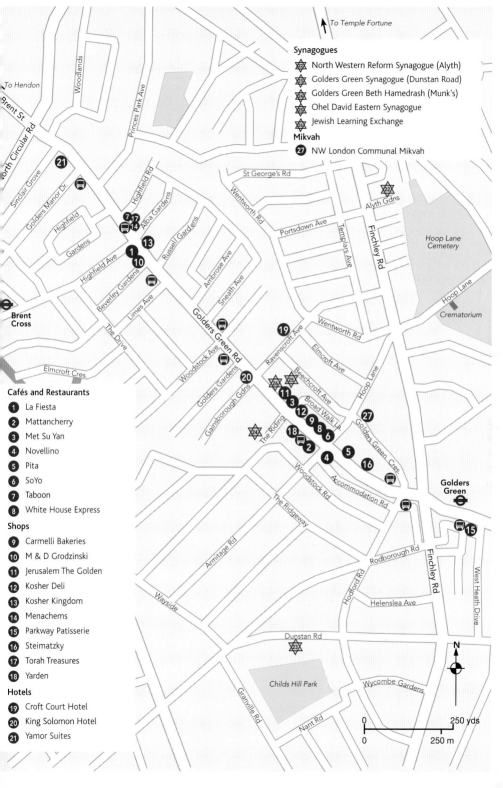

To Temple Fortune

Synagogues

North Western Reform Synagogue (Alyth)

Golders Green Synagogue (Dunstan Road)

Golders Green Beth Hamedrash (Munk's)

Ohel David Eastern Synagogue

Jewish Learning Exchange

Mikvah

27 NW London Communal Mikvah

To Hendon

Brent Cross

Cafés and Restaurants

1 La Fiesta
2 Mattancherry
3 Met Su Yan
4 Novellino
5 Pita
6 SoYo
7 Taboon
8 White House Express

Shops

9 Carmelli Bakeries
10 M & D Grodzinski
11 Jerusalem The Golden
12 Kosher Deli
13 Kosher Kingdom
14 Menachems
15 Parkway Patisserie
16 Steimatzky
17 Torah Treasures
18 Yarden

Hotels

19 Croft Court Hotel
20 King Solomon Hotel
21 Yamor Suites

Golders Green

Childs Hill Park

0   250 yds
0   250 m

NOVELLINO

Italian/dairy ££

103 Golders Green Road, NW11 8EN; ☎ *020 8458 7273; www.novellino.co.uk; open Sun–Thur 8.30am–12am, Fri 8.30am–1 hr before Shabbat, check for opening hours after Shabbat; KF; reservations advisable.* ❹

A popular choice for all ages, this lively dairy restaurant serves mainly Italian and Mediterranean fare, including homemade pasta, fresh fish and a tempting array of desserts. An all-day breakfast is served until 5pm on weekdays. The takeaway service sells homemade breads, fresh sandwiches and cakes.

PITA

Falafel/grilled meat £

98 Golders Green Road, NW11 8HB; ☎ *020 8381 4080; open Sun–Thur 11.30am–11.30pm, Fri 11.30am–2 hrs before Shabbat, Sat night 1 hr after Shabbat–3am; KF.* ❺

Soyo's chandelier.

This small café is great for takeaways. (See p. 195 for main West Hampstead branch.)

SOYO

Dairy £

94 Golders Green Road, NW11 8HB; ☎ *020 8458 8788; open Sun–Thur 8am–12am, Fri 8am–2pm, after Shabbat–3am; KF; credit cards accepted (min. £10); reservations advisable.* ❻

Opened in 2010, this futuristic and funky café, with modern decor including a chandelier made out of 2,000 plastic spoons, is especially popular with a youngish crowd. A good-value Israeli-style breakfast is served until 3pm. Otherwise, the menu includes an assortment of appetizing soups, sandwiches, pancakes, quiches and pastas with a wide selection of salad options. The house dessert speciality is frozen yogurt with a choice of sauce, fruit and sweet toppings.

TABOON

Falafel £

17 Russell Parade, Golders Green Road, NW11 9NN; ☎ *020 8455 7451; tube: Brent Cross – 8 mins; open Sun–Thur 9.30am–12am, Fri 9.30am–12.30pm (4pm in summer), Sat 7pm–12am (in winter); LBD & SKA; no credit cards.* ❼

Totally unpretentious and great value for money, this small falafel bar serves what many consider to be the best falafel in London, complete with a self-service salad bar. Eat in or take away. Their pitta bread is also highly rated.

WHITE HOUSE EXPRESS

Middle Eastern/meat £

102 Golders Green Road, NW11 8HB; ☎ *020 8458 9345; open Sun–Thur 12pm–1am, Fri 12pm–4pm; LBD & SKA; branch in Hendon (see p. 182).* ❽

Offering a reasonably priced variety of tasty grilled meats and burgers, this popular informal eatery attracts a youngish crowd.

KOSHER FOOD SHOPS

CARMELLI BAKERIES

Bakery

126–128 Golders Green Road, NW11 8HB;
☎ *020 8455 2074; www.carmelli.co.uk; open*
Sun–Thur 6.30am–12am, Fri until 1 hr before
Shabbat and 1 hr after Shabbat; Kedassia & LBD;
no credit cards. ❾

Israeli-owned bakery, founded in 1992, with a
wide range of bagels, breads, cakes and
takeaway snacks, Carmelli's is busy all day and
attracts the hordes seeking bagels late at night.
There is a takeaway menu for tarts, fish, quiches
and salads.

M & D GRODZINSKI

Bakery

223 Golders Green Road, NW11 9ES; ☎ *020 8458*
3654; www.grodzinskibakery.co.uk; tube: Brent
Cross – 8 mins; open Mon–Thur 6am–11pm, Fri
6am–2 hrs before Shabbat, Sun 6am–10pm
Kedassia & LBD. ❿

Affectionately known as 'Grodz' (see p. 46 for
history), this bakery established in 1888 retains
a loyalty to heimishe-style baking. There's also a
good choice of freshly made sandwiches, salads
and hot snacks to take away.

KOSHER DELI

Butcher/deli

132 Golders Green Road, NW11 8HB; ☎ *020 8731*
6450; www.kosherdeli.co.uk; open Sun–Thur
7am–10pm (Thur 11pm), Fri 7am–2pm (4pm in
summer); LBD; branches in Temple Fortune, Hendon
& Edgware. ⓬

Kosher Deli is a long-established family business
offering fresh meat and poultry as well as a
wide range of cooked meat, fish and vegetable
dishes, and pre-packed salads and cold cuts.
Ready-cooked rotisserie chicken and potato
kugel are good buys for Shabbat.

KOSHER KINGDOM

Supermarket

7 Russell Parade, Golders Green Road, NW11 9NN;
☎ *020 8455 1429; www.kosherkingdom.co.uk; tube:*
Brent Cross – 8 mins; open Sun–Wed 7am–10pm,
Thur 7am–12am, Fri 7am–5pm (summer) and until
2 hrs before Shabbat in winter, Sat night in winter
1 hr after Shabbat to 11pm; LBD. ⓭

This is a large modern kosher supermarket and a
one-stop shop for all your kosher requirements.

MENACHEMS

Butcher/deli

15 Russell Parade, Golders Green Road, NW11
9NN; ☎ *020 8201 8629; tube: Brent Cross – 8 mins;*
LBD; open Sun 7am–3pm, Mon 7am–5.30pm, Tue
7am–6pm, Wed 7am–7pm, Thur 7am–8pm, Fri
7am–1.30pm. ⓮

Menachems is a friendly and popular family
business selling an extensive selection of fresh
meat and poultry, tasty ready-cooked meats
and salads including chopped liver, and
Sephardi-style specialities.

PARKWAY PATISSERIE

Bakery

30A North End Road, NW11 7PT; ☎ *020 8455*
5026; Kedassia & LBD; no credit cards; open
Sun–Thur 8am–5pm, Fri 8am–2 hrs before
Shabbat. ⓯

Conveniently located opposite Golders Green
tube station, this family bakery with two other
branches, in Finchley and Wembley, has been
established for over 50 years. A popular choice
is fluden – a delicious chocolate-topped apple-
filled cake. There are also ready-made rolls and
sandwiches.

YARDEN

Mini-supermarket

121–123 Golders Green Road, NW11 8HR; ☎ *020*
8458 0979; open Sun–Thur 7am–11pm (Thur
12am), Fri 7am–2 hrs before Shabbat. ⓲

Owned by a South African family, this well-
stocked kosher supermarket includes a wide
range of South African specialities.

NON-FOOD SHOPS

JERUSALEM THE GOLDEN

Judaica

146–148 Golders Green Road, NW11 8HE; ☎ *020 8455 4960; www.jerusalemthegolden.com; Sun & Thur 9.15am–8pm, Mon–Wed 9.15am–7pm, Fri 9.15am–12pm (winter) & 1.30pm (summer).* **⓫**

Established in Golders Green in 1975, this well-stocked shop is packed with a wide selection of Jewish-themed products including an extensive range of silver Judaica, Hebrew books, gifts, toys and greetings cards. The comprehensive music section includes listening stations.

STEIMATZKY

Bookshop

46 Golders Green Road, NW11 8LL; ☎ *020 8458 9774; www.steimatzky.co.uk; open Mon–Thur 10am–7pm, Fri 10am–5pm (2pm winter), & Sun 10.30am–7pm.* **⓰**

This is the London branch of the famous Israeli bookshop specializing in secular Jewish literature and Israeli writing, both Hebrew and English. There are also Israeli newspapers and magazines, a wide selection of Israeli CDs, videos and DVDs, greetings cards, children's books and toys. A good range of Israeli-made gifts, jewellery and Judaica are also on offer. Its shop windows contain a mine of information for Israelis in London, including accommodation. The staff speak Hebrew and English.

Jerusalem the Golden.

TORAH TREASURES

Judaica/books

16 Russell Parade, Golders Green Road, NW11 9NN; ☎ *020 8458 8289; www.torahtreasures.co.uk; tube: Brent Cross – 8 mins; Sun 9.30am–4pm, Mon–Thur 9.30am–9pm, Fri 9.30am–1pm (3pm in summer).* **⓱**

This shop has a huge range of Judaica and Jewish books, as well as gifts, cards and toys.

HOTELS

CROFT COURT HOTEL

£

44 Ravenscroft Avenue, NW11 8AY; ☎ *020 8458 3331; www.croftcourthotel.co.uk.* **⓳**

Recently renovated, this small and reasonably priced bed and breakfast is popular with kosher and Shabbat-observant guests (Shabbat keys are available). A Kedassia-supervised continental breakfast is included in the room rate and kosher meals can be ordered for Shabbat. It is well located for kosher shops, restaurants and synagogues. En suite rooms include a TV, safe, fridge, hairdryer and Wi-Fi access.

KING SOLOMON HOTEL

£

155–159 Golders Green Road, NW11 9BX; ☎ *020 8201 9000; www.kingsolomonhotel.com; email: info@kingsolomonhotel.com; tube: Golders Green/Brent Cross – 10 mins.* **⓴**

A budget hotel with 80 rooms over three floors (no lift) conveniently located close to Golders Green's kosher facilities. There is a kosher dairy restaurant on site. En suite bedrooms include a TV, safe, hairdryer and Wi-Fi access. Shabbat keys are available.

YAMOR SUITES

£

Golders Green Road, NW11 (exact address given on booking); ☎ *07968 387 499; www.yamor.com; email: Office@stonelinkinvestments.com; tube: Brent Cross – 5 mins.* **㉑**

Established for 14 years, these well-located self-catering suites are ideal for Orthodox visitors. En suite air-conditioned rooms include twin beds, kitchenette (microwave, fridge and hot plate), TV, safe and hairdryer. There is Wi-Fi access and Shabbat keys are available.

SYNAGOGUES

GOLDERS GREEN BETH HAMEDRASH

(known as Munk's)

The Riding, Golders Green Road, NW11 8HL; ☎ *020 8455 2974; www.ggbh.info; tube: Golders Green – 13 mins.* ㉔

Known as Munk's after its founding rabbi, this Ashkenazi 'Yekke' independent Orthodox community was established in 1934 and moved to its premises in 1956. Its website lists service times and a daily lecture programme, and contains a form for visitors seeking Shabbat hospitality. Visitors should be aware that the congregation does not support the use of the eruv (see below).

GOLDERS GREEN SYNAGOGUE

(known as Dunstan Road)

41 Dunstan Road, NW11 8AE; ☎ *020 8455 2460; www.goldersgreensynagogue.co.uk; email: office@ ggshul.org.uk; tube: Golders Green – 12 mins.* ㉓

This United synagogue was the first in Golders Green, consecrated in 1922, and today has 500 member families. On Shabbat there is a formal service at 9.15am in the main synagogue, and the smaller, more informal and participatory 'New Minyan' starts 15 minutes later. There is a weekly kiddush. Shabbat hospitality can be provided with prior notice.

JEWISH LEARNING EXCHANGE

152–154 Golders Green Road, NW11 8HE; ☎ *020 8458 4588; www.jle.org.uk; tube: Golders Green – 13 mins.* ㉖

For the 20–35 crowd, this Orthodox outreach organization provides synagogue services as well as a daily programme of educational and social opportunities. See website for further details.

NORTH WESTERN REFORM SYNAGOGUE

(known as Alyth)

Alyth Gardens, Finchley Road, NW11 7EN; ☎ *020 8455 6763; www.alyth.org.uk; email: mail@alyth. org.uk; tube: Golders Green – 15 mins; office open Mon–Fri.* ㉒

This large Reform community founded in 1933 moved to its current premises in 1936. With around 3,300 adult and young members the congregation is thriving, with social and educational programmes for all ages. Each Shabbat, shul members welcome visitors at the door. Friday-night services are at 6.30pm, and Shabbat Shacharit is at 10.30am. There is a weekly kiddush. Email for information on services or hospitality requests. The website contains an excellent guide for visitors on what to expect from a Reform Shabbat service.

OHEL DAVID EASTERN SYNAGOGUE

4–14 Broadwalk Lane, NW11 8HD; ☎ *020 8455 3491; www.oheldavid.org; tube: Golders Green – 5 mins.* ㉕

Established in 1959, this is an independent Sephardi Orthodox congregation with daily services.

MIKVAOT

NW LONDON COMMUNAL MIKVAH

40 Golders Green Crescent (entrance via No. 42), NW11 8LD; ☎ *020 8731 9494 / 020 8457 5900; tube: Golders Green – 8 mins; open daily.* ㉗

This is one of the two most modern mikvaot in London. The other is in Maida Vale (see p. 194).

ERUV

The NW London Eruv was erected in 2003 and covers most of Golders Green, Hampstead Garden Suburb, Hendon and Finchley. For coverage see *www.nwlondon eruv.org.*

SMOKED SALMON AND CREAM CHEESE BAGELS

The quintessential Jewish food experience for a bite to eat is the smoked salmon and cream cheese bagel, sometimes spelled beigel.

Bagels originated in Poland where the raw dough was boiled and then baked, and came to London with the influx of Jewish migrants in the 19th century. They were sold displayed on thin wooden poles or, as many remember, from the bagel ladies in Brick Lane, straight from the sack.

Bagels go well with everything but perhaps the perfect filling is smoked salmon with cream cheese. Two salmon smokeries, Goldstein and Forman, both having origins back to 1905, still operate in London. Wolfe Goldstein, English but of Portuguese descent, became the most skilled salmon filleter and curer in London. The first Goldstein smokery opened in Leyden Street, off Petticoat Lane, post-WWII, moving to Stepney in 1960. Using traditional methods, it remained there until 2000 when it moved to Stanmore, North-west London. Goldstein Salmon, run by Ian, Wolfe's grandson, is strictly kosher.

Aaron (later Harris) Forman, a Russian immigrant, also established his business in East London, where it can still be found. Based until 2008 in Stratford, it had to relocate as part of the project for the London 2012 Olympic Games. Its new salmon-pink premises, including a restaurant and art gallery, overlook the new Olympic stadium. Like Goldstein, it is still in family hands. The current MD, Lance Forman, is the fourth generation to run the business and is proud of his family's heritage. In 1934 his grandfather, Louis Forman, was pictured with the biggest salmon ever sold at Billingsgate. By then, Forman's concentrated on the luxury trade, supplying top stores and

Salmon smoking at Forman's.

Selection of bagels, Hendon Bagel Bakery.

Above: Louis Forman, Billingsgate 1934.
Top: Carmelli Bakeries.
Right: Beigel Bake Brick Lane Bakery.

hotels such as Fortnum & Mason and The Dorchester. They still do so today.

There have been great changes in the smoked-salmon business. Originally, smoked and cured fish were used by immigrants as provisions for their journey. On arrival, with no refrigeration in their homes, they became essential foodstuffs.

Salmon was originally imported from the Baltic but it was also found in Scotland and sold at Billingsgate fish market close to the East End. Smoked salmon became and remained a luxury item well into the 1970s. Nevertheless it was still sold by many East London delicatessens.

Subsidies to Norwegian salmon suppliers in the 1980s and technological advances for adding flavour made the price more affordable and smoked salmon became available in the supermarkets.

The taste of traditionally smoked Scottish salmon cannot be beaten. Lance and Ian both describe the process as using just three ingredients – salmon, salt and smoke. Goldstein Salmon (*www.gold salmon.co.uk*) is available in kosher outlets and other selected stores. Forman's smoked salmon is hand-sliced and available via mail order and the Internet (*www.formanandfield.com*). Panzers (*www. panzers.co.uk*), St. John's Wood, stock four grades of smoked salmon, all hand-sliced.

WHERE TO BUY

To buy ready-filled bagels, try one of these kosher outlets:
Carmelli Bakeries, Golders Green (see p. 169)
Hendon Bagel Bakery, Hendon (see p. 182)
Daniels Bakery, Temple Fortune (see p. 176)
Beigel Bake Brick Lane Bakery (see p. 29) is open 24/7, it is not supervised

NORTH-WEST: HAMPSTEAD GARDEN SUBURB

To the east of Golders Green and 11km (7 miles) from Central London, leafy Hampstead Garden Suburb (HGS) was established in 1907 by philanthropist Dame Henrietta Barnett, the wife of an East End vicar who had seen at first hand the cramped housing in which people lived. Her aim was that rich and poor would live together in uplifting and beautiful surroundings. Bordering Hampstead Heath, it is a fine example of early 20th-century domestic architecture and town planning. Today it is an affluent community and popular with Jewish families.

Most of HGS is a 15–30 minute walk from Golders Green tube station, so it is easier to reach the area by taxi or buses 102 or H2 from the station.

KOSHER FOOD SHOPS

GREENSPANS

Butcher/precooked dishes

9–11 Lyttleton Road, N2 0DW; ☎ *020 8455 9921; open Sun, Mon & Fri 8.30am–1pm, Tue– Thur 8.30am–5.15pm; LBS.*

This popular butcher sells an interesting range of fresh meat and poultry and hot rotisserie chicken, with hot salt beef available on Sunday morning from 11am–1pm. Frozen ready meals include chilli and chollent.

KINGS BAKERY & PIZZERIA

52 The Market Place, Kingsley Way, NW11 6JB; ☎ *020 8458 6060; open Sun–Thur 6am–6pm, Fri 6am–3pm; LBD.*

Kings sells traditional baked goods, and there's also a small coffee shop offering soup, pizza, sandwiches and cakes.

KOSHER FOOD CO

Mini-supermarket

56 The Market Place, Kingsley Way, NW11 6JP; ☎ *020 8455 0558; open Sun 7.30am–6pm, Mon–Wed 7.30am–8pm, Thur 7.30am–9pm, Fri 7.30am–2pm.*

This is a small kosher grocery store for all your basic kosher needs, including wine.

HOTELS

HOLIDAY INN EXPRESS

(see p. 178)

Located in Temple Fortune, this is the nearest hotel for HGS, a 5–10 minute journey via bus 102, or anything between a 5 and 25 minute walk away, depending on where you're visiting.

SYNAGOGUES

HAMPSTEAD GARDEN SUBURB SYNAGOGUE

(known as Norrice Lea)

Norrice Lea, N2 0RE; ☎ *020 8455 8126; www.hgss.org.uk; email: office@hgss.org.uk; tube: Golders Green, then Bus H2 to Norrice Lea; office open Sun–Thur.*

This United synagogue was formed in 1933 and today numbers around 1,800 adult members and more than 1,000 youngsters under 21. Members are designated to greet and welcome visitors on Shabbat. Congregants dress smartly. Whilst the main service is Ashkenazi, there is a separate Sephardi minyan. There is a weekly kiddush. Shabbat hospitality can be provided on prior notice.

ERUV

The NW London Eruv covers most of HGS (see p. 171).

NORTH-WEST: **TEMPLE FORTUNE AND FINCHLEY**

Linking Golders Green and Hampstead Garden Suburb, Temple Fortune has a sizeable Jewish population, with numerous kosher shops and eateries. Located along Finchley Road, its main artery, this is a bustling shopping area, particularly on a Friday morning.

Finchley lies just to the north of Temple Fortune. They are both easy to reach by public transport. Golders Green (Northern line) is the nearest tube station for Temple Fortune and frequent buses (Nos 82, 102 or 460) travel from there along the Finchley Road, taking 5–10 minutes. Alternatively, a taxi will take about five minutes from the station. For drivers, parking is easier than in Golders Green. Finchley Central tube station (Northern line) is best for most destinations in Finchley. The listings are in the Temple Fortune area, unless otherwise stated.

KOSHER CAFES AND RESTAURANTS

BURGER BAR

Burgers £

110 Regent's Park Road, N3 3JG; ☎ *020 8371 1555; open Sun–Thur 12pm–11pm, Sat 1 hr after Shabbat in winter–11pm; KF & SKA; no credit/debit cards.* ❶

Rated as one of the best places to eat a kosher burger in London, this informal restaurant offers a variety of huge 300g (10½oz) burgers. Chargrilled to order, they are served with a large mound of chips or onion rings. There are also tortilla wraps filled with a burger, chicken, falafel or steak. Eat in or take away.

FISH FISH

Fish ££

30 Temple Fortune Parade, NW11 0QS; ☎ *020 8458 2375; open Sun–Thur 12pm–10pm, Fri 12pm –3pm, Sat night after Shabbat–10pm in winter; SKA.* ❷

With nautical decor, this unambiguously named restaurant serves perfectly cooked fish (in matzah meal or batter) and chips. Appetizers include whitebait and anchovies, and main courses offer freshly grilled, roasted, poached or pan-fried fish. The lunch special menu is great value.

MATOK BAKERY

Bakery/dairy café £

1 Bridge Lane, NW11 0EA; ☎ *020 8458 0280; open Sun–Thur 7am–7pm, Fri 7am–2 hrs before Shabbat; KF.* ❸

Opened in 2010, Matok is a modern bakery, takeaway and café. Appetizing quiches, salads, stir-fries and fish dishes are available in the café or to take away. The bakery sells a wide selection of breads, including sundried tomato or vegetable herb, challot and an assortment of tempting rugelach and borekas.

ORLI

Dairy café £

108 Regents Park Road, N3 3JG; ☎ *020 8371 9222; open Sun–Thur 8am–11pm, Fri 8am–1 hr before Shabbat, Sat night in winter 1 hr after Shabbat– 12am; KF & SKA; no credit/debit cards; branches at Hendon (p. 180) and Edgware (p. 186).* ❹

Orli is an established café serving a buffet breakfast in the morning and an extensive all-day menu including salads, pastas, pizzas, tortillas and toasted bagels. Portions are more than generous.

Rugelach, Matok Bakery.

KOSHER FOOD SHOPS

Daniels Bakery.

THE BAGEL PLACE

(known as Avi's) Bakery

10 Thornfield Parade, Dollis Road, Finchley, NW7 1LN; ☎ 020 8922 9454; tube: Mill Hill East – 10 mins; open Sun 8am–1pm, Mon–Thur 9am–4pm, Fri 7am–2pm; LBD.

Israeli owned, this shop attracts a cult following wanting to buy the delicately shaped and pleasantly chewy challot and delectable rugelach.

CREME DE LA CREME

Bakery/patisserie

5 Temple Fortune Parade, Bridge Lane, NW11 0QN; ☎ 020 8458 9090; www.cremedelacreme. org.uk; open Mon–Thur 8am–5pm, Fri & Sun 8am–3pm; Kedassia & KF. **6**

Opened in 1995, this bakery is one of the best kosher outlets in London. Although pricier than others, it produces delicious croissants, quiches, cakes, ice cream and handmade chocolates. The selection on offer in store is smaller than the range available to order.

DANIELS BAKERY

Bakery

12–14 Hallswelle Parade, Finchley Road, NW11 0DL; ☎ 020 8455 5826; www.danielscatering.co.uk; open Sun–Wed 7am–9pm, Thur 7am–10pm, Fri 7am–6pm (in summer), 1hr before Shabbat (winter). LBD; credit cards accepted (min. £10). **7**

Daniels is renowned for its bagels and challot, which are considered by many to be the best available. Cakes and biscuits include rugelach, Danish pastries and gingerbread. There are also salads, sandwiches and hot soup to takeaway. Daniels catering menu offers a wide choice of platters and appetizing desserts.

KOSHER DELI

Butcher/deli

9a Hallswelle Parade, Finchley Road, NW11 0DL; ☎ 020 8458 7933. **9**

See p. 169 for more information, including opening hours.

KOSHER PARADISE

Mini-supermarket

10 Ashbourne Parade, Finchley Road, NW11 0AD; ☎ 020 8455 2454; open Sun 8.30am–10pm, Mon–Wed 8am–10pm, Thur 8am–12am, Fri 8am–2 hrs before Shabbat. **10**

This is a well-stocked shop with a full range of kosher produce, wines and sandwiches.

LUXURY DESSERTS

Bakery

105A Ballards Lane, Finchley, N3 1XY; ☎ 078 8259 3415; tube: Finchley Central – 10 mins; open Sun–Thur 10am–4pm, Fri 10am–1 hr before Shabbat; SKA; no credit/debit cards.

Luxury Desserts claim to be the first Armenian kosher bakery in the world. It is a family-owned bakery that produces handmade Armenian specialities made mainly with honey instead of sugar.

MATOK

Bakery **3**

See p. 175.

PARKWAY PATISSERIE

Bakery

Gateway House, 326/328 Regents Park Road, Finchley, N3 2LN; ☎ 020 8346 0344; tube: Finchley Central – 6 mins.

See p. 169 for more information, including opening hours.

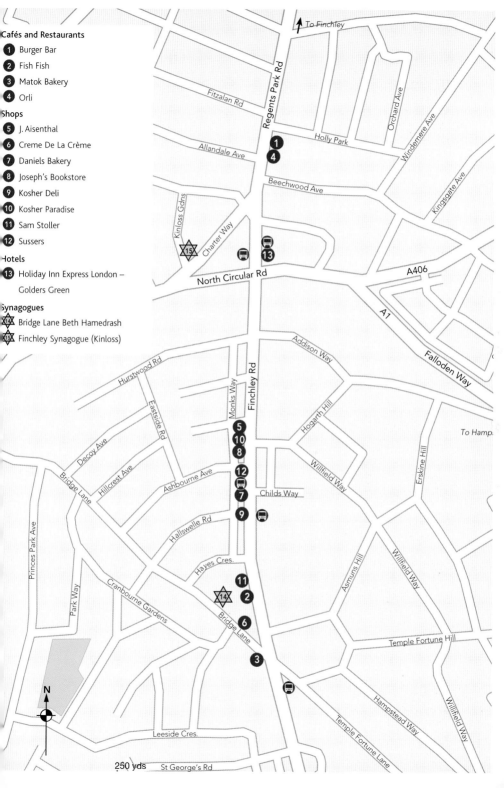

Cafés and Restaurants
1. Burger Bar
2. Fish Fish
3. Matok Bakery
4. Orli

Shops
5. J. Aisenthal
6. Creme De La Crème
7. Daniels Bakery
8. Joseph's Bookstore
9. Kosher Deli
10. Kosher Paradise
11. Sam Stoller
12. Sussers

Hotels
13. Holiday Inn Express London –
    Golders Green

Synagogues
14. Bridge Lane Beth Hamedrash
15. Finchley Synagogue (Kinloss)

SAM STOLLER

Fishmonger

28 Temple Fortune Parade, Finchley Road, NW11 0QS; ☎ 020 8455 1957; open Sun 8am–1pm, Mon 8am–2pm, Tue–Thur 7am–5pm, Fri 7am–4pm (summer), till 12.30pm (winter); SKA; credit cards accepted (min. £10). **11**

Established in 1947, Sam Stoller sells a wide selection of fresh farmed and organic fish as well as an assortment of precooked fried fish and poached salmon.

SUSSERS

Wine merchant

15 Hallswelle Parade, Finchley Road, NW11 0DL; ☎ 020 8455 4336; open Sun 10am–2pm, Mon–Wed 10am–6pm, Thur 10am–6.45pm, Fri 8.15am–4pm (summer) and 2hrs before Shabbat (winter). **12**

Sussers sell an excellent range of kosher wines and spirits.

OTHER SHOPS

J. AISENTHAL

Bookshop and Judaica

11 Ashbourne Parade, Finchley Road, NW11 0AD; ☎ 020 8455 0501; www.aisenthal.co.uk; open Sun 9.30am–2pm, Mon–Thur 9am–6pm, Fri 9am–4pm (summer), till 1pm (winter). **5**

Long-established and well-stocked bookshop that also sells gifts, Judaica and toys.

JOSEPH'S BOOKSTORE

Bookstore

2 Ashbourne Parade, 1257 Finchley Road, NW11 0AD; ☎ 020 8731 7575; www.josephsbookstore. com; open Sun 10am–5pm, Mon–Fri 9.30am–6.30pm. **8**

A lovely neighbourhood independent bookstore with helpful and knowledgeable staff offering a great collection of Jewish-interest and secular books together with greetings cards and calendars. There are regular authors' events and occasional small art exhibitions.

HOTELS

HOLIDAY INN EXPRESS LONDON – GOLDERS GREEN

£

58 Regents Park Road, N3 3JN; ☎ 020 8371 6060 (reservations 0871 423 4896); www.hiexpress.co.uk; 82/460 buses stop right outside. **13**

This good-value modern hotel with 83 rooms is located on the corner of the North Circular Road and Regents Park Road, opposite Finchley Synagogue, and within walking distance of the kosher facilities at Temple Fortune. The room rate includes a kosher continental breakfast. A non-electronic key is available for Shabbat and whilst there are automatic doors to enter the hotel, staff are aware of the need to open these for the observant on Shabbat. En suite bedrooms include a TV, iron, hairdryer and Wi-Fi access. Room rates are discounted by 20 per cent when booked and paid for more than three weeks in advance.

Selection of wines at Sussers.

Joseph's Bookstore.

SYNAGOGUES

BRIDGE LANE BETH HAMEDRASH

44 Bridge Lane, NW11 0EG; ☎ *020 8458 6059; www.blbh.org; email: gabbai@blbh.org.* **14**

An Orthodox synagogue affiliated to the Adath movement housed since 1976 in a building formerly occupied by the Ebenezer Baptist Chapel. A new synagogue is being built, so visitors should check the website before visiting. The community is vibrant and a hub of Torah learning. For hospitality, visitors should email or inform the warden at the Friday night service. There is a kiddush once a month.

FINCHLEY REFORM SYNAGOGUE

101 Fallow Court Avenue, North Finchley, N12 0BE; ☎ *020 8446 3244; www.frsonline.org; tube: West Finchley – 8 mins.*

This Reform congregation, with over 700 family members, was founded in 1960, and their synagogue inaugurated in 1973. They are a friendly community and welcome all individuals regardless of their Jewish background. Friday-night services are at 6.30pm. The main Shabbat morning service is at 10.30am and attracts about 150 members. Visitors are welcomed at the entrance and there is a weekly kiddush.

FINCHLEY SYNAGOGUE

(known as Kinloss)

Kinloss Gardens, N3 3DU; ☎ *020 8346 8551; www.kinloss.org.* **15**

Finchley Synagogue has been a member of the United Synagogue since 1935. The community is thriving, with more than 1,500 members and five different services on Shabbat. As well as the main Ashkenazi service with a chazan, there is a separate Sephardi minyan, an informal and participatory alternative minyan attracting 250 people, a youth minyan and an early-morning service. Members greet visitors at the entrance. There is a weekly kiddush. Shabbat hospitality can be provided on prior notice.

NEW NORTH LONDON SYNAGOGUE

80 East End Road, N3 2SY; ☎ *020 8346 8560; www.nnls-masorti.org.uk; tube: Finchley Central – 15 mins.*

This Masorti community was established in 1974. It moved to The Manor House site in Finchley in 1987. The community grew at a phenomenal rate during the following 25 years, due mainly to its exceptional rabbi, Jonathan Wittenberg, whose scholarship, both religious and secular, attracted a large number of followers. With around 2,500 members, the community made the decision to build a new synagogue and community centre to meets its needs for the 21st century. The new building was opened in 2011.

There are weekly traditional Shabbat services with separate seating and egalitarian services with mixed seating. The atmosphere is welcoming, relaxed and participatory. The main traditional Shabbat service is at 9.30am and attracts around 400 people. There is a weekly kiddush. Shabbat hospitality can be provided on prior notice.

ERUV

The NW London Eruv covers Temple Fortune and Finchley (see p. 171).

New North London Synagogue.

NORTH-WEST: HENDON

Hendon is a sprawling suburb lying to the north of Golders Green. The Jewish population grew substantially after the underground reached here in 1923, and today there is still a sizeable Jewish presence. The Orthodox community predominates and Brent Street serves as its backbone with kosher eateries (around 16 at the time of writing), food outlets and gift shops. In 2010, Hendon really came into its own when London's first kosher boutique hotel opened, within walking distance of Brent Street.

At the time of writing, Hendon is the location of the fascinating Jewish Military Museum, although this may relocate in 2012.

Unless otherwise stated, the listings below are conveniently located in or around Brent Street, within a 10–20 minute walk of Hendon Central tube station (Northern line) or perhaps more easily reached by the 183 bus from Golders Green tube station (Northern line).

KOSHER CAFES AND RESTAURANTS

ADAM'S

Middle Eastern/meat £

2 Sentinel Square off Brent Street, NW4 2EL; ☎ *020 8202 2327; tube: Hendon Central – 15 mins; open Sun–Thur 12pm–12am, Fri in summer 12pm–5pm, Sat night in winter 10pm–2am; LBD & SKA; no credit cards.* ❶

Adam's is a busy snack bar offering satisfyingly tasty and good-value fast food that can also be taken away. Charcoal-grilled meat and shawarmas in homemade pitta or laffa bread with hummus and a choice of salads are popular and filling options. A wide choice of prepared dishes is available for Shabbat.

BEIT HAMADRAS

Indian/meat ££

105 Brent Street, NW4 2DX; ☎ *020 8203 4567; www.beithamadras.co.uk; tube: Hendon Central – 14 mins; open Sun–Thur, lunch 12pm–3pm, dinner*

5.30pm–11pm, and 1 hr after Shabbat in winter to 12am; KF. ❷

A popular Indian restaurant with a diverse selection of spicy curries, tandoori specialities, and biryanis served in comfortable and relaxing surroundings. Customers can choose their dish's 'heat' level. Lunchtime specials and set meals in the evening are especially good value.

EIGHTY SIX BISTRO BAR

French/American/meat ££/£££

86 Brent Street, NW4 2ES; ☎ *020 8202 5575; tube: Hendon Central – 12 mins; open Sun 12pm–3pm & 5.30pm–11pm, Mon–Thur 5.30pm–11pm; KF & SKA; reservations advisable.* ❸

From foie gras to entrecôte steaks, spaghetti Bolognese to burgers and fries, the menu here is eclectic. Whilst prices are slightly higher than an average bistro, portions are more than generous.

KAIFENG

Chinese ££/£££

51 Church Road, NW4 4DU; ☎ *020 8203 7888; www.kaifeng.co.uk; tube: Hendon Central – 16 mins; open Sun–Thur 12pm–2.30pm & 5.30pm–10.30pm, Sat night after Shabbat in winter; LBD; takeaway menu available.* ❹

Named after Kaifeng, the capital city of China in the 10th century that welcomed Jewish settlers, this restaurant was established over 25 years ago and serves a well-presented array of Chinese delicacies including crispy aromatic duck and sizzling meat dishes. Prices reflect the generous portions and the Sunday buffet lunch represents great value.

ORLI

Dairy café ££

96 Brent Street, NW4 2HH; ☎ *020 8203 7555; tube: Hendon Central – 12 mins.* ❺

See p. 175 for more information, including opening hours.

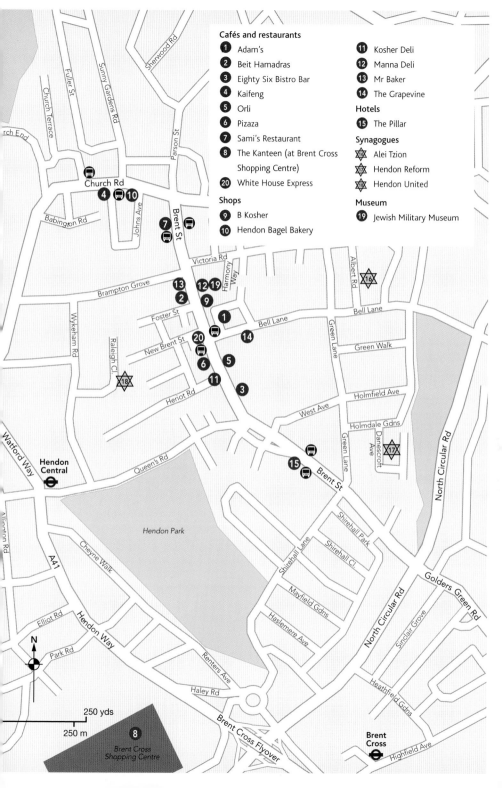

Cafés and restaurants
1. Adam's
2. Beit Hamadras
3. Eighty Six Bistro Bar
4. Kaifeng
5. Orli
6. Pizaza
7. Sami's Restaurant
8. The Kanteen (at Brent Cross Shopping Centre)
20. White House Express

Shops
9. B Kosher
10. Hendon Bagel Bakery

11. Kosher Deli
12. Manna Deli
13. Mr Baker
14. The Grapevine

Hotels
15. The Pillar

Synagogues
16. Alei Tzion
17. Hendon Reform
18. Hendon United

Museum
19. Jewish Military Museum

PIZAZA

Pizza bar £

53 Brent Street, NW4 2EA; ☎ 020 8202 9911;
www.pizaza.com; tube: Hendon Central – 12 mins;
open Sun–Thur 12pm–12am, Fri 12pm–3pm, Sat
night after Shabbat–3am; KF; credit cards accepted
(min. £10). ❻

Popular Pizaza serves tasty pizzas that are large
enough to feed two people. There are various
fillings and a choice of different crusts. The
decor is modern and bright orange and suited to
its mostly younger customers who enjoy sweet
milkshakes for dessert. Service is friendly and
helpful. The six tables each seat a maximum of
four. Eat in or take away.

SAMI'S RESTAURANT

Middle Eastern/meat ££

157 Brent Street, NW4 4DJ (entrance in Lodge Road);
☎ 020 8203 8088; tube: Hendon Central – 15 mins;
open Sun–Thur 12pm–11pm, Sat night in winter, 1½
hrs after Shabbat–11pm; LBD & KF & SKA. ❼

Established over 25 years ago, Sami's serves
mainly Middle Eastern fare in unpretentious
surroundings. Grilled charcoal chicken and steak in
freshly baked pitta are favourite choices. Service is
swift and portions are generous. Takeaways are
especially popular with free local delivery.

THE KANTEEN

Dairy café/bakery within Brent Cross Shopping Centre £

Brent Cross Shopping Centre, NW4 3FP – on Lower
Mall at side of John Lewis store; ☎ 020 8203
7377; tube: Brent Cross – 15 mins; open Mon–Thur
9am–8pm, Fri 9am–before Shabbat, Sun
11am–6pm; KF. ❽

Bustling with shoppers from breakfast through to
evening, this pleasant café serves a vast selection
of light bites and tasty mains providing
something to please everybody. Freshly made
sandwiches and salads are available to take away.
The bakery sells challot, cakes and biscuits.

WHITE HOUSE EXPRESS

Middle Eastern/Thai/meat ££/£££

63 Brent Street, NW4 3EA; ☎ 020 8203 2427; tube:
Hendon Central – 13 mins; open Sun–Thur
12pm–11.30pm, Fri in summer 12pm–4pm, Sat
night in winter 1 hr after Shabbat–11.30pm; LBD &
SKA; branch in Golders Green. ⓴

See p. 168 for more information.

KOSHER FOOD SHOPS

B KOSHER

Mini-supermarket

144 Brent Street, NW4 2DR; ☎ 020 3210 4000;
tube: Hendon Central – 14 mins; open Sun & Mon
8am–9pm, Tue & Wed 8am–10pm, Thur
8am–11pm, Fri 8am–6pm (summer), 1hr before
Shabbat (winter). ❾

This store is very well stocked with fresh meat,
dairy products and baked goods plus a good
selection of wines and liquors.

HENDON BAGEL BAKERY

Bakery/coffee shop

55–57 Church Road, NW4 4DU; ☎ 020 8203
6919; tube: Golders Green, then take 183 bus to
Church End (approx. 10 mins), then 1-min walk, or
Hendon Central – 17 mins; open Sun–Thur
7am–10pm, Fri 7am–1 hr before Shabbat; KF; no
credit cards. ❿

This modern bakery is crammed with excellent
bagels in a variety of flavours (including hard-

Hendon Bagel Bakery.

to-find pumpernickel), great challot and a huge choice of tempting cakes and biscuits. To eat in or take away there are also filled bagels, a selection of salads, quiches and borekas. There is also a catering menu for parties.

KOSHER DELI

43–43a Brent Street, NW4 2EA; ☎ 020 8202 0402; tube: Hendon Central – 12 mins. **⓫**

See p. 169 for more information, including opening hours.

MANNA DELI

146 Brent Street, NW4 4DR; ☎ 020 8201 7575; www.mannakosherdeli.co.uk; tube: Hendon Central – 15 mins; open Sun 11am–3pm, Mon 11am–7pm, Tue 10am–8pm, Wed 9am–8pm, Thur 9am–10pm, Fri 8am–4.30pm (summer), check for winter. LBD. **⓬**

Manna Deli offers a delicious range of meat and parev takeaway dishes, including a wide choice of soups, salads, couscous and stuffed vegetables – the aubergine is particularly recommended.

MR BAKER

Bakery/café £

119–121 Brent Street, NW4 2DX; ☎ 020 8202 6845; tube: Hendon Central – 14 mins; open Sun–Thur 7am–12am, Fri 7am–2.30pm (winter), till 6pm (summer); KF & SKA; credit cards accepted (min. £10). **⓭**

This is a large, bright bakery with tempting piles of rugelachs and borekas, and delicious sweet Middle Eastern pastries. The café serves snacks including pizza, salads and soups.

THE GRAPEVINE

Kosher wines and spirits

20 Bell Lane, NW4 2AD; ☎ 020 8202 2631; www.thegrapevineuk.com; tube: Hendon Central – 14 mins; open Mon–Wed 9am–6pm, Thur 9am–8pm, Fri 9am–2pm, Sun 10am–4pm; branch in Stamford Hill (see p. 200). **⓮**

Opened in 2006, The Grapevine claims to stock the largest selection of kosher wines, spirits and liqueurs in the UK. Their wines come from all the main global wine-producing areas.

HOTEL

THE PILLAR HOTEL

££

19 Brent Street, NW4 2EU; ☎ 020 8457 4000; www.thepillarhotellondon.com; email: info@the pillar.co.uk; tube: Hendon Central – 12 mins, or from Golders Green station take 183 bus which stops outside hotel; KF; ample parking. **⓯**

Built in 1893, this beautifully converted 22-room kosher boutique hotel opened in June 2010. Many of the rooms are located over two floors around the original quadrangle modelled on a 15th-century Oxfordshire almshouse, now a peaceful garden.

The tastefully decorated en suite rooms retain their original architectural features and include cable TV, safe, hairdryer, Wi-Fi access and Shabbat light. Shabbat keys are available. There are two duplex suites (which can be interconnected), each with a sitting room, a kitchenette (including a microwave, fridge and Shabbat kettle) with dining table and chairs and two bedrooms; perfect for families.

A kosher continental breakfast is included in the room rate, and hot drinks and snacks are available all day for guests. A hot plate can be provided for Shabbat.

It is close to and convenient for Hendon's kosher shops, restaurants and synagogues.

Top: Hotel garden. Above: Hotel bedroom.

SYNAGOGUES

ALEI TZION

London School of Jewish Studies, Schaller House, 44a Albert Road, NW4 2SJ; ☎ *020 8343 5691 / 07531 668512; www.aleitzion.co.uk; email: info@ aleitzion.co.uk; tube: Hendon Central – 20 mins.* ⓰

This is a friendly, religious Zionist, United Synagogue community established in 2004 mainly for the 25–35 age group. Around 150 people attend on Shabbat morning when it is best to arrive early to find a seat. Whilst the atmosphere is relaxed, the focus is on davening with no talking during the service. Friday-night services tend to attract a more religious crowd. There are also daily services. Visitors are greeted at the front door where help is given with directions and finding a siddur.

There is a weekly kiddush with kugel every week and often chollent too.

Alei Tzion has a unique Shabbat meal exchange scheme on their website – meals can be requested or offered. Anyone can also email a meal request, and early contact is welcomed. However, visitors seeking hospitality on Shabbat morning can usually be hosted and an announcement is made at the end of the service indicating who to speak to.

Hendon Reform Synagogue, stained-glass windows.

HENDON REFORM

Danescroft Avenue, NW4 2NA; ☎ *020 8203 4168; www.hendonreform.org.uk; tube: Brent Cross (Northern) – 16 mins; office open Mon–Fri.* ⓱

Hendon Reform was founded in 1949. The current synagogue was consecrated in 1968. It is a warm and welcoming community with both men and women participating in services in which Hebrew and English are used. The synagogue has two walls comprising over 60 stained-glass windows depicting Judaica and biblical scenes, and there is a particularly large stained-glass window in the foyer (see p. 12).

Friday-night services are at 7pm and Shabbat morning at 10.30am. On Shabbat, members welcome visitors at a desk in the foyer. Around 80 members regularly attend, far more if there is a simcha. There is a weekly kiddush and hospitality can be provided on prior notice.

HENDON UNITED

(known as Raleigh Close)

18 Raleigh Close, NW4 2TA; ☎ *020 8202 6924; www.hendonsynagogue.com; tube: Hendon Central – 6 mins; office open Sun–Fri.* ⓲

The Hendon United community formed in 1928 and moved to its current location in 1935. Today, it is thriving with a membership of around 1,000 families ranging from traditional to Modern Orthodox in outlook.

On Shabbat there are various minyanim. The main service at 9am attended by over 200 is mainly for the older community members. There is also an informal, more participatory alternative minyan at 9.30am (known as RCAM), as well as services for children and youths. There are also daily services.

Visitors are welcomed at the front door and there is a weekly kiddush. Shabbat hospitality can be provided on prior notice, or speak to the rabbi or wardens at the service.

ERUV

Hendon (including all the places in this section) is within the NW London Eruv (see p. 171).

JEWISH MILITARY MUSEUM

Shield House, Harmony Way, off Victoria Road, Hendon, NW4 2BZ; ☎ *020 8201 5656; www.the jmm.org.uk; tube: Hendon Central – 20 mins, or Golders Green, then Bus 183 or 240 to Sentinel Square; open Mon–Thur 10am–4pm, Sun by appointment; donations welcome.* **⑲**

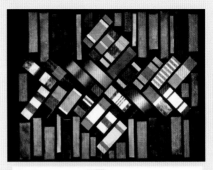

A hidden gem, this museum, founded in 1996, tells the story of the British Jewish contribution to the British Armed Forces over the past three centuries, from campaigns against the French in the 18th century to Afghanistan in the 21st century. More than 115,000 British Jews served in two world wars and nearly 6,000 died. Eight were awarded a Victoria Cross. With so few ex-servicemen alive today to tell their stories, this museum provides the visitor with a reminder of the immense debt we owe to those who served for the freedoms we enjoy today.

Top: Abram Games memorial window. Above: Haggadah used at a Passover Seder in Italy during WWII with signatures of the attendees.

The collection includes absorbing documents, intriguing photos, audio testimonies, uniforms, medals, weaponry and letters which tell the inspirational personal tales of the Jewish soldiers, chaplains and others involved in British military conflicts.

Highlights include:-

A cape worn by WWII Jewish nurse, Doris Benjamin, showing the lining where she had sewn some 200 shoulder flashes given to her by servicemen she had nursed in the military hospitals in Dorset and Oxfordshire.

Poignant letters from the WWI trenches written by **Lt Marcus Segal** to his parents. He complains about the lack of kosher food and asks for a copy of *The Jewish Chronicle*.

A beautiful **memorial window** composed of medal ribbons in the shape of a Star of David. It was designed by Whitechapel-born **Abram Games**, who served as Official War Artist in WWII.

The Record of Honour – visitors can search online for records of family members who served in the forces. Representing the 150–200 Jewish soldiers serving in the forces today, a **desert-issue uniform** of a Jewish officer who served in Afghanistan in 2007.

Guided tours from ex-servicemen can be requested. The extensive archive is available for research.

In 2012, the museum is hoping to relocate – so be sure to call or check the website before visiting, for current location and opening hours. **Visits should be booked in advance.**

NORTH-WEST: EDGWARE AND STANMORE

In 1924 the Northern line reached the North London suburb of Edgware, and subsequently a considerable Jewish community developed. It is now one of the most thriving Jewish communities in London, with 36 per cent of the local population giving their religion as Jewish in the 2001 census. The arrival of a large ultra-Orthodox presence has led to a proliferation of kosher shops, eateries and a wide choice of synagogues, providing an atmosphere not unlike that of Golders Green, but on a smaller scale.

Stanmore, nearby, is a leafy and affluent area situated at the end of the Jubilee line. The Jewish community here developed later than Edgware, following the station opening in 1932.

KOSHER CAFES AND RESTAURANTS IN EDGWARE

AVIV

Israeli/meat ££

87/89 High Street, HA8 7DB; ☎ *020 8952 2484; www.avivrestaurant.com; tube: Edgware – 8 mins; open Sun–Thur 12pm–2.30pm & 5.30pm–10.30pm, Sat nights Oct–Apr; KF.* ❶

This popular and bustling eatery is London's longest-established kosher restaurant. Specialities include the huge range of hors d'oeuvres and charcoal-grilled meats. A wide choice of set meals are great value.

MET SU YAN

Pan-oriental/meat ££

1–2 The Promenade, Edgwarebury Lane, HA8 7JZ; ☎ *020 8958 6840; Tube: Edgware – 7 mins; open Sun–Thur 12pm–3pm & 6pm–11pm; KF.* ❷

See p. 166 for more information.

ORLI

Dairy café £/££

295 Hale Lane, HA8 7AX; ☎ *020 8958 1555; tube: Edgware – 7 mins; open Sun–Thur 8am–11pm, Fri 8am–4pm in summer (check for winter), and after Shabbat in winter; KF.* ❸

See p. 175 for more information.

PAPALINA

Churrascaria and grill ££/£££

313 Hale Lane, HA8 7AX; ☎ *020 8958 7999; www.papalina.co.uk; tube: Edgware – 6 mins; open Sun–Thur 12pm–3pm & 6pm–11pm (Sun 5pm–11pm), & 1½ hrs after Shabbat Oct–Apr; KF.* ❹

Opened at the end of 2010, popular Papalina is a carnivore's paradise. The Brazilian concept has waiters bringing unlimited skewers of different meats direct from the rotisserie to your table and continuing to do so until you ask them to stop. Unlimited breads, salads, potatoes, rice, corn and fried onion rings accompany the meats, all for a set price plus service.

UNSUPERVISED CAFES AND RESTAURANTS IN EDGWARE

B & K

Salt-beef bar £

11 Lanson House, Whitchurch Lane, HA8 6NL; ☎ *020 8952 8204; tube: Edgware – 8 mins; open Tue–Sun 12pm–3pm & 5.30pm–9.15pm.* ❺

This well-established and popular small informal restaurant specializes in generous portions of salt beef, fish balls, chicken soup and other kosher-style foods.

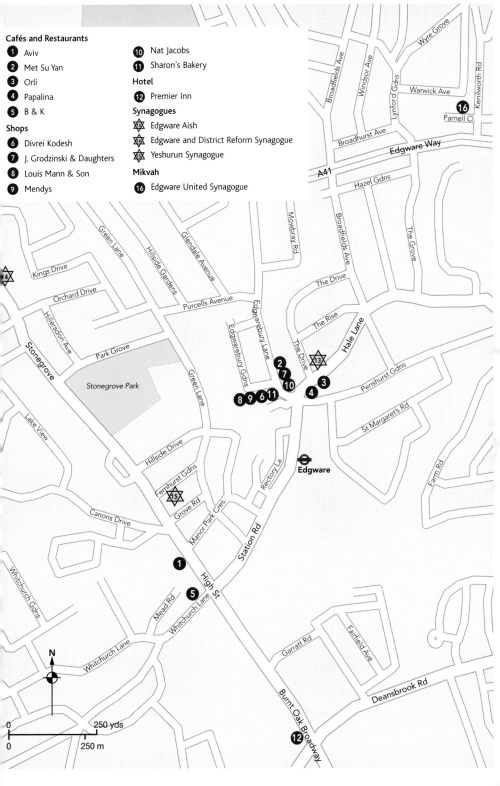

Cafés and Restaurants

1. Aviv
2. Met Su Yan
3. Orli
4. Papalina
5. B & K

10. Nat Jacobs
11. Sharon's Bakery

Hotel

12. Premier Inn

Shops

6. Divrei Kodesh
7. J. Grodzinski & Daughters
8. Louis Mann & Son
9. Mendys

Synagogues

Edgware Aish
Edgware and District Reform Synagogue
Yeshurun Synagogue

Mikvah

16. Edgware United Synagogue

KOSHER FOOD AND OTHER SHOPS IN EDGWARE

There is a convenient cluster of stores in Edgwarebury Lane that sell everything the kosher shopper desires, all within six minutes' walk from Edgware tube station. They include:

DIVREI KODESH

Books/Judaica

13 Edgwarebury Lane, HA8 8LH; ☎ *020 8958 1133; www.divreikodesh.co.uk; open Mon–Wed 9.30am–5.30pm, Thur 9.30am–8pm, Fri 8.45am–1pm (winter) & 2pm (summer), Sun 9.30am–3.30pm.* ❻

This bookstore offers a huge selection of Judaica, gifts, toys, Israeli CDs and cards.

J. GRODZINSKI & DAUGHTERS

Bakery/café

5–6 The Promenade, Edgwarebury Lane, HA8 7JZ; ☎ *020 8958 1205; www.grodzinski.co.uk; open Mon–Thur 7am–7pm, Fri & Sun 7am–3pm; Kedassia & LBD.* ❼

As well as a large selection of baked goods, there's a small café offering quick bites.

LOUIS MANN & SON

Butcher

23 Edgwarebury Lane, HA8 8LH; ☎ *020 8958 4910; open Sun, Mon & Fri 7am–1pm, Tue–Thur 7am–5pm; LBS.* ❽

This friendly butcher provides an excellent array of fresh and organic poultry and meat.

MENDYS

Mini-supermarket

17–19 Edgwarebury Lane, HA8 8LH; ☎ *020 8958 3444; open: Sun 8am–7pm, Mon & Tue 7.30am–7pm, Wed 7.30am–9pm, Thur 7.30am–11pm, Fri 6.30am–1pm (3pm summer).* ❾

A comprehensive range of kosher groceries and wine is stocked.

NAT JACOBS

Fishmonger

7 The Promenade, Edgwarebury Lane, HA8 7JZ;
☎ *020 8958 5585; open Sun 8am–12.30pm, Tue–Thur 8am–5pm, Fri 8am–1pm (winter) and 8am–12.30pm (winter); LBD.* ❿

Both fresh and ready-fried fish are sold here.

SHARON'S BAKERY

11 Edgwarebury Lane, HA8 8LH; ☎ *020 8958 4789; open Sun 7am–8.30pm, Mon–Thur 6am–8.30pm, Fri 6am–5pm (summer), 2hrs before Shabbat (winter); LBD.* ⓫

This bakery offers a wide selection of bagels, breads and cakes with takeaway sandwiches and salads.

KOSHER SHOPS IN STANMORE

Several of Stanmore's kosher shops are centred around Canon's Corner HA8 8AE, 10 minutes' walk from Stanmore tube station, with Bonjour bakery (LBD) at No. 2, Ivor Silverman, butchers (LBS) at No. 4 and Steve's Deli (LBD) at No. 5.

HOTEL

PREMIER INN

£/££

435 Burnt Oak Broadway, Edgware, HA8 5AQ; ☎ *0871 527 8652; www.premierinn.com; email: londonedgware.pi@premierinn.com; tube: Edgware – 8 mins.* ⓬

With 114 comfortable and modern en suite bedrooms, this hotel welcomes Shabbat-observant guests and is 10 minutes' walk from Yeshurun Synagogue. The entrance door is manual, and whilst the bedroom keys are electric, staff will assist with opening doors on Shabbat. Stairs are accessible and rooms on lower floors should be requested – email the hotel in advance (see above).

SYNAGOGUES

EDGWARE AISH

Services are held at 296 Hale Lane, Edgware, HA8 8NP (in hall above Tesco next to Vishnitz Shtiebel), entrance in car park on The Drive; ☎ *020 8457 4410; www.aishedgware.com; tube: Edgware – 10 mins.* ⓭

Challot.

This is a young, welcoming and vibrant orthodox community. The main Shabbat service is at 8.50am and around 60–70 people attend. There is a weekly hot kiddush – chollent and kugel every week. Shabbat hospitality can be requested via the website, or by calling Rabbi Sandler (☎ 07967 822283) by the Thursday prior to Shabbat.

EDGWARE AND DISTRICT REFORM SYNAGOGUE

118 Stonegrove, Edgware, HA8 8AB; ☎ 020 8238 1000; www.edrs.org.uk; tube: Stanmore – 15 mins. ⓮

Founded in 1935, this is now the largest synagogue in Europe, with a membership of approximately 2,000 families. Their services reflect the more traditional wing of Reform Judaism and are in both Hebrew and English. There is a choir, and both men and women play prominent roles in leading services.

Friday-evening services start at 6.30pm and the main Shabbat service is at 10.30am followed by kiddush.

YESHURUN SYNAGOGUE

Fernhurst Gardens, Edgware, HA8 7PH; ☎ 020 8952 5167; www.yeshurun.org; tube: Edgware – 6 mins. ⓯

The flagship congregation of the Federation Synagogues, this is a warm Modern Orthodox community. There is a meet-and-greet programme to welcome visitors and Shabbat hospitality can be provided on prior notice. The main Shabbat Shacharit service is at 9am, followed by kiddush. There are also daily services.

STANMORE AND CANONS PARK SYNAGOGUE

London Road, Stanmore, HA7 4NS; ☎ 020 8954 2210; www.sacps.org.uk; tube: Stanmore – 4 mins; office open Sun–Fri.

Visitors should contact this United Synagogue before Shabbat if they wish to attend or if they require Shabbat hospitality. The main Shabbat service is at 9.15am. Visitors are welcomed at the entrance, and there is a weekly kiddush. Members dress smartly. There is a Sephardi service fortnightly.

MIKVAH

Edgware United Synagogue; Parnell Close, HA8 8YE; ☎ 020 8958 4488/8358 7822. ⓰

There is a Mikvah in the grounds.

ERUV

Most of Edgware and Stanmore are covered by an eruv – see *www.edgwareeruv.org* and *www.sacps.org.uk.*

NORTH-WEST: ST. JOHN'S WOOD

This upmarket and unique suburb lies a couple of miles north of Central London. In the 1960s, it was designated a conservation area and many of its houses were listed by English Heritage, ensuring a continued atmosphere of calm and privacy.

Before WWII, many wealthy European Jewish refugees settled here, and it became a fashionable Jewish area after the war. The area continues to attract affluent and prominent Jewish families. It is home to the residences of both the Chief Rabbi of Great Britain and the Israeli ambassador.

The nearest tube stations for most of these listings are St. John's Wood (Jubilee line) and Maida Vale (Bakerloo line).

RESTAURANT

HARRY MORGAN'S

'Kosher-style' deli/restaurant £/££

29–31 St. John's Wood High Street, NW8 7NH; ☎ *020 7722 1869; www.harryms.co.uk; tube: St. John's Wood – 10 mins; open daily 9am–10.30pm (Sat & Sun from 10am); unsupervised.* ❶

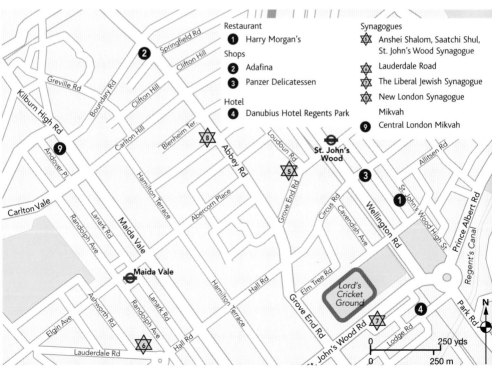

Restaurant
❶ Harry Morgan's
Shops
❷ Adafina
❸ Panzer Delicatessen
Hotel
❹ Danubius Hotel Regents Park

Synagogues
✡ Anshei Shalom, Saatchi Shul, St. John's Wood Synagogue
✡ Lauderdale Road
✡ The Liberal Jewish Synagogue
✡ New London Synagogue
Mikvah
❾ Central London Mikvah

Established in 1948 by Harry Morgan, this is a popular and comfortable restaurant with many traditional Jewish specialities including chicken kneidlach soup, chopped liver, hot salt beef sandwiches, lockshen pudding and New York cheesecake. A takeaway service is also available.

SHOPS

ADAFINA

Kosher traiteur

67 Abbey Road, NW8 0AE (nr Boundary Road); ☎ 020 7624 2013; www.adafina.co.uk; Tube: St. John's Wood – 15 mins; open Mon–Thur 8.30am–7.30pm, Fri 8am–3 hrs before Shabbat; LBD & SKA. ❷

Adafina was the traditional meat stew eaten by Sephardi Jews in medieval Spain for Shabbat lunch. This shop is a kosher deli and caterer, voted one of London's top 10 delis by *Time Out* in 2008. Its wide range includes fresh bread, charcuterie, smoked fish and dairy products as well as a tempting menu of freshly cooked Ashkenazi- and Sephardi-style dishes.

The website includes a special menu of dishes available for delivery to hotels with 24 hours' notice – call or email to order. Adafina has a separate counter in Selfridges Food Hall (see p. 162) and supplies sandwiches to John Lewis, Waitrose and Budgens supermarkets, and runs the Jewish Museum café (see p. 116).

Adafina.

PANZER DELICATESSEN

13–19 Circus Road, NW8 6PB; ☎ 020 7722 8162/8596; www.panzers.co.uk; tube: St. John's Wood – 5 mins; open: Mon–Fri 8am–7pm, Sat 8am–6pm, Sun 8am–2pm. ❸

Established since 1955, this popular mini-supermarket has a large selection of kosher products including challot, cakes and biscuits, meat, fish and ready-made convenience meals, plus traditional but unsupervised specialities like herring, bagels and smoked salmon from four different suppliers.

HOTEL

DANUBIUS HOTEL REGENTS PARK

££

18 Lodge Road, NW8 7JT; ☎ 020 7722 7722; www.danubiuslondon.co.uk; tube: St. John's Wood – 10 mins. ❹

This is a modern four-star hotel with 365 rooms that is around 10–15 minutes from the synagogues in the area. As the bedrooms have electronic doorkeys, the hotel will arrange for doors to be opened for guests on Shabbat. There is a manual entrance door to the hotel.

The London Marriott Regents Park (see p. 196) is also convenient for St. John's Wood.

SYNAGOGUES

There are several long-established, large synagogues in the area that have responded to the change in demographics and the demands of younger worshippers, by generating or hosting new or alternative communities within their premises.

ANSHEI SHALOM

37/41 Grove End Road, NW8 9NG; www.anshei shalom.org.uk; email: info@ansheishalom.org; tube: St. John's Wood – 5 mins. ❺

Established in 2003, with over 130 members, this is a welcoming and friendly Sephardi synagogue with many French members, mostly under the age of 40. There is learning every evening and regular social and educational programmes with renowned speakers. Services are held in the St. John's Wood Synagogue building. Shabbat Shacharit is at 8.50am with kiddush after the service. Contact the synagogue by email for Shabbat hospitality.

LAUDERDALE ROAD

2 Ashworth Road, Maida Vale, W9 1JY; ☎ *020 7289 2573; www.lauderdaleroadsynagogue.org; tube: Maida Vale – 7 mins.* ❻

This is one of the synagogues belonging to the Sephardi Spanish and Portuguese Jews' Congregation. See p. 103 for history.

On Shabbat, visitors are greeted at the door. Around 100 people attend, with far more for simchas. There is a weekly kiddush, with a special kiddush held on the Shabbat before Rosh Chodesh when chollent is served. There are also frequent guest speakers. Shabbat hospitality can be provided on prior notice. Daily services are also held.

THE LIBERAL JEWISH SYNAGOGUE

28 St. John's Wood Road, NW8 7HA; ☎ *020 7286 5181; www.ljs.org; tube: St. John's Wood – 10 mins.* ❼

The synagogue was founded in 1911, and is Britain's oldest and largest Liberal synagogue. A building on the current site was opened in 1925 with seating for 1,350 worshippers. It was heavily damaged in WWII and renovated by 1951. It was completely rebuilt between 1988 and 1991, retaining the original portico. The Sanctuary is lined with Jerusalem stone and the Ark doors are made of interwoven metals, set in a frame of bronze. There is a Holocaust memorial by Anish Kapoor in the entrance (see p. 130).

The community has about 2,000 members and is affiliated to the World Union for Progressive Judaism. Shabbat services are held on Fridays at 6.45pm and Saturdays at 11am. The community is welcoming and friendly. Members greet visitors at the door and at the weekly kiddush. On the first Friday of each month there is a Chavurah supper with a guest speaker. A thriving Religion School meets on Shabbat mornings.

The Liberal Jewish Synagogue, the Sanctuary.

NEW LONDON SYNAGOGUE

33 Abbey Road, NW8 0AT; ☎ *020 7328 1026; www.newlondon.org.uk; email: office@newlondon. org.uk; tube: St. John's Wood – 10 mins.* ❽

The current community was established in 1964 and led by Rabbi Louis Jacobs (see right). Whilst it is a Masorti congregation, men and women sit separately and worship with the prayer book used by the United Synagogue. For most services, women can sit either upstairs, or downstairs in the left-hand block parallel to the men. There is a mixed choir once a month. There is also an egalitarian service on the first Shabbat of the month. The community is friendly and visitors are greeted at the door. There is a weekly kiddush. Shabbat hospitality can be provided on prior notice by email to the office.

SAATCHI SHUL

37/41 Grove End Road, NW8 9NG; ☎ *020 7289 2367; www.saatchishul.org; email: samuel@ saatchishul.org; tube: St. John's Wood – 5 mins.* ❺

The Saatchi Shul was opened in 1998 by Charles and Maurice Saatchi to honour their parents, Nathan and Daisy (see p. 153). Its aim was to attract disaffected young Jews. It is an independent orthodox community that is informal and inclusive.

There are monthly Friday-night dinners with a speaker. Shabbat Shacharit is at 9.30am in the Beth Hamedrash located just across the courtyard from St. John's Wood Synagogue,

NEW LONDON SYNAGOGUE

This Grade II listed building, designed by H. H. Collins, was built in 1882 by the United Synagogue and named St. John's Wood Synagogue. The courtyard in front of the Italianate red-brick and terracotta exterior contains a sculpture by Naomi Blake (see pp. 18, 62, 129 and 137). The interior, with original light fittings and ornate cornicing, was redesigned in chocolate brown and cream. The synagogue has a particularly interesting collection of Judaica including excellent contemporary silverwork. The community moved to new premises in the early 1960s and the building was scheduled for demolition.

New London Synagogue, Abbey Road.

It was at this point that 'The Jacobs Affair' erupted. Rabbi Louis Jacobs was a Talmudic scholar. His prodigious depth and breadth of knowledge, both religious and secular, was such that many saw him as a future Chief Rabbi. In 1960, he resigned as rabbi of the New West End Synagogue, becoming Moral Tutor at Jews' College but the publication of his book in 1957, *We Have Reason To Believe*, where he questioned the divine authorship of the Torah, was to have enormous repercussions.

In 1964, the New West End Synagogue again had a vacant pulpit and wanted Rabbi Jacobs to return but, due to his, as some saw them, non-fundamentalist beliefs, this could not be sanctioned by the United Synagogue. His supporters at the New West End decided to form a breakaway community. After a series of temporary homes, salvation came from a totally unexpected quarter. Despite fierce opposition from the United Synagogue, the empty building in Abbey Road was purchased by supporters of Rabbi Jacobs for their New London Synagogue. Battles still had to be fought against the Jewish establishment to permit weddings and burials to take place under the auspices of New London Synagogue but these were eventually won. Regular services began that autumn, and New London grew and became a vibrant synagogue, led by Rabbi Jacobs for almost 40 years. It was the founding community of what has become the Masorti movement. See p. 9.

Rabbi Jacobs influenced Judaism well beyond the boundaries of St. John's Wood. In a poll organized by *The Jewish Chronicle* in 2005, he was voted the 'Greatest British Jew' since the readmission of Jews to England in the 17th century. Rabbi Jacobs, when asked his opinion on the poll, said in his slight Mancunian twang 'barmy'.

In October 1967 all four Beatles attended the memorial service for their manager Brian Epstein held at New London. Rabbi Jacobs officiated at the service where congregants also included other artists managed by Epstein, including Cilla Black and Gerry Marsden. A stone's throw away from the synagogue is Abbey Road Studios with the famous zebra crossing photographed for the Beatles's *Abbey Road* album of 1969.

Ronnie Cohen, Executive Director 2001–11

St. John's Wood Synagogue – stained-glass window, ark and curtain.

and each week there is a nosh 'n' drosh during the service. There are fortnightly free Shabbat lunches. Welcoming guests is an integral part of the community – for Shabbat hospitality email (see p. 192) or use the form on the website.

ST. JOHN'S WOOD SYNAGOGUE

37/41 Grove End Road, NW8 9NG; ☎ *020 7286 3838; www.shulinthewood.com; tube: St. John's Wood – 5 mins.* ❺

In 1876, this was the first congregation to join the five original members of the United Synagogue. It moved to its current location in 1965 and is one of the largest in London and is often used for high-profile communal events. It contains outstanding stained glass by David Hillman showing Festival and Shabbat images.

Today it has 1,300 members and around 200 attend the main Shabbat service led by a chazan, joined by a choir once a month. Visitors are greeted at the door and there is a weekly kiddush, that includes chollent and kugel when a simcha is being celebrated. Dress is generally smart. Shabbat hospitality can be provided on prior notice. There are also daily services.

MIKVAH

CENTRAL LONDON MIKVAH

21 Andover Place, NW6 5ED; ☎ *020 7372 7237/07870 696570 for appointments on Sun/Tue, 07989 858615 for appointments on Mon/Wed/ Thur; www.mikvah.org.* ❾

This is a modern Mikvah for the Spanish and Portuguese community. By prior appointment only.

ERUV

At the time of writing, the outcome of an application for an eruv is awaited. See *www.northwestminstereruv.org.*

NORTH-WEST: HAMPSTEAD, BELSIZE PARK AND CRICKLEWOOD

These pleasant residential neighbourhoods close to Central London became home, during the interwar years, to many Austrian and German refugees fleeing Nazi Europe. Housing was then both available and affordable. Today, accommodation here is expensive, but the areas are popular with young Jewish professionals and Israelis. The proximity to the centre of the city, a wide range of synagogues and cultural venues makes this an ideal area for Jewish visitors to stay.

KOSHER CAFES AND RESTAURANTS

PITA

Falafel/grilled meat £

339 West End Lane, NW6 1RS; ☎ 020 7435 5554; tube: West Hampstead (Jubilee) – 10 mins; open Sun–Thur 11.30am–11pm, Fri 11.30am–2 hrs before Shabbat, Sat night 1 hr after Shabbat–3am; KF; branch in Golders Green.

Pita is popular with a local cosmopolitan crowd for quick meals or takeaway – the menu is sensibly short and reasonably priced with generous portions. Perfectly crisp falafel, hummus with warmed pitta and shishlik with salads are all freshly prepared. Service is swift and the environment is pleasant with unobtrusive ambient world music.

UNSUPERVISED CAFES AND RESTAURANTS

MANNA

Vegetarian ££

4 Erskine Road, NW3 3AJ; ☎ 020 7722 8028; www.mannav.com; open Tue–Sun 6.30pm–10.30pm, Sat–Sun 12.00pm–3pm; reservations advisable.

Opened in 1966, this vegetarian restaurant is the oldest in London. The menu changes seasonally offering globally influenced innovative dishes such as satays, empilladas and tempura as well as pasta and quiches. Leave room for the delicious fruit crumble.

OLIVER'S FISH & CHIPS

95 Haverstock Hill, NW3 4RL; ☎ 020 7586 9945; www.oliversfishandchips.com; tube: Chalk Farm (Northern) – 5 mins; open Tue–Sun 12.15pm–2.30pm & 5pm–10.15pm; reservations advisable; home delivery available.

Whilst this popular traditional fish and chip shop is unsupervised, there is no meat or shellfish served and the fish is fried in vegetable oil. Takeaway or eat in – cod, haddock or plaice in batter or matzah meal with chips are the most popular choices. There are also inviting desserts like sticky toffee pudding and apple crumble.

SHOPS

There are no kosher food shops in this area. However, kosher provisions are available from the larger supermarkets in the area: Budgens, Haverstock Hill, Belsize Park, NW3; Sainsbury's, O2 Centre, Finchley Road, NW3; and Waitrose, Finchley Road, NW3. Sainsbury's and Waitrose stock kosher challot and bread. Kosher shops in Golders Green are easily accessed by public transport.

HOTELS

Shabbat facilities – with advance notice, the following hotels will arrange for guests' bedroom doors to be opened as keys are electronic, and will heat guests' kosher meals. These hotels all have manual entrance doors. Rooms on lower floors should be requested.

BRITANNIA HOTEL

£/££

Primrose Hill Road, NW3 3NA; ☎ *0871 222 0043;*
www.britanniahotels.com; tube: Chalk Farm
(Northern) – 10 mins.

Great value, convenient for Primrose Hill and
five minutes' walk from South Hampstead
Synagogue, this hotel has 121 comfortable en
suite bedrooms. The bedrooms have manual
door keys. Visitors may want to request one of
the 20 ground-floor bedrooms which were
refurbished in 2010.

CROWN MORAN HOTEL

£/££

142–152 Cricklewood Broadway, NW2 3ED;
☎ *020 8452 4175; www.moranhotels.com; tube:*
Willesden Green (Jubilee) – 15 mins.

Convenient for Brondesbury Synagogue, about a
20-minute walk away, this is a modern four-star
hotel with 116 spacious en suite rooms with a
gym and swimming pool amongst its amenities.
Rooms booked on 'Advance Purchase' on the
hotel's website are particularly good value. They
stipulate that only kosher meals provided to
guests by outside caterers will be heated.

LONDON MARRIOTT REGENTS PARK

££

128 King Henry's Road, NW3 3ST; ☎ *020 7722*
7711; www.marriott.co.uk; tube: Swiss Cottage
(Jubilee) – 8 mins.

This luxurious four-star hotel is 10–15 minutes
walk from either South Hampstead Synagogue
or St. John's Wood Synagogue. It has 304
modern and comfortable large en suite
bedrooms as well as a gym and swimming pool.

QUALITY HOTEL

£

5 Frognal, NW3 6AL; ☎ *020 7794 0101; www.*
qualityhampstead.com; tube: Finchley Road
(Jubilee, Metropolitan) – 8 mins.

This hotel is about 10–15 minutes' walk from
Hampstead Synagogue and Shomrei Hadath. It
has 57 en suite rooms. The hotel can keep an
exit door open on Shabbat.

SYNAGOGUES

BELSIZE SQUARE SYNAGOGUE

51 Belsize Square, NW3 4HX; ☎ *020 7794 3949;*
www.synagogue.org.uk; tube: Swiss Cottage
(Jubilee) – 5 mins.

This unique community founded in 1939 by
German refugees was originally affiliated to the
Liberal movement and its first chairman was
Lily Montagu (see pp. 99–101). Its services are
based on the German Unified Prayer Book with
music used in German services and composed
in the 19th century. The synagogue became
independent in 1989.

Visitors are welcomed at the door but should
bring their passports for security purposes.
Friday-night services are at 6.45pm and
Shabbat Shacharit is at 10am. Around 80
members attend the main service, many more
for a simcha. There is a weekly kiddush.

BRONDESBURY PARK SYNAGOGUE

143/145 Brondesbury Park, NW2 5JL; ☎ *020*
8459 1083; www.bpark.org; tube: Willesden Green
(Jubilee) – 12 mins.

One of the fastest-growing communities in the UK,
this welcoming, young and informal United
Synagogue community is led by the friendly and
dynamic Rabbi Baruch Levin, son of the rabbi at
South Hampstead Synagogue. Visitors are
welcomed at the front door. The morning service is
at 9.30am and around 120 people attend, with
many children attending the four children's services
at 11am. There is a weekly kiddush. Shabbat
hospitality can be provided on prior notice.

HAMPSTEAD SYNAGOGUE

(known as Dennington Park Road)

Dennington Park Road, NW6 1AX; ☎ *020 7435*
1518; www.hampsteadshul.org; tube: West
Hampstead (Jubilee) – 6 mins.

The community combines modern orthodoxy with
a tolerant and welcoming outlook. Shabbat
Shacharit is at 9.15am and visitors are welcomed
at the entrance. There is a weekly kiddush. See
opposite.

HAMPSTEAD SYNAGOGUE

The synagogue in Dennington Park Road, West Hampstead was founded in 1892 by professional, intellectual and artistic Jews wishing to modernize the rituals and liturgy of the United Synagogue. In part, this was to discourage the emergence of a separate Reform movement. They wanted to remove repeated sections in services, omit the Blessing of the Priests, adopt two Shabbat morning services, establish a mixed choir and allow confirmation services for girls. Rejected suggestions included adopting the triennial reading of the Torah and having organ music. The congregation joined the United Synagogue, and Hampstead would become its largest and most radical constituent. Hampstead women were given a vote in synagogue business by 1914, long before the United Synagogue allowed it in 1954.

The original building was designed by Delissa Joseph and expanded in 1901 when the community grew. It was the first orthodox synagogue to combine the Ark and Bimah and the sanctuary featured an octagonal dome with lantern. Later decoration included wonderful stained-glass windows and a new magnificent red-veined marble Ark.

From the 1950s the congregation dwindled as young couples found the spacious houses in the neighbourhood too large for modern living. However, there has been a contemporary revival in its fortunes led by Rabbi Dr Michael Harris, (son of the late Rabbi Cyril Harris, Chief Rabbi of South Africa). The building has recently undergone an award-winning multi-million-pound restoration and the membership has become increasingly less formal and more youth orientated.

SHIR HAYIM

Hashomer House, 37a Broadhurst Gardens, NW6 3BN; Rabbi Tabick – ☎ *020 8959 3129; www.shirhayim.org; tube: Finchley Road (Jubilee, Metropolitan) – 5 mins.*

This is a small and welcoming Reform community. Services are held at 6.15pm on Friday nights and 10.30am on Shabbat morning with a weekly kiddush. Services may be held elsewhere for simchas so visitors should call to check the location.

SHOMREI HADATH SYNAGOGUE

64 Burrard Road, NW6 1DD; ☎ *020 7435 6906; www.shomrei-hadath.com; tube: Finchley Road (Jubilee, Metropolitan) – 15 mins.*

This small friendly Federation synagogue holds Shabbat services and Shacharit on Sundays, Mondays and Thursdays. There is an excellent weekly kiddush. Shabbat hospitality can be provided on prior notice.

SOUTH HAMPSTEAD SYNAGOGUE

21/22 Eton Villas, Eton Road, NW3 4SG; ☎ *020 7722 1807; www.southhampstead.org; tube: Chalk Farm (Northern) – 5 mins.*

A United Synagogue led by charismatic Rabbi Shlomo Levin, who transformed this declining community when he became its rabbi in 1984. This vibrant, thriving congregation now has around 840 members, with a larger proportion than most of young singles. The shul is friendly, informal and, above all, inclusive. There are services for children and youth. The rabbi's sermons are always thought-provoking. Members welcome visitors at the door on Shabbat and there is a hospitality programme offering Shabbat lunch to visitors. There is an excellent kiddush with an occasional sit-down nosh'n'drosh with interesting guest speakers. There are daily Shacharit and Ma'ariv services and Mincha in the summer.

ERUV

An eruv serving the South Hampstead Synagogue community is due to be erected in early 2012. Check *www.southhampstead.org* for details.

EAST LONDON AND THE CITY

Once the centre of Jewish life in London, there are still synagogues open for prayer and a popular kosher restaurant. While the Jewish population has dwindled to a few thousand, both visitors and Londoners can discover memories of the Old Jewish East End.

KOSHER CAFES AND RESTAURANTS

BEVIS MARKS

Modern European ££/£££

Bevis Marks, EC3A 5DQ; ☎ *020 7283 2220;*

www.bevismarkstherestaurant.com; tube: Aldgate (Circle, Metropolitan) – 5 mins; open Mon–Thur 12pm–3pm & 5.30pm–10pm, Fri 12pm–3pm; LBD & SKA; takeaway and delivery service available.

Considered to be one of the best kosher restaurants in London, this stylish venue, with the chandeliers of the adjoining synagogue seen through its windows, is perfect for entertaining clients or for special occasions. It offers an elegant atmosphere to enjoy inventive modern cuisine together with traditional dishes like chicken soup and salt beef.

HOTELS

HOTEL MARLIN APARTMENTS

££

Reserve by calling ☎ *020 7378 4840 or via www.marlinapartments.com.*

With self-catering accommodation at 58 and 577 Commercial Road, these modern apartments are well located for visiting the East End synagogues.

IBIS HOTEL

£

5 Commercial Street, E1 6BF; ☎ *020 7422 8400; www.ibishotel.com; tube: Aldgate East (District, Metropolitan) – 1 min.*

A contemporary economy hotel with 348 rooms and well located for visiting the East End.

SYNAGOGUES

For the history of the synagogues listed below see East End Synagogues pp. 56–60 and Bevis Marks p. 22–23.

BEVIS MARKS

4 Heneage Lane, EC3A 5DQ (entrance through gate in Bevis Marks); ☎ *020 7626 1274/7628 1188 (office); www.bevismarks.org.uk; tube: Aldgate (Circle, Metropolitan) – 5 mins.*

Services are conducted in the Spanish and Portuguese Sephardic orthodox tradition. Friday-night services are followed by kiddush and a light supper. Shabbat Shacharit starts at 8.30am followed by kiddush at 11.45am.

CONGREGATION OF JACOB

351–353 Commercial Road, E1 2PS; ☎ *020 7790 2874; www.congregationofjacob.org; email: david.brandes@congregationofjacob.org; station: Shadwell (DLR, Overground) – 8 mins.*

This is a small and welcoming independent Orthodox community. Shabbat Shacharit is at 9.10am and around 15 people attend. There is a weekly kiddush, and they have a sit-down lunch with chollent monthly (see website). Visitors seeking hospitality should email (address above) in advance.

EAST LONDON CENTRAL SYNAGOGUE

(known as Nelson Street)

30/40 Nelson Street, E1 2DE; ☎ *020 7790 9809; station: Shadwell (DLR, Overground) – 10 mins.*

Shabbat Shacharit at this beautiful Federation synagogue is weekly at 10am. Nusach Sephardish is used. Kiddush follows the service.

FIELDGATE STREET GREAT SYNAGOGUE

41 Fieldgate Street, E1 1JU; ☎ *020 7247 2644/07939 160843; tube: Aldgate East (District, Metropolitan) – 8 mins.*

Fortnightly Orthodox Shabbat services are planned with a smoked-salmon bagel kiddush – call to check.

SANDYS ROW

4a Sandys Row, E1 7HW; ☎ *020 7377 6169; www.sandysrow.org.uk; tube: Liverpool Street (Central, Circle, Metropolitan) – 6 mins.*

This independent welcoming orthodox community holds Shabbat services fortnightly followed by a kiddush. Mincha is held at 1.30pm Monday–Thursday.

SETTLEMENT SYNAGOGUE

2 Beaumont Grove, E1 4NQ; ☎ *020 8599 0936; tube: Stepney Green (District, Hammersmith & City)*

Call the above telephone number for details of services

STAMFORD HILL

Stamford Hill in the north-east London Borough of Hackney is about 8km (5 miles) from the centre of London. Today it is home to Europe's largest ultra-orthodox Jewish community (known in Hebrew as Haredim). Other smaller Haredi communities are in Golders Green, Hendon and Edgware.

The Haredim began moving to Stamford Hill after 1926 when the Union of Hebrew Orthodox Congregations located to Stamford Hill, followed by ultra-orthodox schools and institutions. The numbers increased before, during and after WWII when many moved there from Central and Eastern Europe.

Today, there are estimated to be about 20,000 Haredim and over 50 synagogues in the Stamford Hill area. The population is rapidly growing, with families having an average of six children, two and a half times the average for England and Wales. The largest Haredi group is the Satmars, who were originally from Hungary and Romania. They have five synagogues in the area.

The Haredim aim to lead modest lives according to the laws of the Torah. Most of the community's first language is Yiddish and they have relatively little contact with modern secular society. Consequently they usually shop in their own strictly kosher and specialized shops where signage appears in Yiddish. In view of their large families and culture, they rarely eat at restaurants and cafés, so there are very few to be found in the area.

The Haredim wear traditional clothes that differ according to their cultural origins. However, generally the men are bearded with sidelocks (payot), and they wear long black coats and large black hats. The women dress modestly covering their arms and legs with long sleeves and skirts and cover their hair with a sheitel (wig) or scarf.

Visitors to the Stamford Hill area should dress modestly.

KOSHER SHOPS

There are many small kosher shops serving the Haredi community in the Stamford Hill area. One of the larger and longest-established shops is The Egg Stores at 4–6 Stamford Hill, N16 6XZ but a typical Haredi shopping area with the full range of essential shops required for everyday living is Oldhill Street, N16 6LU. The shops are staffed by Haredim, and are mostly independently owned with no high-street chains.

As well as a butcher (The Meat Plaza at No. 23), a baker (Indigs Heimishe Bakery at No. 37), a fishmonger (Hoffman's Fish & Delicatessen at No. 92), a grocery shop (Kosher Spot at No. 69), a health-food shop (So Real at No. 43) and a well-stocked kosher wines and spirits shop (The Grapevine at No. 90), there is a Satmar bookshop (Mesoiroh Books at No. 61) packed with religious books and Yiddish children's books, and a clothing store (Roth Clothing at No. 65–67) filled with predominantly black traditional garments. A Kedassia supervised café, Munchies Take-away at No. 48, sells falafel, burgers and hot dogs.

The nearest tube to Oldhill Street is Seven Sisters (Victoria) from which there is a six-minute bus ride from Stop Q on 73, 76, 243, 476, 149 to Lynmouth Road, and then a seven-minute walk to Oldhill Street.

SYNAGOGUE

NEW SYNAGOGUE

The New Synagogue at 87 Egerton Road, N16 6UE was opened in March 1915 having relocated from Great St Helen's in the City of London where it had been since 1838 (see also p. 88). A vast cathedral-like building, the New Synagogue was a famous landmark in its day and one of the original constituents of the United Synagogue, when formed in 1870. Many of its fixtures and fittings were moved to the new building at Egerton Road.

It was a thriving congregation in the 1950s and 1960s, but with many members of the New Synagogue moving to other suburbs in the 1970s and 1980s, a large synagogue was no longer needed and the building was sold in 1987 to the Haredi Bobover community. Today it is one of the two synagogues currently used by the Bobovers.

The remaining members of the New Synagogue meet at the Victoria Community Centre, also in Egerton Road, N16 6UB. For details of service times, the synagogue can be contacted on ☎ 020 8880 2731 on Sunday mornings and Wednesday afternoons.

HOTELS

KADIMAH HOTEL

£

146 Clapton Common, Stamford Hill, E5 9AG; ☎ *020 8800 5960; www.kadimahhotel.com; tube: Manor House (Piccadilly), then 10-min bus ride on 253 or 254 bus to Clapton Common, then 1-min walk or Seven Sisters (Victoria), then a 4-min bus ride on 76, 243, 149, 476 to Stamford Hill Broadway, then 1-min walk; Kedassia.*

For those who want to stay in a reasonably priced kosher hotel in the Stamford Hill area, this long-established bed and breakfast-style hotel is perfect. It has 17 en suite rooms with modern facilities including flatscreen TV, mini-refrigerator, safe, hairdryer and free Wi-Fi access. Kosher continental breakfast is included in the room rate. There is a restaurant where lunch or supper can be purchased. The hotel caters for the requirements of the strictly orthodox over Shabbat.

EDUCATIONAL AND CULTURAL JEWISH LONDON

Until the 1970s, the majority of Jewish activities were centred around the synagogue, and as such, catered in the main for those who were synagogue members. There was little provision for those unaffiliated to a synagogue. However, in response to the shift in demographics, with an increasing number of single households and more people who were culturally Jewish but not necessarily observant, a wide range of cultural and educational initiatives have been established.

EDUCATIONAL JEWISH LONDON

The organizations below are known for providing top-quality educational and cultural programmes. In addition, many London synagogues run their own programmes.

LONDON JEWISH CULTURAL CENTRE (LJCC)

Ivy House, 94–96 North End Road, NW11 7SX; ☎ 020 7457 5000; www.ljcc.org.uk; tube: Golders Green (Northern) – 15 mins.
Established in 2005 in Ivy House, the former home of the ballerina Anna Pavlova, it attracts more than 1,000 students and runs 80 courses and activities each week. Its wide range of events and courses cover current affairs, history, philosophy, art, film and languages. There is a kosher café (SKA).

LONDON SCHOOL OF JEWISH STUDIES (LSJS)

Schaller House, 44a Albert Road, NW4 2SJ; ☎ 020 8203 6427; www.lsjs.ac.uk; tube: Hendon Central (Northern) – 20 mins.

The LSJS runs fascinating courses providing the tools to understand Judaism and its texts. They are also pioneering interactive online courses.

SPIRO ARK

25-26 Enford Street, W1H 1DW; ☎ 020 7723 9991; www.spiro ark.org; tube: Marylebone (Bakerloo) – 5 mins.
Led by Nitza and Robin Spiro, this organization has provided a huge variety of innovative and fascinating Jewish- and Israeli-themed historic, cultural and educational events and courses since 1999. It holds art exhibitions at its West End premises, teaches Hebrew and Yiddish and runs heritage tours and trails.

LIMMUD

Dedicated to Jewish learning Limmud (*www.limmud.org*) holds an incredibly popular week-long annual conference in Warwick at the end of December. Over 3,000 delegates attend sessions on culture, history, music, politics, Israel, film and the Torah, with many presented by internationally known speakers. Day Limmuds run throughout the year at other venues, including London.

CULTURAL YEAR

London's thriving Jewish cultural scene involves diverse arts events throughout the year and internationally prestigious annual book and film festivals. *Jewish Renaissance* quarterly magazine includes advance listings of Jewish cultural events throughout the UK (see p. 206).

Ivy House, home of the LJCC and the Hampstead and Highgate Literary Festival.

January

27 Jan – annual **Holocaust Memorial Day** (see p. 117).

February/ March

Mid-Feb – Jewish Book Week (*www.jewishbookweek.com*). This nine-day festival attracts high-profile authors and speakers from the Jewish and non-Jewish worlds. The programme, released in mid-January, is always eclectic and sometimes controversial. From 2012, the festival will be held near Kings Cross station at Kings Place (*90 York Way, N1 9AG*).

September

Early Sept – Klezmer in the Park (*www.jmi.org.uk; www.klezmerinthepark. org.uk*). Regent's Park hosts a celebration of Klezmer with Britain's finest bands, an exhibition of Jewish life, displays by Jewish cultural organizations and kosher food.

Early Sept – European Day of Jewish Culture and Heritage (*www.jewisheritage.org; www.go londontours.com*). Established in 2000, many Jewish heritage sites in London (and the rest of the UK) are open, some with guided tours. Jewish-themed guided walks and events also take place.

Mid-Sept – Open House London (*www.londonopenhouse.org*). Visitors have the chance to explore, free of charge, hundreds of London buildings, new and old, which are usually closed to the public, including many synagogues.

Mid-Sept – Hampstead and Highgate Literary Festival (*www.hamhighlitfest.com*). A three-day event established in 2009. In 2010 it hosted 50 events with 78 authors, many of whom were Jewish. The festival is hosted at Ivy House, home of the LJCC (see p. 201).

November

Early Nov – UK Jewish Film Festival (*www.ukjewishfilmfestival.org.uk*). Since 1997 this annual festival presents a well-chosen array of Jewish-themed features, documentaries and short films. In 2010, 66 films were shown at 10 screens over 18 days. Film-makers attend some of the events for audience Q&As. For many films this is often the only chance to see a UK screening.

Mid-Nov – AJEX Annual Remembrance Ceremony and Parade (*www.ajex.org.uk*). This annual Association of Jewish Ex-Servicemen and Women (AJEX) event is in remembrance of the British Jews who have died in military conflicts. It takes place one week after the national Remembrance Sunday parade which is held on the nearest Sunday to 11 November.

In 1919 a member of the royal family overheard a remark suggesting that Jews did not serve enough during WWI. The king asked the Chief Rabbi to arrange a parade by Jewish servicemen to show this was not the case. In 2010, over 1,400 people participated in the march from Horse Guards Parade, on Whitehall, to the Cenotaph (the permanent memorial to those who have died in conflicts) where a wreath was laid and the Chief Rabbi conducted a memorial service.

December

Chanukah – Numerous festive events are arranged throughout London.

JEWISH CULTURAL ORGANIZATIONS

Go London Tours (inc. Go Jewish London) Rachel Kolsky (☎ *020 8883 4169; www.go londontours.com*), one of this book's authors, provides a wide range of informative and entertaining Jewish heritage walking tours. These include monthly public tours and bespoke private tours for families, groups and cultural organizations.

Jewish Community Centre for London (JCC)
The JCC (☎ *020 7431 9866; www.jcclondon. org.uk*) currently hosts a variety of cultural events at different venues across London. In

Artist's impression of the new Jewish Community Centre.

2013, a new state-of-the art Jewish Community Centre in Finchley Road, Hampstead, is due to open. The centre plans to provide over 100 hours of activity every week including debates, films, theatre and family events.

Jewish Museum
The museum hosts an events programme, often linked to temporary exhibitions (see pp. 111–16).

Jewish Music Institute (JMI)
The JMI (*www.jmi.org.uk*) presents Jewish music performances in leading UK venues throughout the year and runs Jewish music summer schools for the public.

London Jewish Cultural Centre (LJCC)
See p. 201.

London Jewish Forum (LJF)
The LJF (*www.ljf.org.uk; www.openjewish culture.org*) is dedicated to the promotion of Jewish life in London and launched Open Jewish Culture in 2010.

New End Theatre
This small 84-seat venue (*www.offwestend theatres.co.uk*) in the former mortuary of New End Hospital, Hampstead, has for nearly 40 years presented many shows and plays with strong Jewish themes. In May/June 2010 together with the LJCC (see p. 201) it hosted the first London Jewish Performing Arts Festival showcasing Jewish and Israeli performing arts.

Spiro Ark
See p. 201.

Zionist Federation (ZF)
The ZF (*www.zionist.org.uk*) runs Israel-focused programmes and events throughout the year.

VIEW JEWISH LONDON

Exploring UK film and TV of the last half century looking for markers of Jewish identity, the urban archaeologist will discover a surprising number of works spread across a variety of cinematic formats.

EAST END

'Old Jewish East End' stories made in the 1950s/60s can tend towards nostalgia and tradition. Often, the films depicting this immigrant community mark a bygone era, a myth or both. In *A Kid for Two Farthings* (1956), a Yiddish-accented tailor creates a utopian world for a non-Jewish boy in a story that balances real locations (Petticoat Lane, Fashion Street) with fantasy.

More recently, in *The 10th Man* (2006), a dramatic short, shot in and around Brick Lane, Fieldgate Street and Sandys Row Synagogue, nine very Yiddish-accented elderly Jewish men search for the 10th Jew to create a Minyan, without whom the Kol Nidre prayers cannot take place.

But there is always a reality check to this cosy shtetl view. As early as 1947, in *It Always Rains on Sunday* (1947), there are indicators of people 'moving on', assimilating and transgressing rabbinical codes. Two East End brothers, both wide boys, weave in and out of

The 10th Man on location in Sandys Row Synagogue.

the Jewish community of Bethnal Green (Camden locations but mostly studio-bound), and in and out of trouble. One plays sax in clubs, knows people 'up West' and cheats on his wife with a non-Jewish girl. The second, a 'macher' with a cigar, also dallies with non-Jewish women, while making his way in the arcade business, crime and boxing.

In *The Vanishing Street* (1962), a documentary shot in Hessel Street, the erasure of the older community is complete when a 'Jewish' street is demolished but recorded in fly-on-the-wall objectivity. Further east, in a recent documentary, *All White in Barking* (2008), a Holocaust survivor hangs on in East London, but faces the reality of new ethnic immigration and a rising tide of ultra-Right party politics and racism.

WEST END

In contrast to the East End, the West End on film has been a marker for Jewish modernity, assimilation and transgression. In the musical *Expresso Bongo* (1959), a small-time Jewish agent sleeps with his non-Jewish stripper, drinks espresso, but still leaves himself time to promote a rock 'n' roll singer. This is played out within the confines of Soho (Old Compton Street, Leicester Square and Piccadilly Circus).

In *Night and the City* (1950), a self-styled sports promoter, Harry Fabian (albeit with a WASP makeover for the film adaptation), cheats and steals his way from east (the Docks) to west (Soho again), all photographed in the German expressionist style of cinematographer Mutz Greenbaum (aka Max Greene).

In *An Education* (2009) yet another Jewish con man seduces yet another non-Jewish girl, this time under age, if better educated and from a higher class, in the stylish surroundings of Café de Paris (West End) and the Nash terraces of Regent's Park.

NORTH-WEST

Shifting to the apparently safer and more ideologically stable North-west London, the romcom *Suzie Gold* (2004) is a comedic and clichéd look at the myth of the Jewish suburbs, played out within the affluent areas of St. John's Wood (St. John's Wood High Street, New London Synagogue interior) and Hampstead Garden Suburb (Norrice Lea Synagogue exterior).

But North-west London is not always so safe, so stable. In *Leon the Pig Farmer* (1992), the eponymous hero must leave his family and North-west London (Edgware) community to travel to rural Yorkshire, all in an attempt to reconcile the accident of his birth – his botched IVF origins with a non-Jewish biological father (fewer London exteriors as most location work was in Yorkshire).

In the TV comedy-drama *Bar Mitzvah Boy* (1976), 13-year-old Eliot rejects the models of manhood offered by his father and grandfather, and walks out of his rite of passage ceremony at the synagogue (location Maida Hill Synagogue (now demolished), Maida Vale and environs).

In *Sunday Bloody Sunday* (1971), Dr Daniel Hirsh, a gay man, is also caught up in the anguish of his Jewish identity, as he witnesses his nephew's bar mitzvah (location New London Synagogue).

All these films raise questions around the value placed on the moral and geographic shifts the Jewish community has made in London over the past half-century. Whatever one's conclusions, these films certainly offer invaluable and entertaining routes into a Jewish London psycho-geography.

Searle Kochberg, principal lecturer at the University of Portsmouth, film writer and documentary maker.

READ JEWISH LONDON

Jewish London has always inspired authors. Whether histories, novels, plays or reminiscences, they evoke the East End Jewish communities and beyond.

BOOKS AND PLAYS

To get a sense of how the late 19th-century immigrant community lived in and around Brick Lane, there is no better read than *Children of the Ghetto* (1892) by Israel Zangwill. Almost 'faction' rather than a novel, he portrayed the vibrant Jewish life against the backdrop of the synagogues, shops and markets he actually knew. Arnold Wesker picked up the dilemma between integration and assimilation in his play *Chicken Soup with Barley* (1958) where, within three generations, aspirations and ambitions collide.

Emanuel Litvinoff's collection of short stories, *Journey Through a Small Planet* (1972) and Harry Blacker's *Just Like It Was* (1974), illustrated with his own drawings, both evoke the bustling East End and the array of characters who populated it. A different slant is provided by Alexander Baron's *The Lowlife* (1963), which vividly portrays the gambling underworld of the dog tracks but also the warm camaraderie of postwar Hackney in the 1950s.

Professor William Fishman has written the seminal book on radicals in the East End. *East End Jewish Radicals 1875–1914* (1975). *East End 1888* (1988) also by Fishman, perfectly complements the picture of the immigrant experience portrayed in Zangwill's *Ghetto*. *Rodinsky's Room* (1999) was co-authored by Iain Sinclair, a specialist in urban psycho-geography, and Rachel Lichtenstein who

accidentally stumbled upon the fascinating story surrounding David Rodinsky and the synagogue in Princelet Street (see p. 31). It provides a layered perspective with social history, a detective story and a feel for different memory viewpoints.

Oral history is found in *Kindertransport* (1995) by Olga Levy Drucker, where adults look back to their childhood experience of being sent to safety in the UK, when in many cases, they never saw their families again. The experiences of the 1930s Austro-German refugees in Natasha Solomon's debut novel, *Mr Rosenblum's List* (2010) portray the dilemma of how far to Anglicize and assimilate. Love and the difficulties it can bring are found within *A Morning Gift* (1993) by Eva Ibbotson (see p. 89) and Patricia Friedberg's *21 Aldgate* (2010), which moves its action between the very different worlds of the Jewish East End and Chelsea in the 1930s.

A wide selection of titles is held at the **Jewish Museum** (see p. 111) and **Joseph's** (see p. 178). Otherwise, order online.

The *Jewish Year Book*, published annually since 1896, provides a comprehensive directory of the who, what and where of British Jewry, with London being the largest chapter.

NEWSPAPERS AND JOURNALS

There are several newspapers available, from which to glean the news and current issues facing the London Jewish community.

Alondon: A free magazine for Israelis in London published every one to two months since 1994 and distributed via Jewish shops, eateries and hotels. It is almost entirely in Hebrew with content covering business, opinion, culture and sport.

Hamakor: Published since 2010, this free fortnightly news magazine, mostly in Hebrew, is read by the Orthodox communities in London and Manchester where it is distributed via kosher shops and cafés.

Hamodia: Originally published in Eastern Europe over 100 years ago, this weekly newspaper (☎ *020 8442 7777; www.hamodia. co.uk*) caters for the Orthodox Haredi community. It is widely available in Orthodox areas or via subscription.

The Jewish Chronicle: Established in 1841, this weekly newspaper (*www.jewish chronicle.com*) published each Friday is considered the foremost publication for British Jewry. Content covers news, communal events and coverage of the arts, travel, cookery and sport. There is also a searchable archive via the web.

Jewish Quarterly: Established in 1953, the Jewish Quarterly (*www. jewishquarterly.org*) provides an academic but accessible insight into a range of topics from art and politics to sport and business ethics. It is available via subscription only.

Jewish Renaissance: Quarterly magazine (*www.jewishrenaissance.org.uk*) of Jewish culture published as a non-profit-making concern. The content covers art, music, literature and drama from Jewish communities throughout the world with a detailed listings section for London and the rest of the UK. It is available via subscription only.

London Jewish News: This free weekly newspaper (*www.totallyjewish.com*) distributed via shops and kosher eateries is widely read. Covering local events, heritage, arts and sport its website provides an up-to-date comprehensive listing of London-based community initiatives.

DAY TRIPS FROM LONDON

Kent, Buckinghamshire and Hertfordshire are within easy reach of London and offer wonderful opportunities to discover the country estates of personalities you have met during your walking tours of Jewish London. While Ramsgate offers a poignant ghost of a memory, Broomhill, Hughenden and Waddesdon are wonderful examples of country houses and the lives of the eminent Victorian Jews who lived in them.

BROOMHILL

Broomhill.

David Salomons Estate, Broomhill Road, Southborough, Tunbridge Wells, Kent, TN3 0TG; ☎ 01892 515152; www.salomons.org.uk, www.canterbury.ac.uk/salomons-museum; train: Charing Cross to Tonbridge (trains every 15 mins, fastest journey 41 mins), then taxi from station – 5km (3 miles); only grounds open, house by appt; museum Mon, Wed & Fri 2pm–5pm.

Sir David Salomons (1797–1873) (see also p. 84) acquired Broomhill Cottage, a 'very elegant small villa', in 1829. Between 1850 and 1852 Broomhill was demolished and rebuilt as a substantial Italian-style country house designed by Decimus Burton (1800–81).

A MAN OF MANY FIRSTS

Salomons became the first Jewish Lord Mayor of London in 1855. He had previously been admitted to the Coopers' Company and was elected the first Jewish sheriff of the City of London in 1835 and the first Jewish alderman in 1847. Professionally, he was one of the founders of the London and Westminster Bank in 1832, which, through mergers, became National Westminster Bank.

He was elected MP for Greenwich in 1851, but at that time, in order to speak or vote in Parliament, MPs had to swear 'on the oath of the true faith of a Christian'. As a Jew, he could not take this oath and was unable to speak or vote on behalf of his electors. In 1851 he did speak and was ejected from the Chamber. In 1859, the requirement for the Christian oath ceased, and he took his seat officially as MP for Greenwich. He was instrumental in breaking down the civil disabilities suffered by Jews and other minorities and, in 1869, was made a baronet.

Salomons was a member of the New Synagogue and held several community offices including presidencies of the Board of Deputies, Westminster Jews' Free School and the Jews' Hospital. He married Jeanette Cohen, and after her death, Cecilia Samuel. He died in 1873 and was buried in West Ham Jewish Cemetery (see p. 156).

David Lionel Salomons.

The lighting installation for the stage consists of an array of early dimmers, colour mixing and footlights. The windows are 'blacked out' by ingenious mechanized shutters. Do not miss the Welte organ. It was the largest ever installed in the UK and the only example of its type left in the world. It has 2,000 pipes ranging from 4.9m (16ft) to just 1.25cm (½in) and plays using punched paper rolls. It was restored in the 2000s and is used for public recitals (check website for details).

Outside he built a vast stable block for 21 horses and 12 carriages. It looks like a small French chateau. He later developed a passion for the motor car and there is an extensive range of early garages, complete with spiral staircases to the chauffeurs' accommodation above and inspection pits below. He arranged what is acknowledged to be the first motor-car show in 1895 at Tunbridge Wells.

A small museum houses a collection relating to the two David Salomons. It includes the House of Commons bench from which Sir David spoke before legally allowed to do so. When the House of Commons benches were changed, his friends bought it

MUSIC AND MOTORS

A visit to the David Salomons Estate, originally called Broomhill Cottage, allows you to see another side to him and also provides an insight into his eccentric nephew, **David Lionel Salomons** (1851–1925). Sir David had no children and the estate was inherited by his nephew, an innovative scientist who extended the house to his own designs. Additions included a water tower, photographic studios and a science theatre, built in 1894 so he could share his enthusiasm for inventions with others. The house is said to be the first in Britain to use electricity for domestic purposes.

Science Theatre with the Welte organ.

208

Salomons Museum with the House of Commons bench from which Sir David Salomons was ejected.

as a memento for him. David Lionel amassed a collection of 'ballooniana', also on display.

In 1938 the name was changed from Broomhill to David Salomons House. In the 1990s it was acquired by Canterbury Christ Church College, which became a university in 2005. The museum, house and grounds are open to the public.

ALL SAINTS' TUDELEY

Tonbridge, Kent, TN11 0NZ; ☎ 01732 808 277; www.tudeley.org; just off B2017 running eastwards from Tonbridge to Paddock Wood; open weekdays during daylight hours, check website; voluntary donations welcome.

Not far from Broomhill is the only church in the world with all its stained-glass windows designed by the Russian-Jewish artist **Marc Chagall** (1887–1985). They are a memorial to Sarah d'Avigdor Goldschmid, who died in 1963 at the age of 21 in a boating accident near Rye. The family estate, Somerhill, now a school, was nearby. An avid supporter of modern art, Sarah discovered Chagall's work when his Hadassah Hospital designs were exhibited in Paris in 1961. This, aligned to her Jewish-Anglican family background and Chagall's propensity for depicting Christ in his work, made him the perfect choice for the memorial which was finally completed in 1985. See also the altar cloth, embroidered by congregants. It depicts, in Hebrew and English, the Jewish daily Shema prayer.

HUGHENDEN MANOR

High Wycombe, Bucks, HP14 4LA; ☎ *01494 755565; www.nationaltrust.org.uk; open daily but opening times vary, check website for details & special events; free adm. to park & woodland, adm. fee for house & garden; see right for travel info.*

If you enjoyed exploring Disraeli's London (see pp. 76–9), you might also want to visit his country estate near High Wycombe, which provides a fascinating insight into his private world.

HOME AND 'WORKSHOP'

Benjamin Disraeli (1804–81) purchased Hughenden Manor in 1848. Then leader of the Tory party, 'it was important to represent a county', and county members had to be landowners. He knew the area well as his father's estate was nearby, at Bradenham.

The simple white stucco three-storeyed house, built in the late 1700s, was remodelled under the Disraelis, revealing the original red-and-blue brickwork, and a parapet, pinnacles and ornate window surrounds were added.

Disraeli's study, Hughenden Manor. Photo: Andreas von Einsiedel.

The reception rooms on the ground floor have large windows overlooking the garden and Hughenden Valley.

The Disraelis split their time between their London home, Grosvenor Gate (93 Park Lane), and Hughenden, which became a much cherished home. Visitors can see a large collection of Disraeli's memorabilia covering all aspects of his family and life, both political and domestic.

Books were central to Disraeli's life and the collection here numbers over 4,000, including many of his father's. Portraits include those of his family and depict Disraeli from youth to old age confirming his preoccupation with his appearance. The collection of letters shows the devotion between members of the Disraeli family. The dining room was used frequently for entertaining despite the poor appetites of both Disraeli and his wife Mary-Anne.

The study, 'my workshop' as Disraeli called it, is the least changed room since his death. Here he carried out political business, wrote novels and penned numerous witty letters to his society friends. Hanging in the corridor, outside the Disraeli Room, is the carriage door that shut upon Mary-Anne's hand when she accompanied him to Parliament before an important speech. Disraeli asked that it be kept for posterity.

As Disraeli and Mary-Anne had no children, Hughenden was left to Disraeli's nephew, Conigsby, and he extended the house in 1910.

SECRET HUGHENDEN

The history of the manor post-Disraeli continues to fascinate, with an exhibition relating to WWII when it was used as a secret intelligence base, code-named 'Hillside', creating maps for bombing missions, including the Dambusters raid in 1943, and for planning an attack on Hitler's bunker. The manor was transferred to the National Trust in 1947 and is today open to the public.

The grounds are almost 607ha (1,500 acres) in size. There is a beautiful formal garden designed by Disraeli's wife, with a long terrace at the rear of the house and extensive woodlands to explore.

In Hughenden Park is the Church of St Michael and All Angels. Disraeli's grave is outside the eastern end of the church. Beside him are his wife, brother Ralph, nephew and heir Conigsby ... and Mrs Sarah Brydges-Williams. Of Jewish descent she had begun a correspondence with Disraeli and a close friendship developed. She named him as her executor, which he accepted as a legacy would result. The small print, however, requested she was to be buried alongside Disraeli. So it was done. Inside the church on the north wall is a unique monument, a memorial commissioned by Queen Victoria who was a great friend of Disraeli. No other Englishman has been so honoured by a reigning monarch.

TRAVELLING TO HUGHENDEN MANOR

Bus: Arriva 300 High Wycombe–Aylesbury (services every 20 mins, takes approx. 10 mins from High Wycombe station). There is a long uphill walk to Hughenden from the bus stop.

Road: 2.5km (1½ miles) north of High Wycombe; on west side of the Great Missenden road (A4128).

Train: High Wycombe closest station (3.25km (2 miles) away). If travelling from London take the train from Marylebone to High Wycombe (frequent trains, fastest journey 29 mins) and either take a taxi from the station or the bus.

MONTEFIORE'S RAMSGATE

Sir Moses Montefiore (1784–1885) lived through 100 years that witnessed dramatic changes for the Anglo-Jewish community. Personally, Sir Moses was a lay-leader of his synagogue, president of the Board of Deputies, a member of the Surrey militia, a sheriff of the City of London and a baronet. (Sites relating to Sir Moses Montefiore are also found in the **Old Jewish East End** (see pp. 18–32), **Jewish City** (see pp. 80–88) and **Mayfair and West End** (see pp. 67–73) walking tours.)

HOME AND ABROAD

His marriage in 1812 to Judith Barent-Cohen joined the foremost Ashkenazi and Sephardi families of their day, while Judith's sister, Hannah, had married Nathan Mayer Rothschild. The two couples lived together at the site of the bank, NM Rothschild.

Professionally, his successful career as a broker enabled him to retire in his thirties,

Sir Moses Montefiore, *c.*1840.

from when he devoted his life to philanthropy. His generosity to Jewish and non-Jewish causes was legendary. Protecting the interests of Jews around the world, he journeyed to Romania, Russia, Morocco and Syria petitioning against unfounded accusations and discrimination.

The Montefiores travelled widely. Their first visit to the Holy Land in 1827 reawakened his religious faith and inspired a love for the country; he subsequently visited another six times. He strove to instil there a culture of self-sufficiency. For example, in Yemin Moshe (Hebrew for 'Right Hand of Moses'), now an upmarket area of Jerusalem originally outside the city wall, Sir Moses funded a flour mill for the local community, the design based on the Hereson flour mill in Kent near his home.

Judith travelled everywhere with him and her diaries evoke the aims and aspirations of the trips but also illustrate the couple's piety and humanity. They lived an orthodox life, taking candlesticks and other Judaica to celebrate Shabbat and festivals.

They owned a town house at 99 Park Lane, Mayfair, and a country estate in the fashionable resort of Ramsgate, where his hundredth birthday in 1884 was declared a public holiday. The town was illuminated, streets decorated with 'MM' motifs and extra workers employed to cope with the increased volume of mail and visitors. Synagogues around the world held celebratory services and erected commemorative plaques. Widespread public grief spread around the world when Sir Moses died just months before his 101st birthday in 1885.

EAST CLIFF LODGE

Visiting Ramsgate allows you to experience the personal life of Sir Moses and Lady Judith. Their association began in 1812

during a honeymoon visit. Subsequently in 1822 they rented the late 18th-century **East Cliff Lodge**, which Sir Moses purchased in 1831 with 9.7 ha (24 acres) of land. In 1835, when the Duchess of Kent, mother of the future Queen Victoria, was staying nearby he commissioned a golden key to the gate separating their homes so they could walk through his grounds whenever they wished.

The mansion was demolished in 1954 but one wall remains from the extensive stable block and this can be seen in the **George VI Memorial Park** (*Montefiore Avenue, Ramsgate, CT11 8BD; open summer months*), which was laid out on the grounds of the mansion. Abutting the wall there is an early 1800s glasshouse, known as the Italianate Greenhouse, because Montefiore planted a small formal garden outside the entrance with an elaborate Italian fountain. It is Grade II listed and was restored in the early 2000s.

The Montefiores transformed the lodge into a centre for local Jewish life, also becoming prominent in local affairs. When Ramsgate was inaugurated as a borough in 1884, Sir Moses funded the mayoral chain. The links are formed from the Hebrew letter Mem.

MONTEFIORE SYNAGOGUE AND MAUSOLEUM

Honeysuckle Road, Hereson, Ramsgate, CT11 7EE; Honeysuckle Road is a turning off east side of Hereson Road, walk past pub & turn right, then left, continue 50m (55yd) to reach mausoleum & synagogue; public transport from London: trains run from Charing Cross, St. Pancras & Victoria to Ramsgate (regular service, fastest journey from St. Pancras 1 hr 17 mins) then taxi from Ramsgate station; synagogue not open for public worship except on special occasions; to arrange visit to

synagogue, mausoleum or cemetery, contact *Lauderdale Road Synagogue,* ☎ *020 7289 2573, www.sandp.org.*

Sir Moses bought some land at Hereson, not far from the lodge and commissioned his cousin, David Mocatta, to design a **synagogue**. Dedicated in 1833, the plain stuccoed exterior gives no indication of its purpose and the interior, originally plaster, was marbled in 1912. There is a clock on the facade, which is unusual on synagogues, and the chiming clock is the only example found in an English synagogue.

In 1831, to commemorate their first visit to the Holy Land, Sir Moses obtained some 'terra santa' (sacred earth), from an ancient burial ground in Jerusalem, to be placed under the Ark. The interior was lit originally by the octagonal glass skylight but windows were later added at the ladies' gallery level. The synagogue also has brass chandeliers lit by candles, just as at Bevis Marks in London.

A small private **cemetery** established in 1872 by Benjamin Norden, was later used by the Ramsgate Jewish community (*Ramsgate Jewish Cemetery, Dumpton Park Road, Ramsgate, CT11*

MAUSOLEUM

The **mausoleum** for his beloved wife was stipulated by Sir Moses to be no more than 15 paces from the synagogue. Mocatta was again commissioned and his design resembled Rachel's Tomb, a small domed structure seen en route from Jerusalem to Bethlehem. The Montefiores both lie in vaults covered by marble chest tombs. The interior is lit by a red and orange glass skylight in a starburst design. Outside stands a short stone column, believed to have been brought by Sir Moses from the Holy Land.

7AL) and managed by the Sephardi authorities although Ashkenazis are also buried there. It was extended in 1931 but is now rarely used. In 2008 the Ohel was listed Grade II.

In his wife's memory, Sir Moses endowed the **Judith, Lady Montefiore Theological College** consecrated in 1869. The building was demolished in 1965. See also p. 104.

WADDESDON MANOR

Waddesdon, nr Aylesbury, Bucks, HP18 0JH; ☎
*01296 653226; www.waddesdon.org.uk; train:
regular service from London Marylebone to
Aylesbury, then taxi from station (19.25km (12
miles) away); bus: Arriva – The Shires Nos. 6/17
from Aylesbury; house open Wed–Sun during
summer months until 4pm, garden open at
weekends in winter – check website; adm. fee.*
Ferdinand de Rothschild (1839–98) was a
member of the Austrian side of the family. A
successful politician, country gentleman and
art collector, his personal life was struck by
tragedy and despite building an opulent
country house at Waddesdon, his sadness
was never erased. (See also pp. 67, 143, 145
and 156.)

FERDINAND DE ROTHSCHILD

Ferdinand and his sister Alice arrived in
London following the death of their mother,
Charlotte. Through his close friendships with
the sons of Lionel de Rothschild, his cousins
Nathaniel, Leo and Alfred, he also became a
member of the circle surrounding the Prince
of Wales, later King Edward VII. In 1865 he
married Evelina, daughter of Lionel de
Rothschild but their happiness was short-
lived; she died in childbirth in 1866.

In memory of his wife he funded the Evelina
de Rothschild Hospital for Sick Children in
London and her father, Lionel, assumed
sponsorship of a school for girls in Palestine,
renaming it the Evelina de Rothschild School.

Ferdinand de Rothschild.

Waddesdon Manor, south front and parterre. Photo: Mike Fear.

Loving the country life, hunting and breeding livestock, Ferdinand remained in England. In 1883, he became High Sheriff of Buckinghamshire, a JP and the Deputy Lieutenant to the County in 1866 and then MP for Aylesbury in 1885 when Nathaniel left the House of Commons to enter the House of Lords.

He devoted time to the Jewish community, being treasurer to the Board of Guardians for seven years, warden at the Central Synagogue and funding a technical scholarship at Stepney Jewish School.

A CHATEAU ON A HILL

In 1874 he acquired 1,000ha (2,700 acres) of land in Buckinghamshire for his mansion Waddesdon Manor. The top of the hill was sliced off, water hauled from 22.5km (14 miles) away and a steam railway built to transport raw materials. Designed by Gabriel-Hippolyte Destailleur, the house was a mixture of Ferdinand's favourite French chateaux, built in honey-coloured Bath stone.

As you approach, the towers resemble the Château de Maintenon, the windows the Château d'Anet and the chimneys the Château de Chambord. The house is surrounded by landscaped gardens and woodlands with terraces, aviaries, rockeries and fountains. After his death, Alice inherited the estate and maintained the house and grounds to her exacting 'Miss Alice's housekeeping rules'. After

Waddesdon Manor, The Red Drawing Room. Photo: John Bigelow Taylor.

her death in 1922, their great-nephew James de Rothschild inherited. In 1957 James died and bequeathed Waddesdon to the National Trust. It opened to visitors in 1959.

Visitors marvel at the extravagance of the interior. In Ferdinand's day, weekend party guests included the Prince of Wales and Shah of Persia. In 1890 Queen Victoria paid a visit, subsequently maintaining a friendship with Alice.

Within the 222 rooms, not all open to the public, special note should be made of the Beauvais tapestries, Sèvres and Meissen porcelain and paintings by Reynolds, Gainsborough and Rubens. There is also the delightful new display of buttons, lace and fans amassed by Baroness Edmond de Rothschild, the mother of James. However, the unmissable piece is the Elephant automaton. Complete with howdah, the

Elephant's ears, trunk, tail and eyes all move. It was made around 1774 and, following careful conservation, still plays its five tunes.

EAT, SHOP AND STAY

The **Stables Café** sells fresh snacks and drinks. The **Manor Restaurant** in the Old Kitchen and Servants' Hall provides breakfasts, lunches and afternoon tea.

One of the best National Trust shops is located here, with items and gifts relating to the Rothschilds and the Waddesdon wines from around the world.

You can stay at **The Five Arrows**, by the gates of Waddesdon Manor (☎ *01296 651 727; www.waddesdon.org.uk/five_arrows/*).

GLOSSARY

Adath synagogues – Ultra-Orthodox synagogal movement (see p. 9)

Aliyah – Emigration to Israel

Ark – Where Torah scrolls are kept in the synagogue

Ashkenazi – Jews from Central or Eastern Europe and their descendants

Bar mitzvah – Religious coming of age for a 13-year-old boy

Beth Din – Jewish rabbinical court

Bimah – Elevated area in a synagogue from which the Torah is read

Boreka – Filo pastry triangle with savoury filling

Challah (plural **challot**) – Plaited loaf used for Shabbat and Festival meals

Chanukah – Festival of Lights

Chazan – Cantor

Cheder – Hebrew classes for children

Chevrot (singular **chevra**) – Religious and social welfare organizations found in the Jewish East End

Chollent – Traditional Shabbat lunch stew cooked overnight

Davening – Praying

Ehal – Sephardi name for Ark (see above)

Eruv – Boundary within which Jews may carry during Shabbat

Falafel – Deep-fried balls of ground chickpeas, usually served with pitta, hummus and salads

Gefilte fish – Chopped fish served boiled or fried

Genizah – Storeroom in a synagogue where disused religious books and scrolls are kept

Haham – Sephardi spiritual leader

Haredi/Haredim – Ultra-Orthodox Jews

Havdalah – Ceremony to mark the end of Shabbat and Festivals

Hummus – Chickpeas puréed with sesame paste, garlic, oil and lemon juice

Judaica – Objects used for the practice of Jewish laws, customs and rituals

Kaballah/Kaballist – A body of mystical teachings of rabbinical origin/practitioner of Kaballah

Kashrut – Jewish dietary laws (see p. 8)

Kiddush – Both the blessing made over wine on Shabbat and Festivals, and a range of snacks and wine served buffet-style after the Shabbat and Festival services

Klezmer – Traditional secular music of Ashkenazi Jews

Kneidlach – Matzah balls made from a matzah meal and egg mixture poached in chicken soup

Kol Nidre – Evening service of Yom Kippur (Day of Atonement)

Kosher – Complying with Jewish dietary laws

Kugel – Savoury pudding usually made of potatoes, eggs and onions

Laffa – Large pitta bread

Lockshen – Noodles

Ma'ariv – Evening prayer service

Macher – An influential person who is also an excellent organizer

Matzah meal – Finely ground unleavened bread (matzah), often used to coat fried fish

Maven – A trusted expert (from the Hebrew word meaning 'to understand')

Mezzuzah – Religious scroll inside a case attached to door frames

Mikvah (plural **Mikvaot**) – Jewish ritual bath

Mincha – Afternoon prayer service

Minhag – Custom

Minyan – Ten men required for certain prayers to be recited in Orthodox services

Nosh 'n' drosh – Lecture with food

Ohel – Chapel in a Jewish cemetery

Parev – Food that contains no dairy or meat ingredients

Payot – Sidelocks worn by Orthodox Jewish men

Rabbi – Spiritual leader and teacher

Rimonim – Ornaments that adorn Torah scrolls' cases or rollers

Rosh Chodesh – the first day of each Jewish month

Rugelach – Small, crescent-shaped pastry filled with a sweet filling such as chocolate or cinnamon

Schmatte – (Yiddish) Rags or cheap clothes

Seder – Story of the Exodus and Festive meal at Passover

Semicha – Ordination to become a rabbi

Sephardi – Jews from Spain, Portugal, North Africa, the Middle East and their descendants

Sephardish – Differing styles of service incorporating both Sephardi and Ashkenazi customs

Shabbat – Jewish day of rest, lasting from Friday sunset for just over 25 hours

Shacharit – Morning prayers

Sheitel – (Yiddish) Wig worn by religious married Jewish women

Shishlik – Grilled marinated skewered meat

Shtiebel – (Yiddish) A small room or synagogue used for Jewish communal prayers

Shtetl – A small Jewish settlement in Eastern Europe

Shul – Synagogue

Siddur – Prayer book

Simcha – A celebration

Talmud Torah – Hebrew school

Tevah – Sephardi name for Bimah (see separate entry)

Torah – The Five Books of Moses, written on scrolls. In its widest sense Torah can also refer to Jewish law and teachings

Yekke – Nickname for a German Jew

Yiddish – Language based on German, Hebrew and other languages

INDEX

CREDITS

b – bottom, c – centre, f– far, i – inset, l – left, r – right, t – top

© Canterbury Christ Church University, Salomons Museum: pp. 84, 207, 208tl, 208br, 209; © John Challicom: p. 121; © Crown Copyright/NMR: p. 23; © Czech Memorial Scrolls Museum: pp. 6, 122–3; © Marion Davies: p. 179; © Dorich House Museum, Kingston University: pp. 107tr, 107br; © English Heritage Photo Library: pp. 2, 58; © Estate of John Allin, courtesy of Portal Painters: p. 26bl; © Lance Forman: p. 173tl; © Jeremy Freedman: pp. 5fr, 24, 57; © Lucian Freud, private collection, on loan to the National Portrait Gallery, London: p. 132tr; © Freud Museum: p. 93; © Jonathan Gestetner: p. 148tr; © Gunnersbury Park Museum: p. 110; © Hampstead Synagogue: p. 197; © Jewish Military Museum: pp. 185tr, 185br; © Jewish Museum: pp. 31tr, 37, 38bl, 48br, 56, 66, 101tr, 111, 112–13, 115bl, 115br, 116, 117, 140, 211 (courtesy of the Spanish & Portuguese Jews' Congregation); © Rachel Kolsky: front cover t, pp. 5fl, 5c, 5c, 6–7, 10, 11, 20, 21, 22, 25, 26tl, 27, 28, 29, 30 (picture taken with the permission of the Rector of Christ Church Spitalfields 2011 Rev. Andy Rider), 31br, 32, 34, 35, 36, 38tl, 39, 40, 42, 43, 44, 45, 46, 47, 48bl, 48tr, 49, 51, 52, 53, 54, 55, 59, 60, 61, 62, 64, 65, 67, 69, 70, 71, 72, 77, 78, 79tr, 81, 82, 83, 84–5, 86, 88, 91, 92, 95, 97, 98, 99, 101br, 102, 103, 108–9, 114, 125, 129, 134, 135 (with permission of Ruth Rosen and by courtesy of the Royal Society of Medicine), 136tr, 136bl, 137, 142tr, 144tl, 145, 146, 147, 148tl, 149, 153, 154, 155, 156, 170, 172, 173c, 178bl, 193, 206; © Steven Kyte: pp. 151, 152tl, 152b, 173tr; © The Liberal Jewish Synagogue: pp. 100, 192, 194tr; © National Portrait Gallery: pp. 76, 131, 132tl; © NTPL/Andreas von Einsiedel: p. 210; © NTPL/Dennis Gilbert: p. 94; © NTPL/John Hammond: p. 79; © The National Trust, Waddesdon Manor: pp. 214, 215, 216; © The Neighbourhood: p. 203; © Nemon Estate: p. 136c; © Jon Rawson: front cover b, pp. 8, 12, 73, 74–5, 105, 126, 127, 128, 130, 158, 165, 168, 175, 176, 178br, 182, 183, 184, 189, 190, 191, 194, 202, back cover; © RISE Films: p. 204; © The Rothschild Archive: pp. 141, 142tl, 143bl, 143br, 144br; © Spanish & Portuguese Jews' Congregation: p. 213; © Spencer House/Mark Fiennes: p. 142br; © Beverley-Jane Stewart: pp. 14–15, 108i; © Tate Britain: p. 134; © Trustees of the British Museum: p. 138; © Victoria & Albert Museum: p. 139.

ACKNOWLEDGEMENTS

Space does not allow us to name everyone individually, but particularly we thank our commissioning editor Guy Hobbs and our editor Clare Hubbard, who have enabled the idea of *Jewish London* to become a reality. We are also grateful for the input and time given by museum curators and synagogue representatives: Eli Ballon at the New West End Synagogue; Maurice Bitton at Bevis Marks; Michael Burman at The Liberal Jewish Synagogue; Kathy Chaney at Salomons Museum; Ronnie Cohen at New London Synagogue; Neil Evans at the National Portrait Gallery; Vanda Foster at Gunnersbury Park Museum; Jeremy Freedman at Sandys Row Synagogue; Evelyn Friedlander at the Czech Memorial Scrolls Museum; David Glasser of Ben Uri Gallery; Brenda Goldberg, Niki Goorney and Nicola Webber at the Jewish Military Museum; Gabriel Herman at Hampstead Synagogue; Louise Hofman at the Victoria & Albert Museum; Brenda Martin at Dorich House Museum; Beverley Nenk at the British Museum; Jane Rick at Spencer House; Rabbi Lionel Rosenfeld at the Western Marble Arch Synagogue; Suzanne Saragoussi at Holland Park Synagogue; Elizabeth Selby at the Jewish Museum; Ilana Tahan at the British Library; Jennifer Weider at St. John's Wood Synagogue; and Nicholas Witherick at Hughenden Manor. Archivists Melanie Aspey at the Rothschild Archive and Miriam Rodrigues-Pereira at the Spanish & Portuguese Congregation were also unstinting in their assistance. Special thanks are also due to Ronnie Cohen, Pam Fox and Searle Kochberg for their contributions.

We are also grateful to the following for their help and ideas: All Saints Tudeley, Sami Benisty, Daniel Bratt, Ashley and Amy Donoff, Joe Dwek, Lance Forman, Howard Gerlis, Ian Goldstein, Anna Kochan, Steven Kyte, Rabbi Michael and Sharon Laitner, Charlie and Daisy May, Phillipa Neidle, Sue Nyman, Joe Nyman, Chuck Plumpton, Mr S, Ruth Swindon, Ben Tankel, Susan and Danny Tarragin, Clare Thompson, Ruth Velenski, Lady Young and Martin Wolff.

Rachel also wants to take this opportunity to thank those at all the Jewish heritage sites, synagogues and cemeteries who have so gladly welcomed her groups over the years.

In addition, we thank the following who kindly donated and gave permission for images to be used: Canterbury Christ Church University, Salomons Museum; Czech Memorial Scrolls Museum; Marion Davies; Dorich House Museum; Lance Forman; Jeremy Freedman; Lucian Freud; Jonathan Gestetner; Gunnersbury Park Museum; Hampstead Synagogue; King's College, London; Steven Kyte; Jewish Community Centre; Jewish Military Museum; Jewish Museum; The Liberal Jewish Synagogue; National Portrait Gallery; the Nemon Estate; Jon Rawson; RISE Films; Ruth Rosen; Lord Rothschild; The Rothschild Archive; Society of Friends; Spencer House; Beverley-Jane Stewart; and Waddesdon Manor.